ENGLISH RECUSANT LITERATURE
1558–1640

Selected and Edited by
D. M. ROGERS

Volume 178

ALEXIS DE SALO

*An Admirable Method to
Love . . . the B. Virgin Mary*
1639

ALEXIS DE SALO

An Admirable Method to Love,
Serve and Honour
the B. Virgin Mary
1639

The Scolar Press

1974

ISBN 0 85967 153 4

Published and printed in Great Britain by
The Scolar Press Limited, 59-61 East Parade,
Ilkley, Yorkshire and
39 Great Russell Street,
London WC1

1791783

AN ADMIRABLE
METHOD
TO LOVE, SERVE
AND HONOVR THE
B. Virgin MARY.

With diuers practicable Exer-
cises thereof.

Al inriched with Choice Examples.

Written in Italian by the R. F. A L E X I S
D E S A L O, *Capuchin.*

And Englished by R. F.

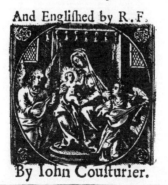

By Iohn Cousturier.

M. DC. XXXIX.

TO THE NOBLE

AND VERTVOVS LADY

the Lady Audley.

MADAM,

I present you vvith this translation, not to remaine in your hãds, but through them to paſs vnto the publick. So ſhal it dou-

bly

bly bee aduantaged : First,
more gratefully accepted of,
comming immediatly from
one so worthy as your self,
and next be beleeued worthie
the acceptation, that J dare
offer it to your sight, so wel
verst in al the Original
Languages. So, Madam,
goe my obligations multi-
plying to the Jnfinite, whilst
J cannot think of paying you
one curtesy but I receiue for
it two ; The whilst I must
euer remaine.

Your most obliged, R. F.

A SVMMARY
of the whole contenſe of this preſent Booke, for the Readers better comprehenſion thereof.

THE whole ſcope of this preſent Treatiſe is no other then to teach in a deuout and excellēt manner how to Reuerence and adore with profound Inclinations our B. Lady and miſtriſſe the Queene of Heauen; as a preparatiue to which, we haue indeauoured to declare,

ã 3   her

her heroical vertues, greatnesses, excellencies and sublime prerogatiues : And by the way is to be considered that although Adoration be peculiar to God alone, yet according to diuines distinction thereof, it also may be appropriated to the B. Virgin, to Angels, and other Saints and thereby become common to God & Man. As we may cleerly gather from diuers passages of the holy Scripture as namely in Paralip. chap. 26. when it is sayd; *And they inclined and adored first God, and afterwards the King.*

These Adorations then admit a three-fould distinction of Latria, Dulia, and Hyperdulia, where of the first is proper vnto God alone, in regard of his infinit and increated Greatnes; the
second

second hath reference to such creatures as aduance in sanctity and glory aboue the rest, which sanctity and glory arriuing in any on to more sublimity (as in the B. Virgin) with the more sublime honour of Hyperdulia, consequently we are to reuerence them: But before we proceed to the exercise of this Adoration we prefix an exhortation to deuotion towards her, and declare fiue Priuiledges, her seruants are indowed with al, setting down (as preamble to the worke) those conditions and qualities which are requisit in her deuots. Then we pass to the explication of these Adorations, in the first Chapter, declaring their excellency, in the second how grateful and acceptable they are to the B. Virgin, and in the fower

fol-

following ones, fower forcible argumēts are establifhed to proue her deferuing that adoration. The firft deduced from her being the Mother of Almighty God. The next for her being elected aboue al other Saints, and al the Quires of Heauen. The third for her foueraine power and authority, ouer al Creatures: And the fourth and laft for her being an affectionat Mother vnto vs al. Then we come to the practife of thefe Adorations, (or Genuflexions) fhewing how they are deuoutly to be performed, as wel in the interiour as exteriour, and heervpon we take occafion to inlarge our difcourfe touching the Adorations due to God, to his Bleffed Saints and Angels, &c. Imploying the remaine of the following

Chapters

Summary.

Chapters, in setting down diuers practical wayes of honouring the B. Virgin applying to euery on its proper Reuerence and Adoratiõs: but principally we insist vpon those twelue sublime prerogatiues of hers, prefigured by the twelue Starres, in her crowne of which S. Iohn in his Apocalips make mention.

Now this aduertisement is giuen to al that although the choice of many exercises of adoratiõs be proposed in this present worke, notwithstanding they are only to fix on, which they may find most gust and comfort in, and especially to beware-of entergiuing to much at once least they become thereby but more negligent in performance of them, and a too precipitious desir of cõming foon to end, make them but haft too much vpon the way, and performe them without fruit and deuotion.

Wherefore we councel rather to make choice of fome few we may performe with mediocrity of deuotion, then of many with danger of tepidity & diftraction. Notwithftanding when any feaft occurs, vnto which we haue a particular deuotion (as thofe of our Bleffed Sauiour his Mother or the like) we may then multiply our Genuflexions to a hundred a day, (for example) or a thoufand diftributed equally to feueral dayes or nights of the octaue as we pleafe , as we fhal more largely declare in the following Treatife by the affiftance of Almighty God, and the fauour of his

his holy Mother , al which we dedicat to the praiſe of God from whom al Good proceeds , to the Bleſſed Virgin his moſt holy Mother , and to Saint Francis our Glorious Patriarch.

A

A TABLE OF THE
Chapters contained in
this Booke.

A TABLE.

A TABLE.

A TABLE.

The

A TABLE.

Remar-

A TABLE.

A TABLE.

A TABLE.

An

AN ADMIRABLE
METHOD

TO LOVE, SERVE
and Reuerence the Glorions
Virgin Mary our B.Aduocate.

*Or a pious Exhortation to be deuoted
to the Queene of Heauen.*

VERY faithful Chri-
ſtian is to Indeauour
to his vtermoſt to be-
come deuot and duly
reſighned to the ſer-
uice of the Glorious Queene of
Heauen whom the Angels ſerue
the

the Arch-Angels adore , the
Thrones honour , the Cherubins
and Seraphins respect, and in fine
the highest aduāced in the Court
of Heauen account it their Glory
to make Court vnto Knowing
how aduantagious her fauour
would be to them, for if a Courtier heer accounts it for so high a
felicity , to haue the glory of
possessing the heard of some great
Princesse as promissing himselfe
great honours and dignities from
thence, and how much more , if
besides al this he were assured
of that dearer place in her memory as shee could refuse him
nothing but if he chaunced to fal
into disgrace , would vndertake
his defence & reconcile him with
his Prince againe free him from
the punishments he had merited,
obtaine

obtaine his repeal if he were ba-
nifhed from the Court, and not
only reftore him to his former
eftate againe, but aduance him
higher then euer he was before,
what a bleffing what an exceffe
of Ioy would this fortunat fauou-
rit receiue from thence what
would he do, or rather what nor
do in gratitud for fo great an obligation? what meanes what fort of
feruices would he moft inuent to
honour her withal ! affueredly
both night & day, he would haue
no other thought then how to expreffe his thankfulnes to her in
fome particular manner, and then
would be no danger fo great, no
feruice fo painful he would not,
go through with al, to maintaine
himfelf in her better graces ftil.

And yet farr more happy a
thou-

thousand times are the seruants &
fauourits of the Queene of Heauen, in that they are assured she
is perpetually mindful of them
that she beares them an vnequald
loue, that they may hope the
Greatest of fauours from her and
that she cannot be wanting to
them in their afflictions that as a
faithful Aduocate she doth Embrace their protection in al oc-
currences, that she preuails her
self of al occasiōs to render the E-
ternal king her B. Sōne propitious
to them, and what is most of al
deliuers thē from eternal paines,
& brings them in fine to the pos-
fesion of the glory and happines
of the Kingdome of Heauen.

From al which we may gather
fiue rare Priuiledges those truely
deuote vnto the Mother of God
Inioy

Inioy thereby the firſt is that ſhe
loues them with a profound and
cordial affection; the ſecond that
ſhe honours them with diuers
particular fauours ; the third that
ſhe is alwayes ready to aſſiſt them
in their neceſſities as after as they
implore her aide; the fourth that
as a moſt careful Aduocate with
particular ſolicitud ſhe vndertake
their deffence and renders them
propitious the eternal King of
Heauen , reconciling them into
him , when they haue offended
him; the fifth and laſt that ſhe deliuers them from eternal damnation. Let vs conſider then and
examine them on by on which
great exactnes to animat euery
ſoule to the affection of ſo deare
and great a Lady.

THE

THE I. PRIVILEDGE.

How affectionat the B Virgin is to al deuout Christians who serue and honour her with humble reuerence.

ALTHOVGH 'tis true the sacred Virgin being al loue & charity loueth al, & like the Sunn sayes the deuout Saint Bernard) displayes alike the beams of her sweetnes & benignity ouer al the world. Yet certaine it is withal shee beholds those with a more deere regard

A   who

who loue her and render her the most dutiful seruices and are most assidual in reuerencing her. And most laudable and holie is that obsequiousnes by whose exteriour signes is manifested the interiour affections of the hart, for so (as S. Gregory says) the proofe of the affection is the performāce of the thing. Now how reciprocal the B. Virgins loue is to vs againe, her self declares in those words attributed to her by the Holy Ghost; those who loue mee, I loue; as much as to say, I haue a particular loue for those who affect mee with al their hart and soule, and endeauour to render such honour as they imagine the most acceptable; and what fort of loue it is her self declares in another passage of Scripture where shee sayes:

I am

I am the mother of beautious loue; signifying the loue shee affeas her seruāts with, to be firme, compleat at al parts, and truly worthy so diuine and louing a mother.

This glorious Queene tenders vs as her owne Children, in that shee is our Mother, and so neare and strait a bond tyes vs together, as her being a descēdant from our generation, flesh of our flesh, bloud of our bloud, bone of our bone, for which reason shee cannot but affect vs much, especially if wee endeauour to deserue it by our constancie and fidelitie in seruing her. Shee is the Mother of *Iesus-Christ* true God and Man, God is our Father : *Our Father which art in heauen* : his Sonne Iesus-Christ our brother : Go to

A 2   my

my brothers, (fayes he to Mary
Magdalen : Oh infinit fweetnes
of loue !) Go to my brothers and
tel them, I afcend to my father &
your father, to my God and
yours. The Bleffed Virgin is
then our Mother , Iefus Chrift
the increated Word our brother, and the Eternal father our
father.

,, Conforme to this , S. Ber-
,, nard on thefe words, *Ecce mater*
,, *tua,* behold thy Mother, argues
,, thus : If Mary be thy mother,
,, O man , (fayes he ,) then Ie-
,, fus Chrift is thy brother, his
,, father thine , his Kingdom
,, thou haft right to, and Con-
,, fequently the grace of Mary is
,, thy riches , fince the mother
,, Vfually layes vp for the Chil-
,, dren , fo thy neceffities goe
                              vnto

,, vnto her hart; for the mother
,, for thefe wants of her Chil-
,, dren is moued at hart; O take
,, her then for thine. Thus S.
Bernard : that eloquent Doctour. And certainly our condition is moſt great and highly aduantag'd aboue al others, to haue
the Mother of God, Empreſſe of
the Vniuerſe, for Mother, and
her only ſonne, the King of glory,
glory of Kings, and our true God
for brother. An honour the Angels could neuer glorie in; For
when or where (ſayes S. Paul)
did God euer ſay to them as he
ſayd to man, ſpeaking to our
Sauiour Chriſt? Thou art my
ſonne, to day I haue begotten
thee.

These spirits, as happy as they are

haue neuer an Angel of them al, inuested with their Angelical nature, they can say is God; whilst wee inuested with our humane haue the God of Angels himselfe wee cannot only say is man but euen our brother too; nor do wee find it was euer sayd to any of thē as it was to man; Behold thy Mother, in the person of S. Iohn, who (according to the Doctours) personated and stood at the foote of the Crosse for al mankind, whilst the Sauiour of vs al deliuer'd him the pretious treasure of his Mother in trust. Let vs conclude then, that her loue is generally towards al; but in a more particular manner towards those who assume her for their Mother, and by most affectionat wayes seeke out her safeguard and protection.

Moreouer

Moreouer wee muſt conclude
this glorious Queen hath ſhewed
more affection to men, then
euer ſhee did to Angels: In imitation of the eternal Father,
whom in her actions, ſhee of al
others, moſt nearly imitats: and
for proofe that his loue is more
to vs then them, but conſider with
what pretious guifts he hath honoured vs, for ſo the greatnes of
the preſents giuen by the louer
to its beloued manifeſtly declares the greatnes of its affection
to it; and what guifts are thoſe
the eternal Father hath beſtowed
on the ſonnes of the earth! Let
the Angels harke, and the Archangels lend an eare, and al the
heauenly Hierarchies remaine aſtoniſh't at ſo wondrous a liberá-
litie. Behold the infinit preſent,
A 4　　the

the infinit guift with God hath
giuē & prefented the world withal, neuer to be enough vallued
neuer to be æqualled. God hath fo
loued the World, as for it he hath
giuen his only fonne; out of his
exceffiue loue to free it from the
miferie in which it was; and what
on the Angels hath he beftowed
the whilft? nothing but their eternal beatitud merited (as the Diuines hold) by one fole act of
their Wil; another thing it is, and
of other valuation which he hath
beftowed on men, to giue his
owne Sonne to faue them, then
his giuing the Angels their eternal beatitud; fo fayes S. Bonauenture, To giue his only Sonne
for the impieties of men was a
greater matter, then to the merits
of Angels to giue eternal life. Let
                              vs

vs grant then and freely acknowledge the loue of God & his holy
Mother, more splēdidly shinning
on men then Angels, since more
admirable haue been the effects
produced of it, towards them then
these, and more obliging to repay
them reciprocally againe.

But this is not al, nor doth our
gratious Mistris stay heere, to repay affection with affection, but
by the transport of her loue shee
passes to honour her seruants, sometimes with her visits, sometimes to comfort them with her
owne deare presence & her Blessed sonns.

An example of which, amongst
an infinitie of others, wee haue
in the new reformed Mirrour of
Examples, and it is this : There
was a yong Virgin some. 14. yea-

res of age, so deuoted to the Mother of God, as shee employed in her seruice almost al her dayes and nights; in which her pious exercises shee continued for almost seauen yeares space, euer beseeching her deere mistres, & patronesse so to fauour her, as shee might behold her B. Sonn iust as shee had brought him into the world; vntil atlast one night) and 'tis beleued to haue been Christmas night) retiring her selfe into an Oratorie shee had in her fathers house, & there with prayers and teares iterating her petition, behold sodainly there appeared vnto her the Queene of heauen, accōpanied with Myriads of Angels, who gratiously reaching her, from her owne armes to hers, her heauenly Infant, sayd : Behold

hold heer my dear daughter, what
you haue ſo much deſired ; take
him, embrace him, and at your
pleaſure ſolace you with him ; at
this the deuout Virgin tooke him
in her armes, and embracing and
kiſſing him, vſed al the tender-
neſſes à deuout loue could expreſſe an affection in ; when in
the heate of her kiſſes & embra-
ces, the diuine Infant darting a
look at her, had been able to haue
pierc'd a farr harder hart, thē hers
asked her if ſhee loued him ? that
I do, ſaid ſhee, and confirmed it
with a thouſand new blandish-
mēts: but how much do you loue
mee ? more then my body ; and
how much more ? more then my
very hart ; yet, how much more
then that ? alaſſe, ſaid ſhee, it is
impoſſible to tel you that, let it
fond

speak for mee, and so with a profound sigh shee cócluded the dialogue, and with that her life; her hart bursting in the midst, vnable to containe so much of loue was in it, when (we may piously imagine) the B. Virgin tooke her white soule in her armes, & deliuering it into the hands of Angels, they with sweete and melodious harmonie conducted it to heauen. At sound of which celestial musick, those of the house accurring & forceing open the Oratory doore, found the dead corps extended on the ground, and exhaling so much sweetnes, as it seemed al the most pretious perfumes of the world had gon to the embalming it. Amongst the rest, two Fathers of S. Dominicks Order were present

sent, who, as they dissected her, to find out the cause of so sudaine & strange a death, perceiued her hart inscribed with these wordes in golden letters : O my Iesus, I loue thee more then my selfe, for hauing Created, redeemed, and adopted mee by thy holy grace. Whereby wee may perceaue, how great was the loue shee bore to the sacred Mother and her Sonne, and how greatly they are aduantag'd by it, who loue them with such tendernes of affection.

I am inuited by this so excellent an Example, to the recital of one other no lesse excellent, taken out of the first part of our Chronicles of S. Francis, one of the most Exemplar patterns of deuotion to the B. Virgin as euer was. This holy Saint in
visiting

viſiting a certaine Conuent ſomewhat remote, had appointed him for companion one of raw yeares and rawer experience in Religion. They being arriued at their iourneys end, the Saint after ſome light refection, retired himſelfe ſome-what more early then ordinary to his repoſe, the bitter to riſe at the accuſtom'd houre of Mattins with the reſt. Meane while his Cōpanion ſingling out one of the Cōuent of as litle ſpirit as himſelf, began with bitter inuectiues to inveigh againſt the Saint, ſaying (by way of mockery) that he could eate, drinke, and ſleepe with the beſt of them, and euen to paſſion ſeek his owne commodities, the whilſt he kept them ſhort enough, and ſtinted them as he liſted; & after many

many such idle & misbe seeming
speeches, resolued at last to watch
him narrowly that night; whither
he rose at the nocturnal Houres
with the rest or no, and so he did.
When behold, about the second
Vigil of night he might perceaue
him rise & take his way towards
the adioyning Wood, and following him stil with his obseruation,
at last he saw him fal prostrat on
the ground directing many a sigh
to heauen & many a praier wing'd
with the fire of loue vnto the
Queene of heauen, beseeching
her of the fauour to let him see
her B. Sonne iust as he was infan-
ted into the world: scarce had he
vtter'd this, when the B. Virgin al
enuironed with celestial light appeared vnto him & with incredible sweetnes presented him from

her

her owne armes with her B. Sonn:
The Saint rauish't with so high a
fauour, and rendring al possible
thanks for it, began to vie kisses &
regards of him, to the emulatió of
his mouth & eies, whether should
take the more delight in him. This
amorous duel lasted til breake of
day (not only to the exceeding
consolation of the S. himself, but
of that Religious too;) whē being
constrained to restore his pretious
burthen to his Mothers arme againe, the visió rauished. At sight so
this so diuine a miracle, the poore
imperfect Religious man was so
moued & edified, as he threw him
self presently at S. Francis feet,
beseeching him of forgiuenes for
his fault which he humbly there
confest, and dying afterwards to
his imperfections, became to liue

a

a perfect Religious man conſum-
mat in al vertue and perfection.

From theſe two examples re-
ſults an infallible proofe of this
firſt priuiledge, & the B. Virgins
exceeding loue to thoſe who hold
deare her memory, and employ
themſelues for her ſake in works
of piety, whilſt they become each
day more faithful and feruent in
ſeruing her. And theſe are thoſe
ſhee moſt eſpecially doth regard;
theſe are thoſe ſhee moſt particularly doth protect, neuer abando-
ning them (vnleſſe they abandon
her) vntil ſhee hath happily guided her to heauen. Al with the
deuout S. Bernard in theſe few
words doth comprehend: It is impoſſible for you B. Lady to forſake
him, who places his Confidence
in you, ſince you are the Mother
of

of mercie it felfe. Who would not endeauour then, to the vttermoft of his forces, to be deuout to her? who, to gaine the fauour of fuch a Queene, would not count it honour to feeke out al occafions of feruing her? 'tis no fmal one, I grant, to ingratiate ones felfe with an earthly Queen; but with the Queen of heauen 'tis the greateft that can be imagined; an honour not only to be preferred before al the greatneffes of the earth but al wee can receaue from any Saint in heauen. And thus much may fuffice for the firft Priuiledge.

THE

THE II. PRIVILEDGE.

*Is that the B Virgin is most
liberal, and accustomed to
bestovv frequent graces &
fauours on her seruants.*

OVE that is true &
perfect (as daily ex-
perience teacheth) is
neuer satisfied in che-
rishing the thing be-
loued, and obliging it by guifts
and fauours, euen to dispoile it
selfe of al it hath most precious,
to giue vnto it. So, Ionathas loue
to Dauid was so great, as the scripture sayes of him : Ionathas loued him as his very soule ; he
pluck't

pluck't off his richer garments &
gaue to him; & to paint his freind-
ſhip forth in more liuely colours
it adds : He gaue him euen his
ſword, his cincture , and his bow.
Now if worldly loue hath ſuch
force ouer the harts of men, what
hath the diuine ouer the harts of
the Saints in heauen , eſpecially
of the B. Virgin , who excels al
men and Saints together in the
perfection of loue ? Let vs vna-
nimouſly ſaye and acknowledge
then , that ſhee is ſo affectionat
to thoſe who honour her, as ſhee
neuer ceaſeth ſhowring on them
the heauenly draw of the moſt
pretious guiſts and richeſt treaſures there; for which reaſon ſhe
is deſeruedly ſtiled by our holy
Doctours , the Treaſureſſe of al
the riches in heauen, and diſpen-
                              ſatrix

satrix of al the guifts of God : A
dignitie to which his diuine Maiestie hath exalted her in heauen;
an honour to which aboue al his
subiects he hath preferred her.
The keyes of euerlasting riches
are in her hands, the coffers of
Paradise ful fraught with diuine
treasures are at her command, of
which shee is nothing sparing;
but liberally giues to al that wil,
to al that aske, to al that can pretend least right vnto them; shee
being most riche and powerful,
and her wil equaling her power
both in heauen and earth.

To you al power is giuen (sayes
the mellifluous Doctor deuoutly
discoursing with her : both in
heauen and earth, so as you haue
ability to do what you wil, and
so her selfe auowes how riche she
is

is in diuine treaſures where ſhee
ſayes: The grace is in mee of al
way and truth, in mee al hope of
vertue and of life. And knowing
how much they import vs, her
ſelfe inuites vs to demand them
of her: Come to mee al, ſayes
shee, who are deſirous of mee,
and be replenish't with my generations. See how ready our riche celeſtial Miſtris is, to make
vs participant of her celeſtial riches, and ſee how much she affects our good, who offers vs ſo
bountiouſly thoſe goods and honours, as are neither beholding
to Time, nor fortune. Why doe
wee tarry then ? why are wee
then ſo ſlow, why shake wee
not off this dulnes that poſſeſſes
vs ? doe wee feare perhaps a diſ-
dainful repulſe from her ? a difficult

ficult accesse? a fastidious regard?
ah no, shee is so farr from it, as
shee is very sweetnes, meeknes
it selfe, and there is nothing, in
earth or heauen more affable,
more courteous, then shee; as S.
Bernard testifies of her, where he
sayes. What humane fragilitie is
it, that feares to approch & haue
accesse to the Virgin Mary, in
whom is nothing austere or
terrible, but shee is al humanitie,
al ful of charitie and curtesie
towards al.

Let vs then with the common
opinion of Doctors hold for certaine, that whosoeuer hath, recourfe to her in their necessityes,
and duly implore her ayde, are
neuer by her frustrated of their
hopes. O sweet Lady (says the
ancient Theophylact) you are a
powerful

powerful protectrix of man; for
O immaculat Virgin, who euer
plac't his hope in you, and was
confounded, or who amongſt
men, hath implor'd your clemen-
cie, and been abandoned?

Free then from doubt and aſſured of the truth, let vs haue recourſe in our neceſſities to this
moſt powerful and pittiful Lady,
and make our ſelues worthy of
thoſe high fauours and prerogatiues ſhee ſo boūtiouſly rewards
her faithful ſeruants. Withal ſhee
is, as wee haue ſayd, the Treaſureſſe and diſpenſatrix of al the
guifts of God; ſhee is the neck
(ſayd S. Hierom) by which our
Sauiour who is the head, infuſes
into his body the Church al that
ſpiritual ſenſe and motion, by 'tis
animated and ſuſtained; ſhee is
the

the body of the tree by which the roote imparts life vnto the boughs, producing flowers, leaues, fruit, and al that in the tree excels either for ornamēt or vse; Shee is the Concaue of the fountaine which first receaues plenty of its liuing waters of grace, and after distributs them to seueral pipes according to their seueral capacities. Wherefore S. Bonauenture most maturely sayes: it is wonderful what a collection there is in the Virgin of al the pleintines of grace, & how from thence it is deriued to others, as from its proper source so aboundantly as S. Bernard affirmes, al the Citizens of heauen, al the men in the world, al the soules in Purgatory, nay euen in Hel it-selfe, do homage to her as to their

souc-

soueraigne Lady , bowing their knees before her in submissiue & beseeming reuerence. So there is no profession nor estate , but is subordinate to her, especially Religious the glory and richest ornament of the Church , which is euer sheltered vnder the protection of her wings , whose founders haue in particular māner stil been deuout vnto her , by which meanes they haue obtained for th.m and their spiritual children particular fauours stil.

Who is not astonish't at the admirable loue of that great Patriark Saint Dominick to the B. Virgin from whom next to God, his Order acknowledges a dependency, and to haue receaued al its lustre and conseruation. For what remarkable graces and fauours
hath

hath he not receaued by her interceſſion? Of this loue vnto her
ſeruice, although there were no
other proofe, yet that of the inuention of the Roſary were ſufficient.

For how manie thouſand ſorts
may we imagine hath this holy
Saint led by this excellent deuotion to the honour and ſeruice of
the Queen of heauen? how many
Princes and Monarkes of the
world, how many Queens and
Ladyes of worth & honour, how
many of al ſorts and profeſſions,
euen whole people and whole
worlds, (as witnes the new World
Antipodes to ours?) neither can
we paſſe in ſilence the ſurpaſſing
affection S. Francis bare to her,
which was ſo great, as he would
often in amorous paſſion com-

poſe

pose verses to her praise , and
either sing them himselfe , or
cause them to be sunge by his Religious. From whence it came,
that he still obtaine'd whatsoeuer
fauour he demanded of Alm:
God, for himselfe in particular,
or his Order in general , by the
intercession of this beloued
Virgin.

One amongst the rest for its
raritie I cannot but recount , and
it is one of the greatest and most
stupédious miracles of the world,
by which such an infinity of
soules haue been deliuered and
dayly are from the very torments
and paines of Hel it selfe ; And
this is that great and admirable
Indulgence granted at the request
of S. Francis by our Sauiour
Christ in the presence of the B.
Virgin

Virgin and innumerable bleſſed
ſpirits, to the Church of Aſsi-
ſium commonly cal'd Our Lady
of Portiuncula; which by reaſon
al Chriſtendome is ſo much taken
with the deuotion, as alſo it
being ful of rare myſterie and
worthy of general notice, we
wil breifly make you the narra
tion of.

S. Francis once feruently praying for the ſaluation of ſoules,
an Angel appeared to him and
ſummon'd him to the Church,
where it ſaid our B. Sauiour and
his mother, with a world of Angels were expecting him. At this,
he ran thither, where, being arriued he ſaw our B. Sauiour ſeated on the high Altar in a maie-
ſtike ſeate, accompanied by his
Mother, and incircled by multi-

B 3   tuds

tuds of Angels ; When falling
proſtrat at his feete, he was ſoone
excitated by this comfortable
voice of his moſt gracious Lord:
Know, Francis, thy praiers are
arriued vnto mine eares , and for
that I know the affection and
ſolicitud of you and your Order
for the ſaluation of ſoules, demand of me what grace you
pleaſe for their avayle, and I wil
grant it you. S. Francis at firſt al
trembling at ſight of ſuch a maieſtie , by the ſweetnes of theſe
words ſecur'd at laſt waighing the
importance of them , thus anſwered : O Lord, not but that I
am conſcious of my great vn-
worthines to obtayne any grace
from you much , leſſe ſo great an
one , but that you are pleaſed to
add this to the number of my in-
                                nume-

numerable obligations beſides ; I accept your gratious offer , and humbly beſeech of you for the good of euery Chriſtian; that al who viſit this Church , hauing firſt duely confeſt, and communicat ; may obtaine a plenary pardō and Indulgence of al their ſins: And you O glorious Virgin and gracious aduocatrix of euery Chriſtian , I befeech you ioyne your powerful interceſſion with my Petition for it; when in concurrency with it , conuerting her ſelfe towards her B. Sonne she ſayd : My deereſt ſonne , whom I once had the honour to beare in this wombe of mine , grant I beſeech you this his petition to your faithful ſeruants, ſince the ſaluation of ſoules (then which there is nothing you more eſteeme)

teeme) is so much concern'd in it.
Grant it to my Temple heer, to
your honour and the edification
of your holie Church. When his
diuine Maiestie casting a gratious
eye towards S. Francis there prostrat before his throne, saye vnto
him: Francis, though what thou
demand'st be much, yet thy desire
merits much more, in being so
conforme to mine; wherefore I
grant thee the Indulgence thou
desirest, with this condition that
thou haue recourse vnto my soueraigne Vicar, who hath the
free dispose to bind and loose al
heer on earth, and of him demand
from mee the grant of it. So the
vision vanished; when early the
next day S. Francis tooke his
iourney towards Perugia where
Pope Honorius then resided with
the

the Court of Rome ; and there humbly kissing his feete he declared how al had past , and the occasion of his comming there. At hearing of which, the Pope granted him a Plenary Indulgence (in manner afore sayd) for one day in the yeare, though as yet what day in the yeare, was vndetermined , it hauing neither been presixed by his diuine Maiestie nor his Holines, vntil al last vpon this occasion:

S. Francis returned to his Conuent , was once at mid-night in deepe contemplation in his Cel, when the Angel of darknes transform'd in shape and voice appeared to him like an Angel of light, and said: Poore Francis, why are you such a Tirant to your seife ? why wil you destroy nature with

B v   your

your superfluous watchings thus?
Do not you know the night
was ordain'd for man to rest, and
that sleep is the principal stay and
support of life? Alasse, you are yet
in the April of your yeares, haue
a care then of your self & be ruled
by me, if not for your owne sake,
at least for your Orders, whose safety wholy depēds on yours; you
are of a strōg & robustious complexion promising a long life, if
you shorten it not by your indis-
cret austerityes, beleeue it, these
extrauagant deuotions are infinitly displeasing to Alm: God,
who in al things is most delighted
with mediocritie. The Saint hearing this, and by this discouering
the malice of the wicked Enemie
to delude him by a false suggestiō,
suddainly, started vp, and al naked

ran

ran to the adioyning wood, where
he so long rowled him self amōg
the sharpe thornes & bristy thist-
les til the bloud issued amaine frō
euery part of him; when in mockery of his body, now (said he)
had it not been better for you, to
haue attended stil to the suffrings
of your God, then to suffer this,
for attending to the Enemy.

He had no sooner vtter'd this,
but instantly behold a cleer light
spred it-self ouer al the wood, and
chasing darknes thēce; on the one
side he saw the ground al icye (for
it was in the hart of winter) and
on the other close by the thornes
(he embrewed in his bloud) the
white and red rose freshly springing; whilst the Angels in multituds made a lane for him from
that place vnto the Church, singing

ing in triumphant manner as he
went : Goe , happy Francis , goe
where thou art expected by the
King and Queen of Heauen; and
he knew it was no illusion , by
their so miraculously reuesting
him a new; then gathering fower
and twenty of those Roses mixt
of either sort , he went towards
the Church treading on riche ta-
pistry al the way, the Angels (as
we said before) making a lane for
him on the right hand and on the
left ; where being arriued , he beheld our Sauiour seated & accompanied as in the former apparition; when with al low submission casting him as his feete ;
Most sacred Maiestie : (sayd hee)
before whom both heauen and
earth do homage, it pleased your
goodnes to grant mee formerly

a

a plenary Indulgence, in that manner (as I desired it) now my petition is, you would appoint a certaine day for the obtaining of it, and this for your most deare and gratious Mothers sake : Our B. Sauiour thus answered him. Francis, thy deserts are such I can deny thee nothing, wherfore I grant thee thy petition, and appoint the first of August to be it; then the Saint rendring him al possible thankes replied; but how, O Lord, shal this bee divulged vnto the world, or on whose faith wil they take on trust so great a miracle : For that (said our Bl. Sauiour) be it my care to prouide, in the meane while haue you recourse againe to my Vicar heer on earth, carrying with you eye-witnes of this apparition one of your

brothers

brothers with some of those Roses you haue gathered there, and feare not, you shal see your desires accomplished. In this amiable sweet, and admirable manner was granted to Holy S. Francis the famous Indulgence of our Lady of Portiuncula, by the soueraige Monarch of Heauen and earth, a grace so great, a fauour so sublime, as neuer was heard of, neuer mortal man receaued the like. By which, and the fore mentioned Institution of the Rosary by thy great Patriarch Saint Dominick, wherby his Order hath been so much ennobled, may cleerly be perceiued, how extraordinarily this bountious Ladye recompences them, who serue her affectionally and faithfully.

THE

THE III. PRIVILEDGE.

Hovv the B. Virgin helps and Comforts her faithful seruants, in their afflictions.

H<small>E</small> third Priuiledge this heauenly Lady honors her fauourits which is : neuer to be wanting to them in their afflictions, a thing which neither ought nor can be doubted of. For if she loues them, and if she loues by effects to shew it, what greater effects of it, then in their moſt neceſſitous times to

reteine

receiue and fuccour them , or
when is the tyme to declare ones
loue and affection , if not then?
A true frende loues at al tymes
(fayth the holy Ghoſt) and a brother is tried in affliction; and can
wee thinke any in heauen or earth
more true to thoſe she loues then
the B. Virgin is ? or that in her
affection she ſerues the times, &
loues not ſo wel in pouerty as in
riches , in ſadnes as in mirth , in
aduerſity as in proſperity ? Oh,
no , A true freind alwayes loues,
but eſpecially in time of affliction , for that is the touch ſtone
of true freindship indeed , and
then she shews hers moſt. What
a happines , what a felicity is it
then, for thoſe who loue & ſerue
her faithfully to haue ſo powerful a freind as she who when the
burthen

burthen of misery lies heauiest
on vs can lighten vs , when we
are deseruing more of pittie then
of loue , out of pittie loues vs
more ; and who lastly in the dark
passage of death,.where so many
leese their way , leads vs safely
out of it,and not forsakes vs then,
when al the world besides forsakes vs , but comforts vs on our
death-beds , when al in this life
turnes to our more discomfort
which we did most affect ; and
stands vnto vs , when whole legions of diuels are beseidging our
souls , sheilding vs from euery
harme , now defending vs from
impatience by assuaging our
griefes, or fortyfijng our mindes
against it , now from sorrow,
with the ioy she brings vs , now
from despaire with the assured
hope

hope of our faluation, and finally
with a new re-inforcement of
Angels puts al our Infernal enemies to flight.

The glorious S. Antony of Padua (as is recorded in his life)
when he was affalted with any
temptation, vf'd no other weapon
then to repeate this Hymne of
hers: *O gloriofa Domina,* &c. when
prefently he fhould come off with
victory. As it happened one day
when being at his prayers, the
diuel (at defiāce ftil with al good
workes) fet fo furioufly on him,
and ftrayn'd his throat fo cruel
hard, as he had almoft ftrangled
him, til the Saint hauing recourfe
to his accuftomed armes, inforc't
him to leefe his hold. In like
manner al the article of his death
being prepar'd vnto it before
                              with

with al the sacraments, and saying with his brethren the seuen penitential Psalmes, he concluded al Deuotions with that, to which he was euer so deuout: *O gloriosa Domina, &c.* when behold, the B. Virgin appeared vnto him, infinitly cōforting him with her apparition, and adding to the Consolation of it, the sight of her deare sonne and his deare Lord; at which with incredible ioy he deliuered his soule into his Bl. hands. Go reade al histories, search into al records., see if you can find any that euer trusted her with their confidence, and were deceau'd; who inuoked; her in their necessities and were not releiued by her? so as we may wel applye those words of the Wise man to her, and say: Behold al

ye

yee nations of men and Know,
that none hath plac't their truſt in
this ſoueraine Lady ; & been Cō-
founded. And could we but ſee
riſing from their ſepulchers al
thoſe who haue been deuoted to
her and could Demand of them
where euer she had fayld' them at
their need or no ? Infallibly they
would al with one accord ſay with
S. Bernard couerting themſelues
towards her . Let him be ſilent O
Bl. Virgin, who can ſay you wer
euer wanting to them when they
inuoked you in their neceſſityes.

We wil add another Example
taken out of *Scala cæli* , of a high
miraculous ſtraine, exemplifying
this priuiledge to the life , and ſo
conclude it.

A certaine Matron of excel-
cellent endowments , and much
deuo-

deuoted to the Queene of heauen, sending her sonne to serue
a certaine Prince, in whose seruice his father had spent his life,
charg'd him before he went by al
the tyes by which Heauen and nature had obliged him to her, to
be deuout vnto the B. Virgin, in
al his necessities to implore her
ayde, and neuer omit dayly, at
least to say vnto her honour an
Aue Maria, with that short prayer : O B. Virgin, bee propitious to me at the houre of death
This he faithfully promised, and
being at Court inuiolably obserued, though for the rest, Youth
easily falling into disorder, and
the Court being a place most slippery, this yong Gentleman frequenting the ! societies of some
deboished ones, soone tooke the
taint

taint of their focieties, and became as deboish't as they; and (as
there is no ftay in wickednes
when one is falling once) at laft
he was fo deepely plunged in it,
as the Prince when no admoni-
tion would ferue the turne firft
banish't him his prefence then
his Court, and laft of al his ter-
ritory. Impatient for this dif-
grace; and conuerting that was intended for his cure, vnto his great
maladie, what did this defperat
youth but affociat himfelfe with
certaine theeues, who harbou-
ring in the woods infefted al the
Prouinces about, and was foone
chofen their Captain; when hauing a more fpatious feild to exercife his wickednes in, he foone
became fo ingenioufly fierce, fo
wittily cruel, as in fiercenes and
                              cruelty

cruelty he excelled them al , sparing no humane creature , and no
fort of inhumanity. But fee Heauens iuftice , which comes with
the greater force vpon vs , the
greater turne it makes ear it comes at vs. He raigned fome yeares thus , in his wickednes , til at
laft it was his fortune to be taken
and deliuered vp bound hand and
foot to the publick Magiftrate by
them to prifon , where the fame
day he was condemned to die ; of
this hauing fecret intelligence;
(ftrait as if the mafke of his wickednes were but then taken off)he
began to perceaue the vglines of
it, fo as to deteft it , be wayle and
curfe his fortune , and euen waxe
defperat for the greefe and fhame
it had brought vpon himfelf and
his family. When behold while
he

he was in this difpofe of minde,
there entred dungeon a man
of mightie ſtature and horrible afpect , who addreſſing
himfelfe vnto him, Offered, if
he would be ru'ld by him, to
free him thence ; and who are
you (ſayd he) almoſt freed by
his promiſe from the feare of his
apparance , I am the diuel (ſayd
he) ſent hither by my Prince to
deliuer you ; obey but his commands; at hearing this , without
any long delay , the priſoner (as
it is ordinary with wicked men,
to preferr the fafety of their
bodyes before their ſoules ,) anſwered; What-fo'ere you are, you
wil oblige me by ſo great a benefit to what foeuer you demand;
then firſt (ſaid the diuel) you
muſt renounce Ieſus Chriſt , his
merits

merits ; and al the principality
he hath ouer you; I doe (sayd he)
and it suffices to haue found a
Prince of your Maister so ready,
to pleasure me; next you must renounce al the Sacraments & communion with his Church: and that
too, answered he. Then to Mary
his mother, and al your hope of
fauour and assistance from her; at
this he demurr'd, and entring into himself call'd al his thoughts
together in consult of what he
had promised his Mother, & what
he had performed til then; when
resolued at last he answered? that
he would neuer doe, farr be it
from me (sayd he) how neere soeuer my life be cócern'd in it, to offer such an affront to my deare Patronesse, and so to iniure her who
so hath obliged me : No, rather I

C   offer

offer her my self (if she daine to
accept it) whether she would
haue me liue or die , to be wholy
and absolutly at her dispose. Confounded with this his resolution,
the diuel vanished , when he touched vnto the quick with a repentance for his hainous offences a-
gainst his Lord & Sauiour, at first
began to weep & sigh most bitter-
ly, then had his recourse to the ordinary refuge of sinners the Mother of God saying vnto her with
a sobbing voice, a thousand times
interrupted by his greefe: O most
sacred Mother of mercy, haue pitty on me miserable sinner, and do
not quite reiect me from before
your sight; I aske not of you deli-
uerãce from my bonds, I beg not
of you to saue my life, for that cõ-
sidering the heinousnes of my crimes) were too much for me to as-

ke and you to grant; I only hūbly
craue you would obtaine for me
pardō of my sinns of your B. Sōn,
and assist me as I haue often pe-
titioned you at the houre of my
death: in this sorrowful and deuout manner he past al night, and
the day was no sooner come, but
he sent for a Confessours and
confest him of al his sinnes; this
done, he was led forth to execution; the poore soule vpon his
way euer calling vpon the Blessed Virgin his Patronesse to assist
him at that time of neede; On the
way it was his chance to passe by
a litle Chappel, where was erected a statue of our B. Lady, which
he beholding vehemently cried
out sighing in most dolorous māner: O thou hope of sinners help
me; the Image at this aduanc't a

C 2   litle

litle, and in fight of al the people
fauourably beckened vnto him
with the head; which he perceiuing befought the Magiftrate he
might be fuffred to approach vnto
it, and kiffe its feete in thankfulnes for fo great a fauour; which
being graunted him behold iuft
as he bowed downe to kiffe its
feete, the Image laid hold of him,
and held his arme fo faft as al the
force the Officers vfed could not
take him thence, the people beholding fo great a miracle, prefently al cried out, a pardon, a
pardon, & deliuered him whether
the Magiftrate would or no; in
prefence of whom he made the
ful relation of al his paffed life,
prayfing and glorifying God in
his B. Mother for it, whence returned into his Countrey, he became

came so reformed a man, as he became as remarkable afterwards for goodnes and vertue, as he had been before for vice and wickednes.

From this History we may vnderstand, that the Mother of God is neuer wanting to her seruants in their necessities, that she is our refuge, our safegard, our comfort, & remedy of al our paines, greefs and afflictions; for which reason S. German Patriarch of Constantinoble vses these words speaking vnto her : There is none saued without you (sayes he) O Blessed Virgin , none deliuered from their greeuāces but by you, none but by your mediation receaues any guift from God, none but at your suite obtaynes forgiuenes of their sinnes; O Virgin worthy of

al glory and praiſe , who next
to your ſonne takes ſuch an eſpe-
cial care of humane kind , as you;
who defends them more affectionatly then you ? who ſuccours
them more readily then you,
when they are aſſalted by temptations? who extenuats their faults
with greater charitie ? excuſes
them to God , and exempts them
from puniſhment due to their offences.

Wherefore (in continuation
of his diſcourſe) ſayes this holy
Patriarch ; Let the afflicted haue
recourſe to you , let thoſe who are
loſt vpon the Sea of this worlds
miſery in danger to be wrack't,
looke towards you as to their
Pole-ſtarr , that ſhal'ſafely direct
you to their Port. Thus this pious
Saint ; By which , and that which
hath

hath been sayd before, this third
Priuiledge is enough illustrated
which the deuout seruants of the
B. Virgin haue. Let vs passe vnto
the fourth.

THE IV. PRIVILEDGE.

Of the deuoted to the B Vir-
gin, Which is to haue her
in Heauen for their assu-
red Aduocate.

ERTAINLY it is
a great comfort for
poore Widowes and
Orphans, and such
afflicted soules, when
their busines lies at Court on
which depends the safety of their
liues

liues or estates, to be assured of
the fauour of some great one who
hath the Princes eare; but if the
Queene her selfe should take
their affayre so to hart, as to employ her whole authority therein,
an vnspeakeable comfort would
it be to thē? Now how much more
cause of Comfort haue we poore
despicable creatures, Knowing
we haue in heauen for Aduocate
to Alm: God the Queene of Heauen her selfe, who defends our
causes, vndertakes our prote-
ctions, procures faithfully our
saluations, and omits no diligēce
in fine to render our soueraine
Iudge propitious vnto vs. O assured hope, miserable sinners
haue in such an Aduocate with
Alm : God, so as the Church
stiles her in her Antiphon: *Eia*
ergo

ergo aduocata nostra &c. who hauing in her hands the mannage of
our affayres, we cannot but she
wil expedite al to our aduantage,
which made the elegant Cassian
Say : Al the helpe of human-Kind
Consists in the multitud of the
fauours and graces of the Blessed
Mary.

The holy Church to our no
smal cóforts with suffrage of the
common opinion of Saints, attri-
buts to the B. Virgin certaine E-
pithets of honour in expression of
the good offices she doth vs , cal-
lig her Mother of sinners, Mother
of mercy, the vniuersal hope and
refuge of al, Aduocatrix of mortals, as also Redemptrix, Pacifier,
and Mediatrix betwixt God and
man. Nor needs there any other
proofe then experience it selfe,

how much al forts and conditions
of Chriftians are deuoted to her;
the Pilgrims cal her their Mother,
the Pupils their Tutrix , the fick
their Phifician , the fea-faring
men their hauen , the Culpable
their Aduocate , the Trauaylers
their Guide, the Captaines their
deliuerer,the forfake their refuge,
the defperats their Hope , the afflicted their Comfort,the oppref-
fed their Releife; In fine , al the
world acknowledges her,and cals
her the only Refuge of the miferable , and the aime to which al
Chriftian people commonly direct their vowes and ardenteft
defires; knowing for certaine she
can do al she wil, and she wil doe
nothing but what may be beft
for vs.

For which reafon al forts haue
recourfe

recourse to her as to their cheife treasure in Heauen, the source whence al their graces spring, & the gate at which they neuer knock in vayne; In so much as from the middest of the vastest wildernes, from the bottome of the deepest sea, from the iawes of death, seru'd vpon the earth bed to it, to be deuoured, from execution and the very stroke of the hangmans hands, she hath deliuered al those who haue duely inuoked her, and miraculously feed them from the dangers they were in; so sure and gratious a freind she is at need to the affli-cted and distrest.

Soe she incessantly makes suite and instance for vs, at that great Tribunal, where her B. sonne presides as soueraine Iudge for it

(as

(as S. Bernard fayes) thefe three requifit parts of a good Aduocate Firft , a great repute in the Court she pleades in ; and the fauour of the Prince or Iudge' ; next the sufficiencie to plead ; and laftly fuch an affection to the caufe she vndertakes , to goe through with it what ere it coft.

Now to declare vnto the ful, the B. Virgins authority with her fonne , not Only exceeds my capacitie ; but the capacities of al men and Angels. Wherefore let it suffife to fay (leaft in offering at more we fhould incurr but the repute of prefumption) that she is Mother of God ; from whence by Confequence we may gather that she is of vnlimited power with him , and that the leaft inti-mation of her defire carryes with

it

it (as I may saye) the force of a Command. And so the holye Church desires no more of her but , *Monstra te esse matrem*; shew thy selfe a Mother ; And in another prayer we saye : Grant he may eare our prayers , who Was borne for vs , and daigned to be thine. So in our ordinary litanies we supplicats her thrice to intercede for vs, as one who hath more power and authority , with the Blessed Trinity, then al the other saints. S. Gregory of Nicomedia in his Sermons to her prayse , cals her Omnipotent in her aduocation; And S. Peter Damian addressing his speech to her ; It manifestly appeares (sayes he) O B. Lady ; *Quod Dominus fecit tibi magna* : how great things God hath done for you in giuing you al

al Power in this world and the
next, euen to be able to afford
the moſt deſperat a ful aſſurance of their ſaluation; for the
Omnipotent taking fleſh of
you, how can you be leſſe then
omnipotent with him ? and in
continuation of his diſcourſe
he ſayes ; you approch , O
Powerful Lady , to the Altar of
our humane reconciliation , not
in ſuppliant wiſe as do the other
Saints , but with the authority
of a Mother to a ſonne, which
is but to aske and haue.

Touching the ſecond Condition of her Capacity of the
charge in rightly vnderſtanding our neceſſityes, beſides that
she is ſtiled the Mother of mercy and our Aduocat , both,
which

which suppose her abilities for it, this example may suffice out of the Chronicles of the Friers Preachers, whose Order in a special manner is deuoted vnto her.

In the Citty of Marcels there ws a deuout Virgin endow'd with al Saintly vertues: who on a certaine day being present at Compline in the Church of the Dominicans, while they were singing the accustomed Antiphon, *Salue Regina*, was rauished in extasy, during which she sawe fower things of singular remarke : The first, that when they pronounced these wordes : *Spes nostra salue*; hayle our hope ; the Blessed Virgin with a gratious Coun-

tenance

tenance returned them their
falutation : The fecond, that at
thefe word ; *Eia ergo aduocata no-*
*ftra:*O therfore thou our Aduocate with a lowly inclination to her
B. Sonne she feemed to intercede
for them: The third, that at thefe
wordes : *Illos tuos mifericordes ocu-*
los ad nos Conuerte: Behold vs with
thofe merciful eyes of thine : she
caft vpon them a moft deare and
fweet regard : And the fourth
thefe words : *Et Iefum benedictum*
fructum ventris tui nobis poft hoc exi-
lium oftende : and shew vs hereafter Iefus the bleffed fruit of
your wombe : she by turnes prefented him there prefent in her
armes to al the Religious : This
vifion, returning from her extafy,
fhe declared to her Confeffor , a
man both holy , lcarned, and dif-
creet,

creet, with great feeling of deuotion and temdernes. Which
example may moue vs, often to
haue recourse vnto this our heauenly Aduocate, supplicating her
by this deuout Antiphon of hers,
in which she seemes to take soe
much delight and complacence.

The third Condition requisit
in a good Aduocate, is faithfully
to acquit them of their charge; &
it is impossible for vs to comprehend, how faithfully and care-
fu.ly the Mother of God nego-
tiats for vs our affaires in heauen,
or to conceaue the admirable effects thereof. So as shee hath al
these requisite parts of a good
Aduocate. Mary wāts not power
(sayes the deuout S. Bernard)
nor right addresse to obtaine
what shee Petitions for; for she
                                    is

is the Mother of Wifdome; nor
the will to employ her felf to the
vttermoft in our affaires, for fhe
is the Mother of mercy. To which
laft, in being our Aduocat, fhe is
(in manner) bound; For fo the
Iurifts hold they are bound, faithfully to negotiat the caufe they
vndertake. Befides being fo good
as fhe is, & fo affectionat towards
vs, how is it pofsible fhee fhould
not take to hart an affaire of fuch
confequence as is that of our faluation; and aboue al, being our
Mother too, as wel as his, to w-
hom fhe interceds for vs : a fträge
circumftance that fhe should be
both Mother of the King, and fui-
ter, of the Iudge and Criminal, of
God and Man; which muft needs
render her much concern'd in the
affaire to make an attonement betwixt

twixt God and vs; and (as S.Bernard, sayes) be euen impatient til she haue performed it. In being our Aduocat then we must suppose her incessantly pacifying her sonns anger towards vs , and mediating a reconcilement for al those , who haue recourse vnto her and implore her assistance: which may be clearly perceaued from this following Example recorded by Iohn Grithi of the Order of the Minorits.

There was (sayes he) a souldier, a man of most wicked life , and violater of al things sacred and prophane: whose wife not withstanding (a holy and pious woman) had obtain'd of him , by solemne vowe to fast in honour of the B. Virgin euery Saturday, & saye an *Aue Mary* as ofte as he
beheld

beheld her picture: which he did, nor euer omitted to doe. One day, (more to a voyd the vehement heat abrode, then for any heate of deuotion he had within) he entred the Church: where beholding an Image of the B. Virgin, he began to doe as he was accustomed. When behold , he had an apparition of our B. Lady on the Altar holding in her armes her B. sonne al couered ouer with wounds and the abundance of bloud that issued out of them: Moued to pitty at the sight of so pittiful a spectacle, the Souldier (diuinely inspired) drew neerer, and had the boldnes to aske our B. Lady who had so wounded her B. sonne ? Thou , and suche sinners as thy selfe , (replyed she with an angry countenance) who

who exercife more cruelty on him with your daylye crimes, then euer the barbarous Iewes who crucified him. Thefe words ftruck the Soldyer into fo liuely repentance for his finnes, as he replyed with a forrowful hart & weeping eyes: O B. Ladye, it is true indeed, I haue been as great a finner as you affirme; yet do but obtaine for me of your B. fonne a ful pardon and remifsion of what is paft, and I heer vow vnto you to be as obfequious hereafter to him, as I haue been rebellious heretofore,

No, fayd the B. Virgin, I am refolued to heare you no more, nor be any more deceiued by you; for whilft you finners cal me the Mother of mercy, you make me with your finnes the Mother of al greef

and

and affliction : Oh B. Lady (fayd
he)be not fo inexorable I befeech
you to my prayers, but remember
you are the Aduocat of finners,
and haue (in a manner) contrac-
ted by it , an obligation to intercede for them , and confequently
for me the moft greeuous of them
al , and moft needing your inter-
ceffion : Heer the B. Virgin moued to pitty with his words, caft a
pittiful eye towards her fonne &
fayd : Pardon then I befeech you,
O my fonne , this poore finner
who fo humbly petitions you;no,
fayd the facred Infant, his offences are too great to be forgiuen;
but she perfifting ftil to coniure
him by al the charmes she thought
moft powerful to moue him ; at
laft feeing his anger fo refolutly
bent nothing would moue it , she
arofe

arofe and placing him on the Altar went downe ready to caft her felfe vpon her knees before him; which when her B.Sonne beheld, fufpecting her intention, he ask't her what she meant to doe? why, faye she, to caft my felfe heer proftrate at your feete, and neuer rife til you haue granted me my petition; O mother, fay the tēder Infant, you know the force your wil hath with mine; For your fake, I pardō this wicked wretche and in lieu of fatifaction admit him, to kiffe my wounde; encouraged al this by the B.Virgin, the foldier drew neere, and whileſt with incredible Confolation, he kiſt wound after wound behold, vnder the touch of his mouth they al heald vpp. The B.Infant thus recouering, the vifion vanished

nished, when the foldier prefently hafting home; diftributed
al his goods vnto the poore, and
then by common confent, he and
his wife feparated, and entred
into Religion. O happy foules
the while, and happy Conuer-
fion which I would to God al finners would imitate. To cunclude
then, fince we haue fo powerful
an Aduocate in heauen of the B.
Virgin; let vs make no delay but
preferr our fupplications to her,
expofe our necefsityes, and petition her for a redreffe of them;
the meane while, more to inte-
reft her in our affaires, let vs be
affiduous in honouring her, and
ingenious in finding out the way
to do it beft, omitting neither
day nor night to falute her with
humble reuerence, alwayes remembring

membring that a litle of feruorous deuotion is better then a
great deale negligently performed.

THE V. PRIVILEDGE.

*How the Mother of God sa-
ues her deuout seruants,
and renders them worthy
of eternal life.*

HE glorious Queen
of Heauen is not cō-
tented yet, to che-
rish her seruants af-
ter a deare manner,
to enoble them with singular prerogatiues, to succour them in their

D   neces-

necessities, and espouse the care of
their affaires; but with al she deliuers them with her prayers from
merited punishment, and directs
them vnto heauen; which soueraigne fauours ought to oblige vs
perpetually to serue her, especially this last which I esteeme the
principal'st of al, and worthiest of
greatest admiration, in that according to the common opinion
of Doctours, 'tis in a manner impossible, that any one should be
damned who liues & dies deuote
vnto her, be they neuer so farre
gone in wickednes, but they reco-
uer at last, and through the mercy
of God (as we haue a daily experience) make a happy end. Now
if any obiect, that this cannot be
without a præuious dispose of
Grace and a sufficient sorrow for
their

their finnes; I anfweer, it is true, but this the inceffant prayers of the B. Virgin obtaineth for them too, whofe power is fo great with her B. Sonne, as by vertue of that, fhe obtaines for them a perfect Contrition, and entire remiffion of their fins. And this, the deuout S. Ambrofe in thefe words affirmes : O B. Mary, fayes he, you embrace with a mater-nal affection the poore finner def-pifed by al the World, and neuer forfake him til God pacified by your prayers hath receaued him vnto Grace.

Let vs Confirme this verity by the example of a common Curtezen conuerted by the inter-ceffion of our B. Lady. We reade in the great Marial, of a lewd wo-man wholly abandoned to vice

D 2   and

and licentiou{s}nes ; who not with
{s}tanding neuer omitted dayly {s}ea-
uen times to bow downe in reuerence of the B. Virgin , and to
{s}ay an *Aue Maria* in honour of
her ; Now among{s}t her frequent
pro{s}titutions , it happened one
of principal quality haunted her
company , who{s}e wife being a
vertuous Lady and one {s}ingularly
deuoted to the Queene of Heauen ; did beare her hu{s}bands il
demeanour {s}o impatiently, as one
day pro{s}trating her {s}elfe before
an Image of the B. Virgin she
{s}ayd : O mo{s}t {s}oueraine Lady,
mirrour of al purity , how can
you {s}uffer this , to {s}ee one {s}o sha-
mefully abu{s}ed, and an impudent
woman thus glory in my iniury?
I be{s}eech you punish her {s}o exemplarly, that she may be a terrible

rible warning hereafter for al
the reft ; Grant this requeft O foueraine Lady , if not vnto the deferuing of my prayers, and heate
of my feruices, Yet at leaft to the
pitty of my Caufe , and the into-
lerables of my iniurye. When
behold a wonder, the Image thus
anfwered her; deare feruant , it
is impoffible for me to fatisfie
your defire, I know your wrongs
and the iuft caufe you haue to be
offended at them;but know whit-
al , she is fo deuout to me , in
midft of al her wickednes, as I
cannot proceed againft her as you
defire; only this I wil doe , for
your comfort , I wil petition my
Sonne for her, that he would
turne her hart , and that she may
turne vnto amendment ; which
was done , for within few dayes

after there happened a miraculous Change in both the Adulterers, both he and she reforming of their liues, and liuing chaftly & exemplarly euer after. And is not this a rare priuiledge then, of thofe deuoted to the Queene of Heauen, that let them be neuer fo deeply plunged in the abyffe of fins, yet she can deliuer them thence? I cal it a priuiledge, fince for their particular deuotion to the Queene of Heauen they are particularly exempted from the law of other finners.

This affectionat deuotion befides to the B. Virgin is a probable and experimented figne of predeftination, I fay only a probable one, becaufe 'tis true, none knowes whether they be worthy of
loue

loue or hate, and an infallible one in this life there is none.

With what contented harts then should we liue, did we but exercise our selues, in good works and frequent acts of deuotion towards the B. Virgin? and what hope of eternal felicity should our minds be raysed vnto free from al those doubts and feares of their saluation, which those who walke not in the way of God and the seruice of his B. Mother, do meet withal so often? And from hence proceeded the firme Confidence of Saints, grounded on the knowledge they had of the excessiue liberality & promises of Alm; God, to Conquer as it were the Kingdome of heauen by the force of Chrifts merits and their owne coopera-

tions,

tions, by which they were so encouraged in the midst of their
most greeuous sufferances, as nothing could daunt or discourage
them.

S.Bernard in his sermons on
Septuagesima sayd, that although
'tis true no man knowes for certaine whether he be in the grace
of God or no, since in this life no
man hath an infallible knowledge
of his saluation; Yet (sayes he,)
(and 'tis a saying of vnspeakable
comfort those who are perseue-
rant in good) we are not to be
disanimated , nor giue ouer the
working of our saluation with an
anxious feare , since we haue for
our comfort a hope of it arising
from so many euident signes of
it , as it seldome or neuer decei-
ues our trust. Heare himself : le'ts
                                    neuer

neuer trouble our ſelues (ſays he) with any ſuch doubt as this , for we haue ſuch certaine markes & manifeſt arguments of our ſaluation, as in thoſe who haue them, there is no doubt at al.

The Example of S. Hilarion comes wel to the Confirmation of this; drawing towards his end, and being affrighted with the apprehenſions of death in this manner encouraged himſelf; Go out my ſoule, ſaid he , What feareſt thou ? 'tis ſeauenty yeares ſince thou begon'ſt to ſerue thy God, and now art a feard of death? Behold what an aſſurance and firme hope of ſaluation a vertuous life can giue to the ſeruants of God, and how cleere and euident the markes are of eternal ſaluation to thoſe who liue vertuouſly. Let

D v   euery

euery Chriſtian then endeauour to liue ſo, and he ſhal feele in himſelfe the contentment of this ſecurity, which is ſo great, as it exceeds al the other Contentments we can haue in this mortal life. Which S. Francis wel experienced, when hauing had a reuelation, how he was predeſtinated to be ſaued, through exceſſiue ioy for a long tyme he could vtter nothing elſe, but Bleſſed be God, bleſſed be God. And if theſe ſignes of Predeſtination are to be ſeene in any, in a moſt particular manner are they to be ſeene in thoſe who are deuoted to the B. Virgin; which from this following Example wilbe made manifeſt.

S. Anſelme in his booke of the miracles of our B. Lady, recounts
this

this story : how the Diuel (who
out of his inueterat hate to man,
seekes al meanes possible to ruine
him) once putt himselfe in seruice to a noble man, hauing first
taken on him a humane shape;
whose humour he knew so wel to
comply withal, as in short space
he had al the care of his family
committed to his charge ; and
pursuing the aduantage he had
ouer his wil and his affections, he
was still suggesting some mis-
cheife or other to him, now coun-
seling him to wrong this man,
now to murther that , so as no
day past in which he made him
not guilty of some notable wickednes; now it hapned one day,
this noble-man walking in his
woods accompanied with his
crew of ruffians, encountred with

a certaine holy Preiſt, whom he
violently layd hands on and carryed priſoner to his Caſtle; at
night the Prieſt ſignified to him
he had a ſecret to impart vnto
him, in which he was much concern'd, but it muſt be in preſence
of al his ſeruants; the noble-man
with a longing deſire to know
what it was, aſſembled them al
together except this diuel, who
retired himſelf, and tooke for an
excuſe ſome indiſpoſition of
health: the Prieſt by diuine reuelation knowing the craft of the
wicked enemie, told the noble-
man his preſence was ſo neceſſary among the reſt, as without it,
there could be nothing done.
How would you haue him come
-anſwer'd the noble-man, ſince
you heare them ſay he cannot
ſtand

stand on his legs he is so ill? All's
one for that, replied the Preist
againe , some meanes must be
found out to bring him heer.
The noble-man seeing him so re-
solut , commaunded two of his
seruants notwithstanding al his
excuses to see him brought, which
was don, and he came counterfai-
ting the sickman vnto the life ;
when the holy-man before them
al, Coniured him presently in the
name of Alm. God to declare who
he was , and to what end he had
put himself in seruice to that noble-man ? At this , the diuel casting toward him such a looke,
was able to make tremble the bol-
dest there , answered plainly he
was the diuel , and his end of seruing his Maister was , to procure
his destruction which he had long
since

fince effected, had not the B.Vir-
gin interpoi'd her felf : & wherefore, fayd the Prieft? why only
for a certaine cuftome this wicked wretch had (fayd he) dayly
to falute her humbly on his knees
feauen times both morning and
euening, and as oft reherfe in her
honour the Angelical falutation.
Which if I could haue once per-
fwaded him to omit, as I endea-
uored often, I had prefently kil-
led him, and taken his foule to
hel, and hauing vttered this in
fhooting himfelf like lightning
out of the roome, he prefently
dif-appeared, with his hideous
roaring leauing them al in horrible affright, of which the holy
man taking his aduantage, exhorted them al to penance and bitter
life, and efpecially the noble-
                              man,

man, with whom he prevayled fo
much, as he wholly conuerted
him and made him as exemplar
in goodnes, as he had been in
wickednes.

By this example we fee this
Priuiledge, and the exceeding
value of this interiour and exteriour reuerence exhibited vnto
the Queene of Heauen. And if
this hapned vnto one fo wicked
a man as he, how much more
fpecial care wil fhe haue of al
thofe, who ferue her in holines
and purity of life? with what a
Deare tendernes wil fhe vnder,
take the protection of thofe? and
what a watchful eye wil fhee
haue to defend them from the affalts of the Enemy?

Let vs then conclude this holy
and profitable exercife with our
duly

duly honouring the B. Virgin
both with exterior and interior
reuerence affered vpp with al becoming obfequioufnes ; fo shal
we ingratiate our felues , with
our moft deare and bountious
Lady , by whofe meanes we shal
obtaine that quiet and repofe of
hart , which is to be preferred before al worldly things.

* * *

The Conditions requisit in a seruant of the B. Virgin, and first of Humility.

S those who are entettain'd in seruice of any earthly Prince to obtaine their fauours, endeauour to appeare endowed with al those vertuous, parts and qualityes by which they are taken most : so those who would be fauoured by the Queene of Heauen , must whilst they serue her, endeauour to be qualified with those vertues she is cheiflly delighted in; which

are

are principally thofe fhe exer-
cif'd her felf in, whilft fhe was
conuerfant in this mortal life, as
namely *Humility*, *Corporal chafti-
ty*, *and purity of hart*, to which
we may add our diligent frequenting and receauing the Sacraments, the only meanes to con-
ferue vs in internal purity and
to begin with humility, which
is the foundation of al other vertues.

It is certaine, no other vertue
was more perfpicuous in her then
that of humility, though she had
al the reft in their higheft exaltation; and this appeares by the
account which she made of it,
teftifyed by thefe words of hers:
*Becaufe he hath regarded the humi-
lity of his handmayed : therefore al
generations shal call me bleffed :* as
much

much as to say ; that God only in
regard of the lowlines of her humility , had elected her to that
high dignity , of being his Mother. And if to be humble of hart
(according to S. Dorotheus) is
to account abiectly of ones selfe
and preferr al before them , of
what excellency was this vertue
in the B. Virgin , who from those
words of her , *Because he hath be-*
held the humility of his handmaide;
we may suppose (as F. Arias wel
obserues) she had so humble an
opinion of her selfe , as she re-
puted her selfe of al other creatures the most contemptible.

This vertue then shining so
resplendantly in her, we may suppose to haue been that, most took
the eyes of her B. Sonne, & made
him soonest chose her for Mother,

as

as a sonne in this world if it lay
in his choice would soonest make
electiō of her for mother , whom
he sawe endued with those graces and qualities which were most
in account with vs ; and this seemes to be inferred by these words
of the text : For he hath beheld
the humility of his handmayd ;
and as if she would say; the sonne
of his heauenly Father hath cast
a fauourable eye on me his humble seruante , and thought me
worthy of his loue ; not becaufe
I am nobly borne, wise , prudent,
conuersant in the scriptures , and
the like ; not for any beauty or
corporal perfection , but only because of my humility. For so although al her other vertues were
most exceeding grateful to Alm.
God, yet that of her humility was
　　　　　　　　　　most

most of al, it being as it were the foundation of al the reſt. In ſo much as according to Lyr'as interpretatió, it was in her the principal diſpoſition to the conceiuing of the ſonn of God; & ſo ſays S.Hierom. God was rather moued to be incarnat in her womb by her humility then another vertue elſe. In this vertue it was (as S. Mechtild vnderſtood by reuelation) she ſo exerciſed her ſelf and laboured ſo carefully, as she atteined the height & perfection of it; by this ſhe came to ſo abſolute a knowledge of her ſelf; by this she would leſſen her own proportion cópared either vnto God or man. And diſclaiming wholy from her owne deſerts; by this she came to attribute al the fauours ſhe receiued to the ſole benignity of Alm.

God

God, and rendred him thanks
for them acordingly ; by this in
fine she came neuer to vtter word
in her owne prayse, or to giue
willing eare to others praises,
neuer to take vain-glory in any
thing, but to attribut al the glory
to Alm : God, incessantly magni-
fiyng and praising him, with rendring him infinity of thanks for
his great fauours towards her; and
so she begins her Canticle ; *My*
soule doth magnifie our Lord, and my
spirit exults in God my Sauiour. And
to the model of this excellent
vertue of hers, are al her deuout
seruants to conforme their actiõs,
and expresse the portraiture of it
in their soules ; when how grateful wil thy appeare in the eyes of
this glorious Queene, when they
present themselues before her in
this

this riche equipage. Certainly
there is none hath any vnderstanding or difcourfe in him, that wil
not humble himfelfe vnto the
ground and thinke him the moft
abiect of al other things , who
fhal but confider how profoundly
humble the B. Virgin was euen
in that exalted ftate of hers of
being Mother of God, more holy
then the Angels , and more pure
then the very fun-beames themfelues. And who confidering his
owne vilenes and extraction only
from a litle earth , his being fubiect to fuch a world of faults and
imperfections , his becoming
through finne enimie to God, and
companion of the diuel , wil not
in imitation of the B. Virgin caft
themfelues into the bottome of
humility , from the topp of pride
and

and prefumption, whereon they
ftand

A great and neere Imitator of
this humility of hers, was her
great feruant S. Francis, who
was ambitious of nothĩg fo much
on earth, as to be accounted the
moſt abieĉt of al his brethren and
for his owne part he eſteemed
himſelfe no better then a colla-
tion of al the abhominable vices
in the world, and one of the moſt
greeuous finners as euer was;
which in one fo great a Saint and
in whom fo many vertues were
aſſembled, was the more rare,
and worthy the greater wonder
and imitation.

And although this in general
might fuffice to affeĉt vs to this
excellent vertue, yet I wil fett
you downe in particular a Method

thod for the attayning it, giuen
by B. Tecelam a Religious of the
third Order, to a certaine freind
of his : who demanding of him
by what meanes the vertue of
Humility was to be acquired, he
answered; Contemne thy selfe,
and al thou hast in the world;
esteeme euery one more perfect
then thy selfe; and haue a slight
opinion of none ; make great
esteeme of thy faults, and litle of
thy vertues & perfections: count
litle al the good thou dost to
others, and the harme thou dost
for great ; and thou shalt be in a
faire way to Humility. To this
we may add S. Bonauentures ad-
vice for the attayning this holy
vertue; Abase thy selfe as lowly
as thou canst (sayes he) ; Imagine al men thy betters, and thy
E   self

felfe hardly worthy to be their?
flaue, and fo thou shalt arriue to
a tranquillity of mind, and neuer
be molefted with offence or mo-
ved to impatience. By which excellent documents we may learn
to find out true humility and the
wayes that lead vnto, a Iourney fo profitable for our foules
which our B. Sauionr perfwads
vs to vndertake faying : Learne
of me to be meeke and humble
of hart. And thofe feruants of the
B. Virgin who are fo indeed, efpecially women-kind are to shew
it in their exterior comportments
as they goe abrode in publique,
shewing neither pride nor vanity
in their lookes nor apparel, and
compafing both according to the
exact rules of vertue and decency
For what an vnworthy thing
                            were

were it in them, to appeare in
the B. Virgins sight lesse vertuously adorn'd or decently be-
haued, things which she in her
selfe so much abhorr'd as S. Epi-
phanius testifies of her together
with diuers others, that her owne
habit was euer plaine and simple
without al affectation of riches
or novelty, and (which is an
euident signe of her owne purity
(neuer subiect to any spott or
stayne, but stil the more whit (as
it wer) for her wearing it, This
humility in their habits then let
women learne of her, euen for
the loue of our B. Saiuiour Christ
who died naked on the ignominious Crosse for vs, and let not
such vanity vnworthy of a Christian appeare in their habits and
exterior garbe.

Surius in the life of S. Elizabeth daughter of Andreas King
of Hungary and wife of the Lant-
graue of Turing, recounts a storie that comes wel to purpose
here. She (says he) one day attired in her Maiestick robes in
al her pompe and brauery entred
the Church, where beholding iust
at the entrance a Crucifix, she sodainly made a stand, and in great
bitternes and compunction of
hart, began in this manner to enter into comparison of her self
with it; Shal, my Lord and Sauiour, remaine al naked nayled
to this hard Crosse, & shal I miserable sinner as I am, go at pleasure vested in these costly robes,
curiously embrodered with gold
and precious stone? Shal my
sweet Redeemer haue these diuine

uine hands of his faftned to the
Croffe with cruel nayles, & fhal
I weare on mine, al the delica-
cies that can be gott? O my Iefus,
fhal I fee thee, the only Spoufe
of my hart, haue thy head tranf-
pearc't with thofe fharp thornes,
& fhal I with fuch magnificence
weare a crowne on mine? Alas,
and can I behold him abandoned
by al his freinds, and inhumane-
ly left for a prey, to the outragious vfage of his enemies, and
fett vp as a marke for them to
fhoote their horrible blafphe-
mies at; whilft I my felf go with
fo great a trayne, wayted vpon
and honoured at euery turne? O
miferable, moft miferable as I
am, is this the loue I beare to my
Sauiour Chrift, are thefe my ac-
knowledgment and gratitud for
E 3   a

al his benefits? And in saying this
a sodaine palenes, ouercast her
face, and a greeuous fainting cast
her in a trance : when returning
out of it, she firmely purposed
neuer to admit of superfluity a-
gaine in any thing she wore, &
de facto euer after she went so
mortified in her apparrel, as most
commonly she had vnder it a rug-
ged hayre cloth, and as often as
the Dukes occasions absented
him from her, she would be so
coursly attired, as no poore woman but went better clad.

And certainly it is a deplorable
thing euer with teares of bloud,
to see what excesse of apparel &
voluptuousnes raignes amongst
women now a dayes, so as they
seeme to place al their their felicity (as it were) in a newfangled
fashion

fashion or attire. I would they knew or considered how displeasing it is to Alm : God, or how many soules their vaine curiosities and foolish pride haue precipitated and cast downe to Hel, and what lamétable harmes haue had their origin from thence; for they are not only the cause of their owne sinnes, but also of others participation with them, whilst in regarding them the bayte hath been but layd by the Enemy to draw thousands vnto hel. Which perhapps we should hardly Credit, did not the holy Ghost it selfe affirme it : Turne away thy face (sayes he) from a woman Curiosity adorned, for many haue been taken by the beauty of women, and become reprobate ; a horrible thing to

E 4   ima-

imagination. And how many
Religious men haue we seene
drawne by the attraction of beauty, first to insinuat themselues
into their familiarityes vnder the
pretence of sanctity and spiritual
conuerse, and after by degrees so
deeply engaged in their societies,
as without hazard of their saluations they haue neuer been able
to get out. The whilst with a
deafe eare they haue neglected al
the inspirations of heauen, flattering themselues with certaine
pernicious Maximes grounded
vpon I know not what imaginarie shew of good manners and
curtesy; For what (will they say)
should we turne our backes to
them? and what were that but to
giue them cause to thinke vs
Clownes, and iustly to accuse vs
of

of difcurtefy and inciuility. But happy is the foule the whilft that reiects thefe vaine feares , in a matter in which their faluation is fo much concern'd, and preferr their foules immortal good before 'al other humane refpects. Let women therfore take warning and leaue off in time , al affectation and fuperfluity in their behauiour & attire leaft they incurr as great or greater punifhment then fhe did, whofe ftory I wil here relate, out of the fecond part of the Chronicles of the Frier-Minors.

A Religious man of the Prouince of Sicily, praying one day in the Church of his Conuent , had the apparition of a woman al naked prefented before his eyes, whom he coniuring in the name

of

of God, to declare vnto him what
she was, she anſwered with great
shame and confuſion; I was (ſaid
she a woman of fashion and quality in my dayes, and of plentious fortune, al which I abuſed
ſo, to his offence who gaue it me,
as in al my life I had no other
thought, than how to adorne me
in moſt curious manner, and follow ſtill the faſhions of the time,
till coming to die it, was God Al-
mightyes mercy to me, I ſhould
repent me of my ſinns, and with
true Contrition make an entire
Confeſſion of them, by which
meanes I had them al forgiuen
me on this códition that I should
for penance of my former vanity,
off attire, wander in this manner
naked vp and downe the world;
and hauing ſayd this, she diſ-ap-
peare

peared. Where is to be noted, that
although the poore soule for its
greater Confusion imagined she
was a spectacle to al, yet none
saw her but those whom God Almightie pleas'd to reueale this his
secret iudgement vnto, in whom
it excited rather a holy feare of
the seuere punishments of Alm.
God , then any vnlawful imagination or desire.

Let those then who desire to
render themselues acceptable in
the eyes of the B. Virgin endeauour with al their might to become humble both in the exteriour & exteriour humility being
the only vertue on which God
bestowes his most aboundant fauours. God resists the proud (says
the holy Scripture) and giues his
grace to the humble. And the
most

moſt ſure and infallible way to heauen is true Humility. Humility (ſays S. Auguſtin) is the Queene of vertues, the deſtruction of vice, the mirrour of Virgins, and the throne of the holy Trinity.

In fine, humility is that, which beſt teaches vs both to Know the deceipts of the diuel, & to auoyd them, being knowne; as was reueal'd to S. Anthony, when beholding one day in viſion al the world ſett with ſnares about, he cried out; O Lord, how is it poſſible for one to eſcape al theſe? and he was anſwered by a voice from heauen; by being humble, Anthony; for onely Humility ſtoopes ſo low, 'tis neuer entangled by them. And ſo we reade, how the diuel once appear'd to
                                        S. Maca-

S. Macarius with a mightie scithe
in his hand, threatening him as
if he would haue mowed him off,
& crying out against him; O Macarius, what a cruel strife is there
betwixt vs two, and yet how impossible it is for me to ouercome
thee: I do al that thou doest and
more, for thou watchest sometimes and I neuer sleepe; somety-
mes thou fastest but I neuer eate;
I thinke as obiectly, and sett as
light as by the worlds vanityes
as thou; only one thing there is
in which thou surmountest me,
which is that profound humility
of thine. We see then, what admirable force this Christian Humility hath, to'ouerthrow pride,
and triumphe ouer the stratagems
and forces of the Enemy; a force
so great, as the very mention of
it

it is enough to put al the armies of Hel to flight; which I wil confirme by an example taken out of the Frier Minors Chronicle, and it is this.

In the Conuent of Perufia the Prouince, where S. Francis was borne, there was a Guardian of an auftere life, endowed withal the vertues of a good Religious man; now it happened that a noble man of the Countrey on Chriftmas-Eue fent an expreffe meffinger to defire him to fend one of his Religious the next day to fay Maffe for him, and it hapned iuft at the inftant that two of his Religious returning from a long iourney, weary with trauayling and almoft dead with cold and hunger, he prefently commaunded them to fatisfie the defire of

the

the Noble-man; which they as
presently vndertake without once
murmuring and repyning at his
cōmaund or alleadging for their
excuses their great necessities;
Going then with great humility
and obedience, behold they were
scarce halfe way on their iourney,
but they were ouertaken by night
and inuolued in so thicke a darck-
nes that they could not see their
way; which incommodity ioyned
to that of their hunger and cold,
made their case the more commi-
serable; when seeing themselues
so destitut of al humane helpe,
they had their ordinary recourse
to the diuine helpe beseeching
Almighty God, to succour them
in their so great necessitie, and
in the meane time going on,
though whether right or no they
could

could not tel; at laſt they hard
the ringing of a Bell, and their
eares directing their ſteps; at laſt
they arriued at a Monaſtery (as it
ſeem'd;) where hauing knockt,
the gate was preſently opened,
and al the Religious in flock came
to ſalute them; from thence they
convey'd them to their chamber,
where they had al things prepar'd
for their reſt & refreſhment with
great diligence; At laſt the Religious departing from them exacted of them a promiſe to make
them ſome ſhort exhortation before the next dayes Matins. Wel,
the morning being come, and it
ringing to Matins, the Religious
were al aſſembled, and one of
theſe good Fathers an excellent
Preacher began to make them an
exhorta-

exhortation taking for his text
these words of the Prophet E-
saias : A child is borne vnto vs,
and a sonn is giuen vs; on which
he discoursed most diuinely of
our Sauiours humility in descen-
ding so low to take vpon him our
humane nature , and whilst he
was in the heat of his exhortation he might perceiue al the Religious one after another slinking
away till at last there was only
left the Abbot in the Quire. Whe
al amazed demanding of him the
reason why his Monkes had left
him so ? your self are the cause,
sayd he , how is that possible answered the good man againe ?
Why (sayd the Abbot) you haue
discourst in such manner of I
know not what humility of the

sonne

sonne of God, as they neither
would nor could endure to heare
it prayſ'd and extolled ſo much:
for to diſcouer the truth vnto you,
we are not (as we ſeeme) Religious men but diuels, who in reward of your prompt obedience
to your Superiour haue been, cō-
ſtrayn'd to giue you that aſſiſtance
you haue receiued of vs to night,
and hauing, ſayd this, both he &
the Monaſtery and al diſ-appea-
red, leauing the good Religious
men mightily aſtoniſh't at ſo
wondrous an accident and in the
ſame place where they firſt hard
the Bell, from whence they tooke
their iourney towards the Noble-
man, al the way thanking and glorifying God for his great fauours
& benefits beſtowed vpon them.

Many other examples of this
great

great vertue I could recount, and
especially that of the B. Virgin,
who when the Highest had chosen
her for his mother profest her
selfe the lowlyest of his seruants,
& in her greatest honors went in
visitation of S. Elizabeth, and serued her for three space moneths;
then with what greater humility can be imagined? besides
how lowly did she matche her
self, onely to a poore Artificer, to
whom she continued dutiful and
obedient euen to death, comforting her selfe alwayes with those
who were most poore and humble; as we may gather by the mariage she was present at of that
poore couple at Cana in Galilee,
neither refusing her company to
the most greeuous sinners such as
was S. Mary Magdalen and the
like,

like; and al this humility in one, who was exalted to so high a dignity, as to be mother of God, and Queene of heauen & earth, was so much the more admirable and rare, that she should neuer boast her of any honour she had, nor be the more exalted in her mind for being so high exalted in dignity; but neither on this nor any other example for the present wil I further enlarge my selfe, not to exceed the limits of that breuity I haue proposed to my self.

of

Of the second Condition which the deuout seruants of the B. Virgin ought to haue, which is Chastity.

AND if the seruants of the B. Virgin be so grateful and acceptable vnto her by reason of their Humility, how great must needs her fauour be towards those, who add to this vertue that of Chastity too, which so purifies and embellishes a soule? in how singular recommendation must she needs haue them, & how tenderly cherish them? Humility and Virginity

nity were so equally in this Blessed Lady, as to which to giue the pre-eminence we do not knowe; so happy was her Virginy in being adorned with such humility, that admitted of no vaine presumption of it, and so happy was her humility in hauing the honour of such virginity, which defended it from al misprision and contempt; and what clearer testimony can there be of this holy Virgins immaculate Chastity then these words of hers; How can this be, seeing I know not man? And of her humility on the other side, then those which presently follow: Behold the handmayd of our Lord; be it don vnto me according to thy word. O what a mariage was heere of these two vertues in the B. Mayd, where chastity became

se

ſo humble, and humility ſo chaſt?
what higher dignity could there
bee, then to be Mother of God,
and yet ſhe profeſt her ſelfe his
humbleſt ſeruant, aba-ſing her
ſelfe as low as he had exalted
her, ſo as S. Antoninus had iuſt
cauſe to ſaye, that it was cheifly
the attraction of her humility,
which drew the ſonne of God
from heauen, to make in her
wombe another heauen on death.

Al then, but cheifly thoſe of
her owne ſexe, are to imitate this
B. Virgin in her Angelical purity, who is propoſed a paterne
and example vnto al. It wa's ſhe;
that firſt aduanced the ſtandard
of Virginity, vnder whoſe white
colours ſo many ſince haue
fought, and firſt ledd the way,
which ſo many Virgine-ſoules
haue

haue followed since, of consecrating theyr virginities vnto God
by vowe; in doing which (sayes
S. Anselme) she sauoured more
of diuine then mortal : neither
did the name of Mother any thing
derogat from the dignity of a Virgin, but rather dignified it the
more, adding the fruit of a mother
to the flower of virginity in a diuine & admirable manner. Where
fore with good reason she is stiled Virgin of Virgins; who began a paterne to al the rest, of
Consecrating their virginityes
to God; a work so grateful to him
and acceptable.

O happy and thrice happy Virgins, then, who perpetuate their
Virginityes by vow vnto Alm.
God, in spight of al resistance the
world doth make; seing besides
the

the many prerogatiues they haue aboue thofe who are wedded to men; they enioy by it fuch a Confolation of mind , as furpaffes al the Comforts in the world.

In confirmation of which , I wil relate the excellent difcourfe of Nereus and Achilles to S. Domitilla in commendation of virginity when they perfuaded her to Chriftianity. Thefe feing her curious in adoring her felf, tooke occafion from thence to difpofe her minde: Madame (fayd they) if you were but as follicitous to adorne your foule with vertues, as you are in fetting your body of , with thefe fuperfluous ornaméts to pleafe your fpoufe Valerian,without al doubt you would take the eies of Iefus Chrift with it , a farr more noble fpoufe then

F   he,

he, and one who would farr more
deserue of you, with whom you
should liue stil in an increase of
beauty : whilst your other would
only liue vpon the spoiles and the
decayes if it; To whom she answered, (yet vnskild in Christian
perfection, and one that knew
nothing but what the world and
flesh dictated vnto her) what can
be more happy fayd she, then the
state of mariage, which compri-
fes in it al that is of honour and
felicity? Alas, Madame, said Nereus againe,) you know no more
then the vaine pleasures which
vanish with this blast of life, and
are ignorant as yet (it seemes) of
those euerlasting ones in the
other life, and waighs the commodities of mariage al if, you
putt not its incommodities in the
other

other fcale , which I would haue
you carefully doe, before you
loofe, a good can neuer once loft
be recouered againe ; And what
good is that , faye she ? your liberty , anfwered he , which with
the litle of Virgin you muft forgoe , changing it for a feruile
eftate and flauish obfequioufnes
vnto one whofe humors you
know not and which perharps
may be fuch , as out of pure Iealoufy he may interdict you the
company of your neareft freinds,
and thofe who you moft efteeme,
behauing himfelfe fo harshly towards you , as no flaue but should
liue a more contented life then
you. Al this, halfe fmiling she
ask't him,whither his general rule
had no exception; for (fayd she)
I grant you Iealoufy is a vice but

too ordinary in men, which my mothers fad experience renders but too manifeſt, yet is it not ſo fatal to al the kind, but there is ſome ſo happy to be exempted from it, and amongſt the reſt, the excellent diſpoſe of my Aurelian promiſes him to be one. Achilles to this replyed, Madam, (ſaid he) be not to confident, for theſe yong louers in the heat of their pourſuite, the eaſier to attaine to their deſires, diſſemble their natural inclinations, and appeare more mild and gentle then they are; but thoſe once attayn'd, off goes the maske of their diſſimulation, and then you ſhal ſee how iealous they can be, how harsh and croſſe in their diſpoſitions, how iniurious to you in words, and not ſeldone alſo in deeds. But

ſup-

suppose them of a more temperat
humour and more gently inclin'd,
what priuiledge enioy they by it?
If you shal giue me leaue, I wil
tel you what: To beare a painful
burthen in the wombe nine moneths together, to waxe leane and
pale with it, to be subiect to a
thousand languors and disguists
the while if you haue no Children. Lord what discontents,
what repinning at it? If you haue
with what danger? and how often in giuing their life do Mothers loose their owne? what care
and trouble in their education?
What feares least al their labours
should be lost, and death make his
haruest of what they had sowne
with paine? then what disconforts
do they bring their parents with
their lewdnes and vntowardnes;

F 3   some

some liuing so as they wish they had neuerben borne ; others dying so, as they wish-they had neuer lived ; so as both a liue and dead, they seeme only borne, for their Parents affliction. At this; Nereus crossing his armes and lifting vpp his eys like one in extasie, concluded thus : O happy then the state of virginity which exempts vs from al these miseries and vnites the soule that is honored with it, to Alm. God O most riche and incomparable treasure, whose possession exceeds al esteeme, and repaires al losse; and O Diuine loue, and more then humane fortitude, by which a weake woman can subdue the flesh, & with a generosity aboue the weaknes of her sexe, wage warr with the world, ouercome

her

her appetites, and vanquish the
forces both of death and hel it-
self; for which they shal one day
enioy a Crowne, with which
none in heauen shalbe honoured
but they. With these speeches of
her deuout seruants, but much
more with those which heauen
spoke to her inward hart, the
Lady was so moued, as she presently consecrated her Virginity
to God, for whose loue vnto the
palme of Virginity she after added that of Martyrdome.

Now we are to note, there are
three sorts of Chastitys in the
Church, by either of which the
B. Virgins deuout seruants may
become grateful vnto her. The
first is Matrimonial Chastity,
when man and wife loyally obserue their Coniugal faith to one
ano-

another : The second is Vidual Chaſtity , when Widowes free from the obſeruance of man , liue afterwards in perpetual continency, & this excels in excellēcy the firſt degree , as S. Paul ſaies ſpeaking of widowes; *Yet they are more happy ſo,* ſayes he, *If you wil Credit me.* The third is Virginal Chaſtity , more excellent then both the other more perfect and more meritorious; and this is, when we cōſerue our ſelues in our integrity of body & mind dedicating our virginities to Alm. God , which, oh , how grateful how acceptable it is to the B. Virgin, who preferrs it before al other oblatiōs. Seing then al theſe three ſorts of Chaſtity, are with proportion both good and laudable , and with the B. Virgin of pretious eſteeme, let

those

those that are deuoted to her, be
they maid, widow, or wife, endeauour in their seueral degrees, to
present her with this gratefull offering, to which end they are to
resolue to fight manfully, for the
Enemies that oppugne it, are
both many and powerful, their
Arts ful of al ambushes, and their
endeauours incessāt for the ouer-
coming of vs: so as S. Augustine
considering the difficulty of the
fight, and rarenes of the victory,
with good reason sayd: *Amongst
al the warrs the Christians had, that
of Chastity was the most sharpe, and
pressed vs most ; where the Combat
lasted alwayes, and an entire victory
was neuer gott attayned vnto ;* and
those that naturely ponder it find
it true. For but consider how few
they are, that fight it manfully

indeed,

indeed, in compare with thofe who cowardly yeild vnto the Enemy, and we may truely faye, the diuel gaines by nothing more then this; for how many of al ages and conditions, of either fexe, doth the Enemy precipitate into this vice, who for the reft ftood firme enough? To which purpofe S. Auguftin hath a feareful faying: *Excepting Infants* (faies he) *this only finne is the occafion that fo few of the reft are faued.* Who at hearing of this, is not aftonished? & conceiues not a pitty of our-miferable eftate, to fee how headlong al runne vnto this vice. And as for the feruants of the B. Virgin, what excufe can they pretend for their exceffes herein? what wayes they to pleafe her, whilft they difpleafe her heere?

Do

Do they thinke, that saying their
beads frequently wil do it? or
their fastings on Saturdayes and
the like? Alas, no, they doe but
deceiue themselues, and the vsur-
pīg such an honourable title as to
be her seruants, whilst they are
such? Doth but more encrease
their damnation, whilst they a-
buse that name to the dishonour
of Chastity by which ought to be
cheefly honoured, and while they
put on the face of wearing her liuery, but weare the badge of her
Enemy in their harts. Alas, how
many may we imagine now in
hel, who were once deuoted to
the B. Virgin as wel as we, till
with a foolish presumption of
their saluation, they with a deafe
eare past ouer her sauing and diuine suggestions & sel: to which

if

if wee desire to be saued indeed,
we must lend an attentiue eare ba-
nishing from our harts, al motions of sensuality, and entertai-
ning al chast ones in their place,
or else we leese her fauour, and
it wil be wo with vs.

But aboue al for conseruation
of our Chastity, it is necessary to
flie al occasions and inducements
to the contrary, for this is such a
kinde of victory, as is best gai-
ned by flight, and they that frequently expose themselues to
daunger in it, are ouercome at
last. Wherefore let none enter into an ouer-wening of theselues
or their forces for any former victory, for they may easily leese in
a moment what they haue been
in an age a getting, and flight
occasion may rauish from them
that,

that , which many difficult ones
went to the obtaining of; and let
no humane or nice reſpect , make
them be wanting heer, to the care
they ought to haue of their chaſtity ; for many out of punctillios
of honour haue ſtood ſo long
vpon it , till they haue falne , and
many by daungerous familiari-
ties haue been deceiued. Rather
let them flie carefully the aſpect
and haunt of thoſe , whoſe com-
panies may endanger them , following the Counſel of our Sauiour in it; *If thy hand or feet ſcan-
daliʒe the , cut them off* , &c. *or if
thine eye, pluck it out* : which counſel ſome Saints haue followed ſo
neer , as S. Bridget in particular,
not only auoided in her ſelf al oc-
caſions of ſinning in this particular , but to auoid it alſo in others,
she

she prayed to Alm. God, he would conuert al the vertue she had into deformity : Others there haue been, that haue disfigured themselues rather then to giue cause to any temptation; and others rather then suffer the effect of it, haue willingly departed with their proper liues. Which I will confirme by an example taken out of the second part off the F F. Minors Chronicle.

A Burgundian Gentelman had a daughter so affected to the seruice of the Mother of God, that secretly from her tender yeares she vowed her virginity to her. This virgin had a corporal beauty, ioyned to the beauty of her foule, so taking, as it attracted to her the harts of al. Among the rest, a seruant of her fathers was

one

one , who omitted no arts nor
induſtries to oblige her to a reciprocal affectiou to him ; But this
not taking, his loue grew deſperat, and at length engaged him in
as deſperat a courſe; For his Lord
and al his ſeruants being gon a
hunting , he ſecretly , returned
home , when his daughter was
either not accompanied at al , or
els ſlenderly only by her maydes;
and taking that opportunity to
execut his wickdnes , went and
foūd her out, where in the Chappel she was proſtrat at her deuotions before a picture of the
Queene of heauen : into which
he entred audaciouſly and without any reuerence to the place, or
reſpect to the perſon , tould the
reaſon of his returne , and how
deſperatly he was in loue with
her

her, coniuring her by al the force
of a wicked eloquence to the ac-
complishmēt of his desires. Whe-
reat the Virgin was so struck at
the first, what with the impudence of the fellow, what
with the horror and vnexpected-
nes of his demand as she remayned a while deuoyd of speech and
sense, til at last rowsing her spirits vp, with a iust disdaine and
bashful anger, she answered him;
Gett hence thou impudent vil-
laine, and seek out some others
more fitt to heare and grant thy
suite then I: and whence is this
insolence in thee? haue you euer
seen any thing in me, that should
thus embolden it? but cease your
boldnes and your insolence, or
I know the way to bring you to
deare repentance of it the fellow

as

at this, growne wholly desperat;
and rageing no lesse for anger
then for loue , drew out his
sword, & fixing the point against
her throte, told her there was but
one way with her , eyther to resolue to dy, or to satisfy his desire;
thy desire (sayd she?) rather then
by me such a wicked desire shalbe
euer satisfied , had I a thousand
liues I would willingly loose
them al ; but you consider better
(said he) for assure your self I am
not in iest; Bee in what mind thou
wilt , replyed she , doe thy worst,
and when thou hast done , goe
vaunt to such as thou art , how
thou hast traiterously murthered
thy Lords daughter in his owne
house in defence of her Chastity.
This put him wholly into the
hands of furye and desperation,

and

and made him at one blow cutt
off her head. When flying instantly to the Vicar of the place who
was his Vncle, he made him ac-
quainted with what he had done;
Who being much troubled at it,
advised him to lye concealed in a
secret place which he shewed
him, til he had don Masse and had
further aduised what course to
take with him. Meane while behold a stupendious miracle. An
Angel sent from heauen presently vnited the trunke of our be hea-
ded Virgin soe properly to the
head againe, as there only remained a red streake about the neck
in memory that it was once cutt
of when she restored to life
againe, had presently recourse to
Church to heare Masse, and render thankes to Alm: God for that
                              mira-

miraculous fauour; Being there, it happened the Curat at the Offertory defcending from the Altar, with much aftonishment efpied her, and beleeuing it rather fome phantafme come to fright him, then her returning to life againe, fufpended his aftonishment and his feares, til after Maffe, when he repaired vnto her more fully to informe himfelfe of what she was; Then she reconted from point to point, al that had hapned to her, greeuoufly a complayning of his Nephewes barbaroufnes, and in particular of his irreuerence towards God and his B. Mother: The good man loft in admiration of the accident, as foone as he had found himfelf, was al in teares, befeeching her to keepe fecret this

hainous

haynous offence of his Nephew,
and pardon it. For my particular,
said she, I doe from my hart; but
how Heauen wil pardon him ; I
know not; For that , said the Cu-
rate, I trust in the infinite mercy
of Alm. God , only yours was al
my feare, and there vpon he produced his Nephew , who on his
knees shedding aboundant teares
besought her of pardon ; when
she rayssed him vpp , and as if she
had forgotten how much he had
offended her, in this mild manner
spake vnto him : My freind , said
she , I haue already past my promise to your vncle that I wil forgiue you ; only procure by penance to purchase the forgiuenes
of Alm. God, and his B. Mother,
or I assure you , a more rigorous
punishment then this world has
any

any, is in ftore for you : Sweet
Miftres, faid he, (making profoūd
reuerence vnto her, and declaring by his fighes; and teares a
more profound greefe & forrow)
how good and gratious you are,
not only to preferue my temporal life, (which if you pleafed to
take it; were forfaited vnto you)
but to take fuch care of my eternal on; yet befides this fauour
I muft needs begg another,
which_is, that from that mouth,
which for fo greeuous a trefpaffe
has pronounc't my pardon, I may
heare what penance I fhal performe for it · Since you wil (faid
she) you fhal ; only take it by
way of councel not of command,
and it is this, That you become
a Friar Minor, and before you are
fo, Confeffe your felfe wholy and
entire-

entirely of al your wickednes: This the sorrowful soule willingly accepted of: and hauing punctually performed what she inioined him, in short space made such progresse in Religion, as he became an example of perfection vnto al. And by this we may perceiue ; how succourable the B. Virgin is , to those who for the Imitation of her , preserue this virginity so carefully , as rather to depart with it , they chose to depart this life.

The third Condition, which is requisit in the honourers of the B Virgin, Of cleannes and purity of mind.

THE sacred Virgin being not only a bright shining mirrour of Humility & Chastity, to its perfection, but also of incomparable purity of mind, wee who make profession of being her seruants, ought to haue her example alwayes before our eyes, to the end the cõtinual Contemplation

of

of thefe three excellent vertues
in her, may excite vs to an affectionat defire of them, efpecially
that of purity of mind, it being
the moft exquifit beauty of the
foule, and an ornament which
moft of al illuftrats it. Now this
purity of mind is nothing els
(according to Albert the great,
as he alleaged by S. Antonine)
but a receffion from al impurity,
which is finne, and an acceffion
to God the foueraigne purity &
in this confifts the true fanctity
of the foule, for the more we
weed it of imperfections, the
more place is left for perfections
to fpring vp in it; and fo S. Dio-
nyfe defyning fanctity fayes, that
it is a perfect purity abftracting
from al finne, and cleanfed from
al impurity; whence we may wel
conclude

conclude, that purity is no other thing, then an exemption from al imperfection.

Let the pious Reader then imagine the purity of the B. Virgins mind, who of al the Children of Adam was not only exēpted from al actual sinne, but also from original; and that becaufe of the conueniency (as S. Anfelme would haue it) that she who was the Mother of God should next to him haue al imaginable purity; which could not be, if she had not been preferued from original sinne. Besides, God hauing predeftinated her to a degree of honour, the higheft that any creature could be capable of, it followed confequently he should endow her with a purity aboue al other creatures, and fo al the fa-

G culties

culties of his power wisdome and goodnes, (we may imagine) were at once imploied in enrit-ching her with such guifts and supernatural preparations, as rendred her of al creatures the most eminent; in such manner as those who had but the eies of spirit open to penetrat into the beautie and perfection of her glorious soule would infallibly more admire Gods workmanshipp, and see more admirable effects of it in her; then in the fabrick and creation of the Vniuersal. Neuer any thing came immediatly out of the hand of God, but it was pure, perfect and compleat; he created the Angels from the purest of the Heauens perfect and pure, he created man likewise soe, of the most pure-parts of the

Earth

Earth , and Eue from the pureſt
fleſh and bone of Adam , whilſt
he was yet in the ſtate of Innocency was created pure ; and the
reaſon is , becauſe the nigher to
the principal of puritie a thing
is, euer the more pure it is. This
being ſo , what can be more reſplendent (ſaies S. Ambroſe)
then she in whom purity it ſelfe
cloſe to abide ? what finally more
vnblemisht , then she whom the
Sóne of God choſe to inueſt himſelfe withal ? And if God hath fauoured other creatures with that
highe prerogatiue to be borne in
grace and exempt from ſinne,
who can doubt but she in a ſpecial manner was borne ſo , and
exempted aboue the reſt ? For
what incongruency els were it to
haue the mother inferior to her

Children

Children the Queene to her fub-
iects and. Seing then the Angels, and both Adam and Eue
more created in grace and in the
ftate of innocency, why fhould
we deny the Queene of Angels,
and the repairer of Adam and
Eues offences, the life prerogatiue? Yet let vs paffe farther, and
affirme the B. Virgin excelling
in purity by infinit degrees not
only al men and women in the
world, but alfo al Angels, Archangels, and the higheft Seraphins in heauen. For this, S. Hilarion affirmes of her addreffing
himfelf vnto her in this deuout
manner. *O fouerainely happy Virgin
aboue al women, and furmounting
euen the Angels themfelues in purity.*

Her fanctity then being fo
great, we may wel conclude of
her

her, that there was neuer in her
any blemish of ſinne, nor the leaſt
shadow of imperfection. Let vs
conſider her then, being ſo immaculate as she was, as an Idea framed by God, of al Chaſtity, as a
liuely paterne of perfection in
women, model of ſupreme purity
and finally ſchoole of al Vertues,
Virgin both in mind and body,
humble of heart, graue in diſco-
uery, prudent in action, neuer
ſtirring abrode til inuited by neceſſity ſober and mortified, wearing alwayes in her Contenance
a holy bashfullnes, her gate wel
ordered and compoſed, ſimple in
Clothing, moderat in her voice,
neuer laughing but weeping often, ſparing of ſpeech, alwayes
wel imployed, hauing ſtil in hand
ſome profitable booke, aſſiduous

in

in prayer, during which she seemed stil in extaſy; more abhor-
ring ſinne, then al the men of the
world together as one who better
then them al together knew,
how hateful and deteſtable it was
to Alm. God: she was of a ſpirit
perpetually attentiue to the exerciſe of vertue and holy life, holding in a generous diſ-eſteeme
al the honours dignityes and riches of the world, as knowing
how contemptible they were al,
in compare with thoſe of heauen,
whoſe ſoueraigne Queene and
Empreſſe she was to bee: how
was it poſſible then she should
euer fal into any ſinne, being of
ſo excellent a ſoule, and it being
replenished with ſo many diuine
graces & perfections? and From
whence (ſayes Dionyſe the Car-
thuſian.

thusian) we may imagine these
beames proceeded, which shoo-
ting from her countenance rendred her so resplendent and venerable to al that regarded her;
al which were nothing yet in
compare with the inward rayes
that illustrated her mind, which
gaue light vnto the Angels of
light themselues; her regard was
such according to S. Ambrose &
S. Bonauenture) as her bare sight
was sufficient to reclaime euen
those that were furthest gon in
sinne; but that which was most,
admirable in her, and which most
rauishes in astonishment both
men and Angels, was her being at
once both Mother & Virgin, virgin in purity, & Mother in fecun-
dity; A prodigie of al others the
most stupendious, and a preroga-

tiue

tiue only appropriat to this rare
Phenix of perfection ; for to
whom els were attributed euer
these supreme titles of honour,
Virgin before child-birth , Virgin in child-birth , and Virgin
after it? Yet? tis an Article of
faith , and al doubt thereof inter-
dicted by the holy Church ; for
the Consummation of which, we
wil here relate a Miracle happening to B. Giles one of the first
Companions of S. Francis , and
it was this.

A Religious Diuine of the Order of S. Dominick , being once
vehemently tempted by the Diuel sworne Enemy to the B. Virgin) to cal in doubt her vndubi-
table Virginity, and not sufficing
by his owne forces to shake it off,
was resolu'd to vse the helpe of
some

some other, and hearing the fame of B. Giles for sanctity, resolu'd it should be he. Being on his way towards the Conuent where the holy man resided, who by diuine reuelation vnderstood the cause of his iourney, behold he was ready to meete him, and embrace him with al the freindly expressions of a Religious charity; and e're euer the other opened his mouth to communicat with him of his temptation, he sayd vnto him; Brother and freind, assure your selfe, shee was a virgin before child-birth; when raking the ground with a litle wane he had, one Lilly presently sprung vp, then conuerting himselfe to him againe; so assure your self, said he. she was a virgin in child-birth, & a second Lilly sprung vp in con-

firmation

firmation therof; finally, the third
time addressing himselfe to him
he said, assure your selfe lastly
(said he) that she was a virgin
after child-birth too; and this by
the springing vp of a third Lilly,
being confirmed also, the Diuine
remained deliuered from his têp-
tation and rendred infinit thanks
to Alm. God, for his so miraculous deliuery.

Let this suffice for a more ample confirmation of the souerai̅ne
Puritie of the Queene of heauen.
Let those then who desire with a
due purity of hart to serue this
glorious Virgin, endeauour withal their forces to imitat her, in
her admirable purity and Inno-
cencie of life, that is, to haue a
hart vntainted, and free from al
contagion of sinne, especially
                                    such

such as are mortal , since, as the
Angelical Doctour teaches vs;
The farther that purity is remo-
ued from sinne , the purer stil it
growes; so shal wee haue part in
the benediction : *Blessed are the
pure of hart , for they shal see God.*
And to come yet neerer to particulars , those are pure of hart,
whose consciences are free from
mortal sinne; those more pure,
are likewise free from venial; but
those most of al, who accompany
this freedome from sinne , with
the assidual practise of vertue,and
this according to S.Christsostom,
is to be pure of hart. S. Hierome
defines it , to haue a conscience
that can accuse vs of no sinne , at
al , such an one as that of our B.
Ladyes was, who according to S.
Bonauenture , was so pure from
sinne,

finne, as it was reueal'd to a certaine perfon, as her confcience vnderftood not what it meant. O happy and a thoufand times happy are fuch as thofe, whofe breaft being pure,& inuefted with thefe white robes of purity, do ferue in that liuery the foueraigne Queene of heauen; for thefe are truly her feruants, thefe truly her fauorits, and fuch as in the next life fhe peculiary honours and aduances aboue the reft.

We reade of S. Lewis Archbifhop of Tholoufe, who iffue from the Royal bloud of France, and was once a Frier-Minor; how he in his life neuer committed mortal finne; this holy Saint dying at the age of 80. yeares, a certaine Frier-Minor farr from the place of his death, and ignorant:

rant of his infirmity, had a vision iust at the instant of his departure of innumerable Angels bearing his soule to heauen, and singing melodiously on the way; *So are they rewarded who serue God in purity and chastity of hart*; and for his chastity and purity we haue the attestation of al that conuersed with him, that al his actions and wordes fauoured of nothing else.

And as vehemently is the B. Virgin displeased with the contrary vice, as with this vertue she is pleas'd; as witnesseth this following storie recounted by the learned Pelbart; A yong Gentleman of a debaushed life, exercising some deuotions in the honour of the B. Virgin, she one day whilst he inuoked her aide

(being

(being ſtraied in a wildernes &
almoſt famiſhed) appeared vnto
him accompanied with a glorious
train of Virgins, bearing in their
hands al ſorts of delicat meates,
but ſerued in ſo foule and loth-
ſome diſhes, as although hishun-
ger was moſt vrgent, yet for very
loathing he would not eate abitt;
which the B. Virgin perceiuing,
aptly took occaſion to reprehend
him ſaying; euen ſuch are your
deuotions you offer vp to me;
Good in themſelues, but coming
from one ſo foule with ſinne, my
heart ſerues me not to accept of
them; ſo ſhe vaniſhed, and left
him ſo ſtrucken with this repre-
henſion by the bitter ſlaine of his
former life , as for the time to
come he wholy amended it.

Let thoſe then, who haue the
honour

honour to be stiled the seruants
of the B. Virgin, that their seruices may be the more acceptable
to her, endeauour to keepe vp,
to the highest point of this perfection of purity of hart, that is,
to be so farr from the conscience
of any mortal sinne, as euen to
decline venial as farr as it is possible; from the which the farther
they are, the nigher they approche vnto perfection, and the more
they increase in grace and holines of life. Happy is that soule
then, which growing dayly per-
fecter in this purity of hart, shal
finde a ready way to euery grace
and perfection it shalbe desirous
to obtaine, & merit to haue Alm.
God amply communicat them
vnto vs, whose property it is to
be most bountious of his fauour

to

to the pure, to impart himſelfe
vnto them in a particular manner,
and enrich them with his diuine
Conſolations. And this Hart of
ours being a thing of ſuch perfection, each leaſt defect in it,
appeares to be deformity, it being
(as Bro. Giles was vſed to ſaye)
like a bright mirrour which the
leaſt breath would ſett a blemiſh
on; For which reaſon the Wiſe-
man ſo earneſtly recomends vnto
vs the Cuſtody of it. *Looke Care-*
fully to thy hart, ſayes he, *for thy*
life depends on it. And ſo we ſee,
how litle a thing diminiſhes of
its merit and purity; an idle or ri-
diculous word a litle leuity in our
actions, a friuolous Curioſity, a
leſſe modeſt regard, immoderate
laughter, or ſuch like, which we
account of as things light and in-
different

different. Now the better to conserue this purity of hart, we must
be most careful of our Exteriour
senses, our eyes, eares, smell,
touching, tasting, &c. least the
Enemy preuaile himself by them
against our selues.

To expresse the danger of which
F. Iacopen of the holy Order of
B. Francis, hath an apt similitude;
There was (sayes this holy man)
a Virgin of excellent beauty, hauing for her dower a Iewel of inestimable price, who had fiue brothers al poore and necessitous; the
one a Musician, the other a Painter, the third a Perfumer, the
fourth a Cooke, and the fifth a
setter of others chastityes to sake
One day the Musician addrest
himself, vnto her, and with an
accent, as charming, as it was pit-
                                    tiful

tiful, defired her of pitty in his
extreme neceffity, if euer Charity, fayd he, were deare vnto you,
or if euer you knew what pitty
meant, declare it now in your af-
fifting me; giue me your Iewel to
redeeme me from my wants; it
is a bould requeft I grant, both
in regard of the greatnes of its
value, and the fmalnes of my de-
feruings, but the greater honour
wilbe yours, with foe vn-interef-
fed a Charity, to affift a brother
in his neceffity, and the greater
wilbe my obligation; and heer fo
pauf'd a while, as if his greefe had
ftopt the paffage of his fpeech;
But she remaining Inexorable
to his prayers, anfwered him
thus: My deare brother, I would
do much for you, but fatisfie your
demand I cannot; for the fame
Charity

Charity which obliges me to benefit others, firtt of al obliges me
to benefit my selfe; what a folly
were it in me then, by my enri-
ching others, to make my self for
euer poore, you know I haue nothing but it to maintaine my life,
and to depart with it were to expose my life te extreme necessity;
Wel (answered the Musician)
then, since you wil not giue it
me, at least sel it me: and what
wil you giue me for it? I wil take
my Lute, sayd he, and sing you
two of the newest Ayres at Court
at this she laughing, ask't him,
when they were done, what remaines for her to liue vpon? no,
no, sayd she, brother you shal
pardon me, I wil not sell soe pretious a Iewel for so slight a thing.
After him the Painter came vnto
                                   her

her with the fame requeſt, offering one of his beſt peeces, in
exchange, but ſhe refuſed him as
ſhe had don the former. Then
the Cooke, & the Perfumer came
next, this profering for it, one
of the delicateſt perfums he had,
the other the moſt ſauory diſhe
he could inuent; but they as the
former fayling of their pretenſes;
the fift lewd Companion, addreſſing himſelfe vnto her, who knew
wel the arts of perſwaſion, and
how to inſtil his words into the
mind, offred her for it, after a
world of ſmooth and ſoothing
word, her choice of a hundred
Paramours; But being as the reſt
reiected, it hapned not long after, that a mighty King moued
by the fame of this riche Iewel,
came to demand it of her, off'ring
                                    to

to marry her on the condition that he might haue it, & giue her for dowry his Immortal King-dome; when she ouercome by the greatnes of his offers, but much more by the goodnes of the Of-ferer, thus anſwered him; My Lord, it were Impudence in me to refuſe you, wherefore behold I freely giue it you, without any reſerue at al, and deſire no other recompenſe for it, but that you would vouchſafe to accept it; and excuſe the ſmalnes of her merit that giues it you. This ſimilitud the holy man would explicat in this manner; The Virgin is the ſoule, the Iewel, the Free wil she hath; her fiue brothers, her fiue Corporal ſenſes; the King, Alm. God; as for the reſt, is obuious enough.

And

And heere I could take occafion to inveigh againſt thoſe, who
would beheld deuout (forſooth)
to the B. Virgin, and haue no
Care the while of bridling their
ſenſes, but let them run on to al
licentiouſnes; nay, which is worſe
they continue ſo, til the end of
their liues, without any remorſe,
out of a vaine preſumption they
ſhalbe ſaued becauſe of ſome odd
deuotions they exerciſe, then
which what greater folly can
there be, what greater blindnes?
not to ſee how the diuel drawes
them as it were bound hand and
foote to hel. For example, you
ſhal ſee many, (I ſpeake it with
greefe and shame enough) ſo
addicted to the devotion of the
Annunciat, as they would not
omitt it for a world, (and 'tis
com-

commendable in them) but
marke how they abuſe it ; the miraculous effects which they ſo
ſpread of it, makes them preſume
the like ; for what wil they ſay:
neuer tel me of Hel nor of the
paines thereof, though I ſinne neuer ſo much , I ſerue a Miſtres
who hath both wil and ability to
helpe me out of it, and let me but
Confeſſe my ſinnes at the houre
of my death, and I am ſure of
heauen ; ſee how theſe miſerable
wretches talke; drawing a wrong
conſequeuce from an Antece-
dent moſt true, that the B. Virgin
both can and wil ſuccour her ſeruants : but they muſt be ſuch as
make due vſe of her fauours, and
employ thē in working their ſaluation : ſuch indeed ſhe ſometi-
times helpes ſo efficaciouſly, as in
ſhipwrack

shipwrack she keepes then from perishing in the sea, and frees them from al dangers on land of enimyes, theeues, and Murtherers, and al this to bring them to amendment of their liues: But those who rather grow worse by it, or out of presumption of it seeke not to amend at al, for my part I hold their safeties desperat. Then there is a difference of sinners, for some sinne of deliberat wil, and make not due vse of their deuotion to the B. Virgin, nay, as I haue sayd before, euen abuse it to greater licentiousnes of life, and such are in a most dangerous estate. Others only sinne, out of humane frailty, and by giuing too much liberty to their senses, doing it with a remorse of Conscience, and greeuous desire to amend

amend their faults , though they
be neigligent to put their good
defires in excution : and for fuch,
it is eafier for them to difpofe
them felues for grace , and preuayle themfelues of thofe Infpirations the B. Virgin procures
them for the amendment of their
liues , themfelues , both the one
and the other are to honour the B.
Virgin, and reuerence her with al
becoming reuerence ; that she
may obtayne for them of her B.
fonne condigne penance for their
finns, & amendment of their life.
Let them like wife endeauour to
make themfelues partakers of that
laudable deuotion of the Annunciat, fince thofe who haue been
of it, haue been in fine recompen-
ced for it, and I exhort as wel the
Iuſt and thofe of better life to

H   this

this, as alſo ſinners and euil liuers; ſithence if theſe find ſuch
benefit of it, how much more
muſt they, who are intimate
freinds as it were to God and his
B. Mother; as thoſe who are in
deadly ſinne, are capital enimies,
as this ſtory taken out of the
Cronicles of the Friers Minors
doth manifeſt.

A certaine Frier Minor of holy
life, vſing to recommend himſelfe vnto the prayers of euery
one he mett; it happned he entring once into a towne; mett a
woman there of euil fame, and
indeed of as euil life, and deſired
her likewiſe to remenber him in
her prayers to Alm: God and his
B. Mother; At which, quite aſto-
niſhed, ſhe anſwered him, Alas
father! what good wil my prayers
do

do you, who am the wickedeſt
ſinner in the world ? bee what
you wil, ſayd he, your prayers
wil do me no hurt I am confident.
When behold a miraculous accident, the woman entring into
the Church, and Kneeling before
an Image of the B. Virgin to ſay
an *Aue Maria* for him, was rauiſh't in extaſy, and behold the
mother of God humbly ſupplica-
ting her ſonne for him ; and he
demanding of her why ſhe would
harken to the prayers of an Ene-
meys, although it was for a freind
ſhe prayed, Be therefore merciful
to her (ſayd ſhe agayne) and for
your freinds ſake receiue her to
freind ſhip alſo. The poore woman returning from her extaſy,
haſtned to find out the Religious
man, to whom with great wonder

der she recounted what had paſt, and hauing made a general Confeſſion of al her ſins , she liued there after a moſt exemplar life in the ſeruice of that great Patroneſſe of ſinners the Queene of heauen.

Let al who ſerue her then , if they deſire to pleaſe her, carefully avoid al mortal ſinne , and preſerue their hearts pure and innocent ; ſo shal they likewiſe obteyne the fauour of Alm : God, ſince as the holy ſcripture ſayes, they who loue purity of heart, infallibly shal haue the king for freind.

The

✣✣✣✣✣✣✣✣✣✣✣✣✣✣✣

*The fourth Condition requi-
sit in the seruants of the B.
Virgin, for the conserua-
tion of this purity of hart,
Which is the frequentation
of the Sacrament s, espe-
cially of that of Confession.*

ALTHOVGH the pro-
fession of being ser-
uants to the B. Vir-
gin, be a great stay
vnto vs from falling
into sinne; neuerthlesse, standing
on such slippery ground, with
this waight of flesh on vs incli-

H 3   ning

ning vs to fal, we canot but sometimes do it, and contract some
blemish by it, and may need the
wiping away of it. As for Mortal
sinne, by the grace of Alm. God
we may preserue our selues vn-
touched by it; as many good Religious do euen to the vttermost
period of their dayes; but for venial, it is impossible, nor is there
any of Adams descendants, that
at some time or other haue not
falne into it. The Apostles themselues although adorn'd with richest sanctity, were not exempted
from it, only the B. Virgin hath
had this singular priuiledge aboue
the rest, as the holy Church conceiues of her in her Office; *You are*
all faire O B. Mary, and there is no
spot in you. Now our B. Sauiour
for the cleansing vs from the stay-

nes

nes both of venial & mortal ſinne
hath prouided vs of the remedie
of the Sacrament of Confeſſion.
And ſo S. Bernard ſayes : *Ama*
Confeſſionem, ſi affectas decorem.
Loue Confeſſion, as thou loueſt
to be faire ; meaning that it is the
imbelliſhment of a ſoule, and ſo
certainly there is nothing that
more efficaciouſly purges the
ſoule from vice, then to frequent
quent this holy Sacrament.

Al the Sacraments of the
Church, according as the Councel of Trent defines, were inſtitu-
ted by our Sauiour Chriſt himſelfe, and had their firſt origin
from his ſacred ſide, at what time
both blood & water came iſſuing
forth, and are ſo many rindets as
it were, by which his aboundant
grace is deriued vnto vs. Let them
H 4   therefore

therefore who frequent them, make account (especially this of Confession), that they haue recourse by it, to the ouer-flowing fountaine of our Sauiours pretious bloud, by vertue of which their soules are wash't and cleanfed from the foulnes of their sinnes: which the Apostle S. Iohn doth infinnuat where he sayes: *The bloud of our Sauiour Christ purges vs of our sinnes.* O how merciful and gratious hath God ben to vs the whilst? how excessiue his loue, to giue vs so pretious a remedy, by which as often as we please we may be purged and cleanfed from our sinnes: and as often as we are dead in mortal sinne, we may be reuiued and raysed to life againe, passing from the death of sinne vnto the life

of

of grace , from vice to vertue, from eternal paine vnto eternal bliffe.

Of al deformities, mortal finne is that , which renders a foule moft deformed , in fo much as could we but fee a foule in ftate therof, we should euen die for horrour , it would be a fight fo feareful and hideous : whereas no fooner it hath been cleanfed by the facrament of Penance , but it produces againe a new beauty & formofity. So S. Gregory the great fayes : Could we but fee a foule made to the refemblance of God, euen in *puris naturalibus*, we fhould admire it to adoration , & beleeue the Creatours beauty himfelfe hardly fuperiour to it. For which reafon (fayes the lear-ned Tilleman) God hath inclofed

it in this corps of clay, leaft it be-holding it-felf, fhould be in danger of that Luciferian pride, which was fo many Angels perdition. And for this caufe thofe ancient Fathers of the Ægyptian deferts in eleuating their mindes to their foules high, and taking the true altitude of their creatiõs, were as it were alienated from themfelues: In fo much (as we reade of S. Antony) as often as he was called on to pay the debt of nature either in food or fleep, or any fuch corporal neceffity, he euen blufh't for fhame, that fo noble a fubftance as the foule, should be intereffed in fuch bafe reckonings. Now if a reafonable foule be of it-felfe fo beautiful, what great addition muft it needs receiue from the Sacrament of
                    Penance,

Penance, which restoring it to its
natiue luster, add to it besides,
that of God Almighties supernatural grace? Certainly there is no
eloquence in the world can speak
it sufficiently, no liuing imagination can conceiue the hundreth
part of its excellence. The Sunne
(sayes S. Chrisostome) with his
cleare rayes doth not so illuminat the world as the Grace of
Alm. God can do a soule. Which
that of S. Catharine of Sienna wel
declares; who hearing a Preacher
once discoursing of the excellecy
thereof, and how exceedingly it
beautifyed a soule, conceiued an
ardent desire to behold a soule in
Grace, and aduantaged with al
the beauties thereof; Ful of this
desire, she was no sooner departed from the sermon, but she hard

a

a voice from heauen saying vnto
her : *Catherine, presently thou shalt
see the fruite of thy desire*; and retiring her into her Oratory , she
there besought God for the performance of his promise, and sodainly beheld a person of incredible Maiesty al Circled about
with light and shining with clear
splendours; at the sight of which,
she was so rapt in admiration and
reuerence, as she presently prostrated her selfe before its feete
with intention to adore it , had it
not with these words prohibited
her: *Catherine forbeare for I am* not
God, as thou imaginest? and who
then ? answered the Saint ; I am,
sayd it , the soule of a certaine
Murtherer you prayed for not
long since in seeng me ledd to
execution who being new clean-
sed

ſed in the fire of Purgatory , and
going al purified to heauen , after
I ſhal haue left you ſatisfied of
your deſire by the commande-
ment of Alm. God. And after
this time, the holy Saint had a
particular in ſight by Alm. God
beſtowed vpon her , of the natures of each ſoule , and ſhe was
wont to affirme vnto her Gloſtly,
Father , that if he ſawe but the
beauty of a ſoule,ſhe was aſſured,
he would: ſpend 1000. & 1000.
liues for the ſauing of one.

The grace of this holy Sacrament of Penance hath a wondrous vertue , not only to purifie
the ſoule confeſſant from the ſtai-
nes of ſinne , but alſo to beautify
it with good inclinations , and
from a ſlaue of ſinne and vn-
apt for good , to render it free &
expedite

expedite; which we wil declare
by an example out of Cæfarius.
There was a learned Diuine (fay's
he) exemplar in al vertue called
Thomas, who approching to his
end, faw in a corner of his chamber the diuel appearing in a fearful shape; to whom he with an
vndanted courage thus fpake;
What art thou there cruel beaft,
fayd he? tel me, I coniure the,
what amongft Chriftians is the
thing which afflicts the moft? but
he forbearing to anfwer him, the
holy man iterating his admiration, in the name of God charged
him to fpeake : when at laft the
diuel thus anfwered him ; Know
(fayd he) there is nothing in the
Church of God afflicts vs more
then the frequenting the Sacrament of Confeffion, feeing when

a

a man is in mortal sinne, he is as it were bound hand and foote, wholy disabled from doing any good, and when he repayres to Confession those bonds are broken, and he is restored to liberty againe; and so certainly sinnes are nothing else but so many chaines which tye vs as it were vnto the gates of hel, and so the Priest in the act of Absolution sayes: *I absolue thee from thy sinnes* ; and a mighty power the Confessours hath, or rather a mighty loue our Sauiour hath of vs to instruct & furnish them with so great a power as they haue. We see, say the holy Fathers, when a Criminal confessed his sinnes vnto an earthly Iudge, he is condemned for it, but the contrary happens at the Tribunal of the

Church

Church, where the Prieſt preſi-
des and repreſents the perſon of
our Sauiour Chriſt himſelfe : For
thoſe who confeſſe, goe away
wholy acquited and abſolued.

Al good Chriſtians then, as
ſoone as they are falne into mortal ſinne, are preſently to procure
to purge themſelucs of the foule
ſtaine of it at the fountaine of
Confeſſion ; and if we be ſo careful when the leaſt ſpott appeares vpon our garments, to waſhe
it out ; how much more careful
ought we to be to waſhe out the
blemiſhes of our ſoule ? for the
which, although Contrition may
ſuffice accompanied with a firme
purpoſe of Confeſſion, not with
ſtanding who can ſecure his Con-
ſcience whether he hath had true
Contrition or no, or that rather
it

it hath not been a greefe lesse perfect for his sinnes proceeeding
rather from the feare of punishments then a true loue of God
Almighty, as it ought to do; such
as the Diuines cal *Attrition*, neither sufficient of it selfe to deliuer vs from our fins, nor consti-
tute vs in the state of Grace, nor
consequētly to free vs from damnation should we dye in that
state of minde; whereas but ioyne
it with Confession, and it is
aboundantly sufficient, the Sacrament supplying al that was wanting to it of true Cōtrition. Who
sees not then the vertue of this
Sacrament, and how necessary it
is for our saluation? For which
cause, the seruants of Alm. God
were euer exceeding careful to
Confesse them euen of their ligh-
test

teft faults, efpecially night the
article of their deaths, at which
tyme, although they had led fuch
Saint-like liues, as it hath pleafed God to teftifie it euen by miracle ; yet being to approach to
the foueraigne purity, they imagined could neuer be pure enough
And fo a certaine learned Authour fayes, that a foule in Grace
at its feparation from its body if
it fhould but fee the leaft blemifh
of venial finnes adhearing to it,
would be fo afhamed of it, as rather thē to appeare with it before
the face of Alm. God, it would
volūtarily plunge it felf into Purgatory there to be cleanfed from
it; nay, which is more, wōderful,
he fayes that fhould an Angel defcend thither vnto it while it were
fuffering the fharpeft and moft
exquifite

exquisite torments there, & putt
it to its choice to go to heauen
with some blemish of sinñe vpon
it, or remaine there purging
from it til the day of doome; the
soule without any demurr vpon
it, would make election of the
last, thereby to render it selfe
more worthy the sight of God
whom it loues so wel, who cannot
endure any obiect of impurity.
The purity of hart then being a
thing of so singular recommendation with the Queene of heauen,
let al who professe themselues her
seruants seeke to purchase it, and
purchasing it once embrace it
with al their might; to which end
lett them know, that according
to the opinion of al, there is no
more efficacious way to do it,
then that of the Sacrament of
Confession

Confeſſion; the benefits of it are
ſo many, that they are impoſſible
to be reckoned vp; For thoſe who
confeſſe often, heape grace open
grace, purity on purity, beauty on
beauty, and make themſelues the
greateſt treaſure of it in heauen;
thoſe who confeſſe often, haue a
more vigilãt eye to the cõſeruing
of their cõſcience in purity, which
in the fountaine of penance they
ſo lately purified, thoſe who Cõ-
feſſe often haue a ſpecial care, not
to fal into thoſe ſins for ſhame,
from which ſo lately their Con-
feſſors help't them out; thoſe
who confeſſe often, make more
eaſily the examen of their Con-
ſciences, and goe with leſſe difficulty to Confeſſion, and are better diſpoſed to the receiuing of
our Sauiour Chriſt in the Sacra-
                              ment

ment of the Alas. In fine; those who confesse often enioy both day and night great tranquillity of mind which only accompanies a pure Conscience, and is the greatest blessing in the world.

This the sacred Catechisme confirmes where it sayes; *Those who holily and religiously receiue this holy Sacrament acquire by it a great tranquillity of Conscience, accompanied with as great content of mind and hart.* But what needs other testimoneis of this, than experiēce it-selfe? How vnwillingly they go to Confession, who haue their conscience charged with a long reckoning of sins? how ful of sadnes and anxiety? how heauie the burthen of them seemes to be, til being lightened of it at last by Confession

Confession, how great Consolation do they feele then in their
soules? how chearful they are? &
how embraced with the loue of
God for which now they could be
content to die, who before cared
not to liue for it! and if the practise of this do often occurr, Oh!
how happy doe they lead their
dayes on earth euen as they were
in another heauen: to participat
of this so great a benefit no Christian if he ripely considered it; but
would goe a thousand and a thousand miles, rather then want so
great a commodity, how much
the greater shame is it then for
those, who vouchsafe not to stirr
fower or fiue paces out of their
way, to discharge themselues of
the burthen of their sinnes. And
yet in how farr worse estate are
                                those

those, who remaine fiue or ten yeares without this benefit, how may we imagine do the Angels in heauen deplore so great a retchlesnes? of this sort how many wicked liuers are there, who pretend some deuotion to the B. Virgin, as saying their beades, fasting on saturdayes in her honour, and the like: who for the rest neuer think of heauen, or of timely repenting them for their sinnes.

Of whom what should we saie, and of their cruelty to their owne soules, whose cheifest contentment they so lightly prize? Certainly we could wishe they would at least (since they make profession of seruing her) beseech the B. Virgin amongst their other deuotions, to obtaine for them of her B. Sonne a true knowledge

and

and contrition for their finns;
which if they doe with a forrowful hart indeed, without doubt
she wil grant them their requeft,
and it wil be amaine difpofition
for them to obtaine the diuine
Grace, feeing (as the Diuines affirme) the workes of charity although done in mortal finne, haue
yet the force to difpofe the finner vnto Grace, and Confequently vnto eternal life. An example of which, it being ful of rare
document befides, out of the fecond part of the Frier Minors
Chronicles we thought good to
record.

Two Frier-Minors going from
the Conuent of Paris in the depth
of winter, were befides the dirty
wayes fo incommodated with có-
tinual fhowers of raine as the
elder

elder of the two towards the euening wholy tired out, sayd vnto
his Companion; My deare brother, what shal we do? I am so
weary that I am scarce able to
stirr a foote; alas, Father, sayd
the other, we cannot remaine
heere in the middest of this foule
weather and fowler wayes; why?
answered the father againe) it
seemes to me I spye a house some
quarter of a league hence, where
perhaps we may be lodged for
God Alm^s sake; I know it wel,
said the father, but it wil be ill
coming thither for vs, the Maister of it being a wicked man, no
freind to God, nor to his seruants,
and such an enemie to himself, as
for these 30. yeares (as the report goes) he hath neuer been at
Confession; howsoeuer (sayd the

I   Father

Father) let vs goe, for there is no
remedy now, and God is neuer
wanting to his feruants at fuch
neceffitous times as this; So they
fett on towards the houfe, where
being arriued, and asking a lodging for God Alm⁵ fake, the Miftres of the place moued with
compaffion to fee them in fuch
pitious plight, tould them her
husband was forth a hunting, and
for her felfe she was defirous to
accommodat them with al her
hart, but if her husband came to
haue notice of it, either of them
should incurr his greeuous difpleafure by it, she for receiuing
them, and they for being receiued, but come what would she
durft not deny them for God
Alm⁵ fake, and had rather then
fal into his difpleafure, incurr
her

her husbands by it a thousand times; so shee entertained them in
a more remote part of the house,
with the greatest secrecie and
charitie she could; In the meane
time; her husband returning from
the chace, finding al things prepared against his cōming home,
sate downe to supper, where he
was plentiously serued, whilst
the goodnes of his appetite equa-
led the goodnes of the prouision;
his wife considering the wants of
the poore Religious men, in
comparison of the plenty which
was there, could not but expresse
some sorrow for it in her countenance; which her husband obseruing, asked her wherefore she was
so sad? and she a while excusing
her selfe, at last he more & more
importuning her, she plainly
I 2   tould

tould him, vpon his promiſe he
would not be offended with it;
how ſhe had entertayned thoſe
poore Religious men in their ex-
treame neceſsity for God Almˢ
ſake, preferring by it the feare of
God before the feare of him, and
how whilſt they by the fire ſide
were plentiouſly feaſting it, thoſe
poore ſoules pinched with hunger & cold were ready to ſtarue
to death, the cōpaſsion of whoſe
incommodities with reflexion
on their commodities the while,
made her ſo ſad and ſorrowful in
her minde: and hauing this diſco-
uered with teares in her eyes, her
husband was ſo moued thereat, as
he preſently aroſe from the table,
and commanding they ſhould be
fetcht into the roome, he himſelf went out to meete them, and
                                    wel-

welcomed them with such signes
of affection, as for his owne mother he could not haue expressed
more, this moued the wonder of
al that were present there , but
much more that which followeth ; when he seeing their garments hang al frozen stiffe about
them , and their feete and leggs
chapt through the extremity of
cold, was so moued thereat, as he
presently seating them by the fire
caused a bath of hott water to be
brought, and he himselfe washed
their feete : then after he had a
while refreshed them there , he
comanded a chamber next his
owne to be prepared for them;
whither hauing conducted them
he addressing himselfe vnto the
father sayd ; My good father , resolue me I beseech you in cur-

I 3   tesy

tefy; whether one who hath liued al his life a greeuous finner,
and yet hath neuer Confeft him
his &finns, may poffibly be faued?
There is no doubt, Sir, anfwered the Religious man, but whofoeuer with requifite penance for
his finns fatisfies the iuftice of
Alm. God, may arriue at laft to
his faluation, for fo God hath
fayd; *At what time foeuer a finner*
shal repent him of his finnes, he
should liue : If it be fo, replied the
Gentleman, for Gods fake oblige
me fo much as to heare my
Confeffion; the good father exceeding weary and oppreft
with fleepe, confidering it a
worke of much time, to heare
the Confeffion, of fuch a one as
he, encouraging him in his good
defires, defired him to deferr it

til

til morning, when he might at
better leifure examine his Confcience, and confider more maturely of what he was to do ; but
who can affure me, anfwered the
Gentleman, to liue til the morning? but for that, as it pleafeth
God, and fo he retired him to his
reft ; meane while the Religious
man moued with an extraordinary folicitud of this his new Con-
verts faluation, was no fooner at
priuacy in his chamber, but cafting himfelf vpon his knees, he
befought Alm. God to difpofe al
that concerned him for his greater good, and thereupon be tooke
himfelf to his bed ; where in the
profoundnes of his fleepe, he beheld in vifion, the Angels and diuels at great debat about the foule
of this Gentleman newlly decea-

I 4   fed;

sed; the one challenging it to be
theirs, the other denying it; the
diuels alleadging for their side
the many and greeuous crimes he
had cōmitted in his life; the Angels for theirs, some slight and
few good workes which he had
done, but with soe litle successe
as the Iudge was euen vpon the
point of giuing iudgement for his
condemnation, when his Angel
Guardian interposed and sayd: I
beseech your diuine Maiestie, remember (what I had almost for-
got) the charitable entertaiment
he gaue to those Religious men
but yester-night; and I trust it
wil more then incite you to pardon him; at this the Iudge de-
murring, at last in consideration
of this one act of his, he gaue sentence for his saluation, and so his
accu-

accusers departed frustrat of their
intents. Heer the vision vanished,
and the Religious man starting
out of his sleepe , called to his
Companion saying : My brother,
my brother , the Gentleman of
this house is dead , and which is
more, is saued ; and heere he re-
lated to him the whole progresse
of his vision. Hereupon they both
rose and calling to them of the
house , aduertised them of what
had happened , telling them for
certaine that the Maister of the
place was dead : at this , al were
wonderfully amazed , and his
wife the most afflicted woman in
the world , not so much for his
temporal death , as his eternal,
which with good cause she feared,
til the Religious assured her that
he was saued, and that by the same

I v   mea-

meanes he came to the knowledge of his death, by the same
he vnderstood of his eternal life;
So a great part of her sorrow
being taken away, the rest she
bestowed vpon his Obsequies, al
that either knew his life or death,
admiring in it the wonderful mer-
cies of Alm. God.

From this Example let sinners
take Instruction, to be alwayes
charitable to the poore; & though
their sinnes be neuer so many, yet
neuer to despaire of the sweet
goodnes of Alm. God, but cheifly let them learne from hence, to
correspond to the Inspirations of
Alm. God, and preuayle themselues of the occasions offered
them by fauourable heauen, for
their conuersions & eternal good:
for so did this Gentleman both in
wil

wil intreating the Religious by
the Inspirement of Alm. God, &
in conceiuing a firme purpose
for the Confessing of his sinnes,
which nothing but death could
hinder the performance of.

---

*The Continuation of the
Fourth Condition; which
is the frequentation of the
Sacrament of the Eucha-
rist.*

S the seruants of the
B. Virgin then to
preserue their harts
and mindes in puri-
ty, ought often to
Confesse: so likewise to increase
it

it in their soules, the more to illu-
strate their mindes, & vnite their
harts more neare to Alm. God,
ought they to frequent the Sacrament of the Eucharist, where God
is gloriously & ful of al sweetnes
imparting of himself, no other-
wise then he doth vnto the B. soules in heauen. And who can imagine the hundreth part of the
greatnesses, maruailes, and super-
abundant aduantages, which ac-
crew to those who receiue this
ineffable Sacrament, much lesse
expresse it in their discourse and
wordes? for the other Sacramēts,
conferr grace 'tis true, to those
who worthily participat of them;
but this is the fountaine of grace,
from whence it springs, which
consequently in more plentious
manner is communicated heare;
the

the others come from God, but in this is God himſelfe, the Authour of al grace and of al the Sacraments, and the ſource of al our good; others are meanes to bring vs vnto God, but this is the End and brings God vnto vs; al the ſanctity of the reſt only helping to diſpoſe to the ſanctity of this. With good reaſon then S. Dionyſius the Areopagite, ſtiles it, *the perfectiue and conſeruatiue* Sacrament, ſeeing it is the perfection and conſummation of al the reſt.

Amongſt al the motiues that should incite vs to the frequentation of this B. Sacrament, none, me thinks, should be more efficacious, then our B. Ladyes ſo often frequenting it, by which with a zeale incredible she dayly (as it were)

were) en-wombed her B. Sonne
againe ; according to the great
Albert , S. Antonine, Sotus, and
the learned Suarez; nor can any
without ftrange temerity call it
in queftion, who but confiders
her (as fhe was indeed the light
and paterne of thofe primitiue
Times , in which the B. Sacrament was fo frequented, as Saint
Luke writes of them; *They per-*
feuered in the Temple in prayers and
the Communion of breaking bread.

And as for the Apoftles , 'its
certaine they al were Preifts and
Bishops ordained and eftablis-
hed by *Iefus Chrift* and Confequently according to their fun-
ctions confecrated and receiued
the Body of our Lord : *I haue re-*
ceiued of our Lord that which I haue
giuen you , (fayes the great Apoftle

ftle S. Paul of himfelfe; And S.
Andrew anfwered refolutly to
the Proconful exhorting him to
Idolatry : *I facrifice dayly to the
God omnipotent, who is the only true
God; not the fmoke of incenfe, nor
the flesh and bloud of beafts, but the
immaculat Lamb, of whofe flesh and
bloud al the faithful do eate and drink
that which was immolated, yet remayning entire and aliue.* S. Albert
a deuout feruant of the B. Virgin
defcends more to particulars, and
fayes, that S. Iohn was her ordinary Preift, from whofe hands
fhe communicated and receiued
the Sacrament, that fhe continued this deuotion al her life,
and at her death procured to haue
miniftred, vnto her. But who can
imagine the exceffiuenes of her
deuotion in receiuing it? Since if
fome

some Saints were so deuout when they came vnto it, as they rauished the beholders in an admiration, can we doubt but she surpassed them in it, who surpassed them by such infinite degrees in the liuely apprehension and vnderstanding of the thing. S. Catherin of Sienna when she would expresse to her Confessarius the ardent desire she had to communicat of this Sacrament, would only say she hungred, and he vnderstood her meaning strait, and hauing receiued it according to her desire, she would remaine some fiue or sixe houres afterwards in extasie. Our S. Francis did so burne, nay euer dye with the desire thereof, as those who beheld him in the Act of Communicating, were astonished at

his

his feruour in it, and none could
behould him without hauing the
fire of deuotion enkindled in thē-
selues the while he seemed so inebriated with it and transported
with the ioy, and so great was his
reuerence of it, as only it was
that, which made him abstaine
from Preist-hood, when once beseeching Alm. God by ardent
prayer to declare vnto him what
his pleasure was in that particular, an Angel appeared vnto him
with a violl in his hand ful of
pure and christallin liquor saying
vnto him; Behold, Francis, those
who duely administer the B. Sacrament, ought to be as cleane
in hart, and as free from blemish
in their soules, as this liquour is
from al foulnes & impurity. With
which apparition he was so confirmed

firmed in his humility as they could neuer induce him to any further Orders then he had.

And S. Clare of the fame time with him, had no leffe deuotion to this Sacrament; as it appeares in that fhee neuer approched vnto it, but with her eyes drowned in teares, whileft her hart was burning in deuotion. But what wonder that men goe to it with fo profound fubmiffion and reuerence, when euen the Angels & diuels adore and reuerence it.

The B. Brother Stephen (as it is recorded in the Chronicles of our Order, celebrating Maffe one day with great guift and deuotion, the Acolothite who affifted him falling afleep, hauing been ouer-watched the night before; Two deuout women being present

preſent at Maſſe, beheld at the
time of Eleuation two Angels in
moſt beautious shapes with tor-
ches in their hands performing
the Office the while of him that
ſlept; and when the Eleuation
was done, after their moſt profound reuerences they diſappea-
red; This to their great admiration theſe deuout women obſerued.

But what wonder if the Angels honour and reuerence their
eternal King, when euen the Diuels themſelues euen do it, as is
manifeſt in their ſtorye following: In Germany there was a
certaine Virgin poſſeſſed by the
Diuel, who before this lamentable accident was of rare vertue
and ſingular piety; It happened
once as she was iſſuing forth of
the

the Church with diuers others,
a Preiſt paſſed by , bearing the B.
Sacrament to the ſicke , when al
the people fell on their knees
reuerently adoring it , except a
certaine Iew who was there
amongſt the reſt ; which this Virgin ſpying ſhe approached vnto
him, and ſtriking him ſayd ; thou
wicked miſcreant , why doſt thou
not adore the Creatour and Lord
of al ? The Iew replyed (moued
with the indignity of the thing,)
we are obliged to the acknowledgement but of one God a lone,
and why then would you haue
me reuerēce this , of which there
are , as many as there are Hoſts
conſecrated in the world ? the
poſſeſſed perſon hearing this,
tooke a Siue , and holding it before his eies , bidd him regard
the

the Sunne , and then ask't him,
how many Suns he sawe ? whe
ther as many as there were beames that came through the siue,
or only one , from whence al
those beames were deriued?
thinke me not so simple , sayd the
Iew , as not to know there is but
one only Sunne ; more simple
thou art then , answered she
againe , to beleeue that we haue
more Gods then one , though so
many Hosts as thou seest euery
where deriue themselues from
his diuinity ; and at this the Iew
confounded left the place.

The B. Virgin not only adored
this B. Sacrament , on earth,
but now in heauen actually Con-
tinues her Adoration ; which we
may confirme by a storye taken
out of Vincentius his Mirrour
Historial

Hiſtorial the. 17. booke, confirmed by diuers other Authors of
worthy credit: There was, ſayes
he, a Curat of euil life, addicted
to his pleaſures, and one who ſtu-
died more to flay and kil his
flock, then to feed them; It happened in his parish at the ſame
tyme there-fel ſicke a riche Gentleman of prime quality, and a
poore widow of a vertuous life;
the Vicar chooſing rather to viſit
the Gētleman (as one from whom
there was ſome what to be hoped for) left the widow without
help abandoned: and after he had
diſpatch't with him, ſlightly hearing his Confeſſion and admini-
ſtring the other Sacramēts, yet he
remained lingering there ſo long
impertiētly flattering the Gentleman with hope of life, though
                                    he

he euen saw death in his Countenance, (only in hope of some
temporal benefitt) vntil the widow mindful of her eternal good;
sent for him being almost in her
last Agonie: but he sticking fast
there, in hope of gaine, could
not be drawne from thence:
which his Vicar perceiuing, moued with compassion; alasse Sir,
sayd he, suffer not this poore woman to dye thus destitute of help,
but at least send me thither: if you
wil not goe your selfe: Goe, if
you wil, sayd he, for my part I
wil not leaue this Gentleman
where there is hope of some what
to be gott, to visit a begger where
there is nothing but misery: hereupon the Vicar went with the
B. Sacrament for her Viaticum,
to visit this infirme creature, poor
indeed

indeed of worldly riches, but riche in heauenly, without which
al is pouerty: and he was no foe-
ner arriued at the doore, where
the poore foule lay only vpon a
litle ftraw, but he beheld the glorious Queene of heauen, accompanied with innumerable troopes
of Angels and Virgins, affifted
at her happy departure, at the
fight of which the Vicar fufpéded
in his thoughts a while, whether
he should enter or no, at laft re-
flecting from his owne vnwor-
thines on the dignity of him who
was in the Sacrament which he
brought with him, he confidently
entred in, when the B. Virgin
and al her Glorious trayne with
humble reuerence adored it, and
prefently vanished away. When
the good Vicar in extreme confolation

solation approched to the Couch where the poore widow lay, and hauing heard her Confession and communicated her, the happy soule presently loosened from its mortal bones, tooke flight immediatly to heauen.

In the meane wiile, things succeeded cleane cōtrary at the riche mans house; whither the Vicar was no sooner returned, but he beheld the Gentlemans bed, al incircled in with ougly black spirits, with horrible noyse, skree-kings, and roarings affrighting of his soule, whilest he cried out in horrible dismay : helpe, helpe, my freinds, these wicked spirits are haling me, and with their gripes they euen presse me to the hart: alasse ! I am a lost and miserable man : and at last, whilst the

K   Curat

Curat and the reſt were labou-
ring in vaine to comfort him , his
aking ſoule weary of thoſe mo-
mentary and painful gripes , iſſuing out of its body was receiued by thoſe Feinds , and carried
where was nothing but eternal
torments.

Imagine but what impreſſions
the whileſt the concurrancy of
theſe two Viſions made in the
heart of the good Vicar, and how
deuoutly afterwards he reuerenced the B. Sacrament , hauing
ſeene with what deuotion the B.
Virgin did it, and al her heauenly
traine ; At leaſt , the profeſſed
ſeruants of this B. Virgin ought
to make their profitt of this Example , and learne from thence
to reuerence the B. Sacrament;
and alſo to haue the often recei-
                        uing

uing of it in highe esteeme; not
withstanding the friuolous opinions of some, who hold it an irreuerence the often frequenting
of it; not considering that it is
stiled our *dayly bread*; that S. Luke
and S. Denis the Areopagite affirmes it to haue been the Custome of the Primitiue Christiãs,
to receiue it dayly with incredible Consolation. For their better
instruction, let them heare Saint
Ambrose exhorting to the frequent receiuing it: *The seruants of
Alm. God,* (sayes he) *receiue this
bread dayly , since dayly thou hast
need of it for thy Comfort refresh-
ment, and purging thee from thy sinnes*; And the Angelical Doctour
S. Thomas sayes , That whosoeuer experienceth an increase of
grace and deuotion by their of-

K 2   ten

ten receiuing it , both may and ought to frequent it ftill , and that although it be Commendable fometimes for humility to abftaine from it , Yet it is more Commendable out of loue to receiue it often. As witneffeth that example of S. Bonauenture , who in his yonger yeares at his firft entrance into the Order of the Frier-Minors , out of the profoundnes of his humility would oftentimes forbeare to comunicate ; vntil hearing Maffe one day , it pleafed Alm. God to fend him a particle of the Bleffed Hoft by the hands of Angels to communicate withal , by this fingular fauour both rewarding his humility , and encouraging him to more frequent receiuing it.

And

And heere we wil ceaſe all
further Diſcourſe of theſe Conditions requiſit in the ſeruants of
the Bleſſed Virgin, and treate
of the due reuerence which wee
owe to her; and firſt we wil declare the Excellence thereof.

Heere endeth the firſt Part.

K 3   THE

The second Part.

Of the Excellency of those Re-
uerences We are to exhibit
in honour of the Queene
of Heauen.

CHAPITRE I.

 MONGST al the
most noble and ex-
cellent seruices ap-
pertaining to the
diuine honour, that
Adoration which the Diuines cal
Latria, and which is only appropriat to God in regard of the infinit

finities of his Maiesty: holdes the
first ranke and place. This adoration according to S. Iohn Damafcene, consists in an interiour Act
by which the Creature testifies
his submission vnto his Creatour,
by some exteriour signe either of
vncouering the head, bowing the
knee, inclining the body, or the
like. With this supreme sort of
Adoration the three Kings adored the Infant Iesus in his Mothers armes; *And entring the house*
(sayes S. Mathew) *they found the
Infant with Mary his mother, & falling on the ground, they adored him*
words which excellétly wel declare the greatnes of this adoration;
by which the Kings and Monarks
of the earth humbly bow the head
and knee vnto the King and Monarke of the heauens.

K 4 　　　Now

Now to fpeake of the adoration proper to the B. Virgin, the next degree to that of God, himfelfe, the Diuines diftinguish it by the name of *Hyperdulia* from the reft by which al creatures both in heauen and earth count it as honour to adore the facred Queene of heauen.

According to the opinion of fome Diuines, God had no fooner created the Angels, but he let them vnderftand, how his B. Sonne was one day to become man, and this man fhould be their God.

Whereupon the B. Spirits with regard vnto the time, honoured him as fuch, and confequently (as Suares fayes in following Saint Thomas his opinion) they odored his Mother as her who

was

was to inueſt him in mortal fleſh.

And 'tis an approued veritie of al the Doctours and the cheife of them al S. Paul ; that the Sonne of God being come into the world , al the Angels came to adore him. So (ſayes he) *when he ſent his firſt borne ſonne into the world, he ſayd ; Let al the Angels of God adore him :* And S. Bonauenture and other deuout writers ſaye , that when the Infant Ieſus was borne in the Stable , al the Angels in their ſeueral Quiers came to adore him , and that perhaps viſibly in humane shapes, the more to honour his Humanity ; After which they did their ſeueral reuerences to his B. Mother, the one and the other ſinging diuine and melodious Canticles of prayſe.

Now if the B. Spirits with such profound reuerēce adored the B Virgin while she was yet resident in the world, what excessiue honours may we imagine do they render her now in heauen, where next to God she holds the second place? invested with incomparable glorie at the right hand of her B. Sonne? For my part I am of opinion, that their most ordinary exercise is to honour the Sonne & Mother with incessant adoration; and so we read how S. Iohn rauished in extasye beheld the Angels incircling the Throne of God, and falling on their faces before it adoring the B. Trinity, and the sacred Virgin, daughter of the Eternal Father, Mother of the Sonne, and spouse of the holie Ghost: by which

which doth clearly appeare the
excellency of this adoration,
both *Latria*, *and Hyperdulia*, exhibited by al the Court of heauen vnto their King and Queen.

If then their glorious ipirits
honour with so soueraigne and
magnificent a kind of Adoration
the Mother of Alm. God, with
greater reason ought we to honour her, by how much greater
her fauours and graces haue been
to vs, then to them. Let vs then
honour her with al possible reuerence, to shew our selues grateful vnto her for her benefits: Of
which we reade a rare and excellent Example in *Scala cæli*; and it
is this. A certaine holy Monke
in England being much deuoted
to the Queene of heauen, and
amongst other his deuotions v-
sing

sing often to salute her with profound reuerence, and bow downe as often as he hard her name pronounced, this holy name through extremity of age becoming so feeble as he scarce could moue himselfe or so much as stirre him in his bed, the Abbot assigned him one to attend on him in his chamber; but he not being able to be alwayes present to his occasions, it happened that once in his absence he desirous to remoue himselfe, and hauing twice or thrice attempted it in vaine, at last hauing recourse vnto his prayers beseeching the B. Virgins assistance, behold she sodainly appeared to him, waited on by a faire traine of Virgins, two of which by appointment set him in that posture which he desired; when

when the B. Virgin, after she had
most sweetly comforted him (as
a pledge of her deare acceptance
of his deuotion) added vnto his
terme of life twenty yeares, and
restored him to his perfect health
againe. A strange fauour, which
coferr'd not so much vnto the corporal vigour of the man, as it did
to his spiritual in deuoutly seruing her.

But in the laudable exercise
hereof, we are not so much to regard the otward comportment of
the body, as the inward disposition of the mind in framing a
deuout conceipt of the B.Virgin,
imagining her present as often
as we exhibit to her any corporal reuerence, and beholding vs
the while with a deare regard,
whereby this one deuotion will
become

become more familiar to vs, and our remembrance of her more deare and cordial, fo as we fhal take pleafure to fpeake with her and of her, on al occafions, and more confidently preferr our petitions to her in our neceffities; And this affection whofoeuer fhal conceiue of her in his mind, is in a moft happy eftate & may wel prefume of his faluation, and to be one of the number of the elect; whence he cannot but experience an incredible ioy of minde, fince (according to a certaine graue Authour:) *If thou feele in thy hart* (fayes he) *a fingular affection and deuotion to the glorious Virgin, it is a figne of thy Prædeftination to eternal life, and thou mayft wel be glad and reioyce at it.*

These holie motions and pious affects

affects of loue & reuerence were found in that deuout woman, of whom it is recorded in *Scala cęli*; That being of noble birth, though fortune were wanting to her nobility; and hauing two daughters, whom fhee carefully had educated in deuotion to the B. Virgin and the feruice of Alm. God ; It chanced at laft that their pouerty was foe great, as they had nothing to fuftaine their life, nor defend them from the extremity of pouerty ; at which the mother exceedingly afflicted, had recourfe one day vnto the Church, where before an Image of the B. Virgin deuoutly kneeling down, fhe with a voice often interrupted with her fobs and fighes, in this manner deuoutly fupplicated her : *O moft holy Virgin, the refuge*

of

of such miserable creatures as my selfe; behold my two daughters here which it hath pleased Alm. God to bestow on me being brought vnto extreme necessity, whom now I resigne ouer vnto your care and motherly Prouidence, since mine no longer can auayle them; accept them then, and prouide for them as you see best, since al humane protection fayleth mee. Hauing finished her supplication, and being ready to depart the Church; behold a yong may of rauishing feature (wee man wel imagine some Angel sent from heauen) presented her with a hundred poundes saying; This money, Lady, I haue long owed to your deceased husband, pardon my so long delaying the payment of it; So he departed, and she vnto her home; where,

with

with the money she made prouision what was necessary for the adorning her daughters according to their quality; which made the world (euer inclined to imagine and speake the worst) report them to haue by lesse chast wayes arriued at that plēty which it saw they had : the noble mother no sooner had notice hereof , but with teares in her eyes , calling her daughters to her , she sayd vnto them; My daughters, go to the B. Virgin , vnder whose patronage you are , and commend your fame and reputation vnto her, who now is more concerned in it then I , to fetch you faire & clearly off againe; they did so, & with al the attestations as deuotion could suggest, they beseeched their diuine Mistresse , to relieue

leiue them in their fame, as fhe
had in their pouerty; neither was
it in vaine, for in fhort time after,
they became fo vertuoufly repor-
ted of, as the Prince of the countrey moued by the common fame
that went of them, conftituted
them Abbeffes of two feuerall
Monafteries of his foundation.

How

How acceptable to the Bleſſed Virgin theſe reueren-
ces & adorations are.

Chap. II.

HERE is none ſo
ignorant that doth
not know, that the
more we honour
where it is deſerued,
the more we ingratiat our ſelues
with the honoured. This ſuppoſed, we hauing in the precedent
chapter declared the B. Virgins
meriting in the higheſt kinde,
this ſort of Adoration which we
cal *Hyperdulia*, conſequently our
honouring

honouring her therby cannot but
be moſt grateful and acceptable
to her. It is an exerciſe , as we
haue inſinuated , praĉtiſed by the
Angels themſelues in heauen and
who ſoeuer praĉtiſes it on earth,
becomes (as it were) by it,
equale vnto them; Angels of
earth in honouring and reuerencing the ſoueraigne Queene of
heauen. Neither are we to imagine that honour we exhibit vnto her here , leſſe grateful vnto
her , then that which they do
there ; nay , perhaps there are
ſome men on earth ſo zealous in
her ſeruice , who acquit them ſo
wel of their deuotions and with
ſuch vigour of ſpirit goe reuerencing her,that their ſeruices to her
heere , are more grateful then
theirs here, and conſequently in
their

their reward of glory alſo they
ſhal out ſtrip then farr.

Dul-ſighted as we are then,
not to ſee of how great glorye we
depriue our ſelues, when we endeauour not in al we may, to
pleaſe the B. Virgin in honouring her. Certainly, to faſt, to
watch, to weare hayrcloth, ſay
our Beads, Offices, or ſuch deuotions, are very meritorious and
pleaſing vnto her; but it is impoſſible for al the learning and
eloquence of the Quire of Seraphins, to expreſſe vnto the life
the infinit gladnes and extreme
pleaſure ſhe receaues from theſe
Adorations proceeding from the
interior of the minde, and accompanied with the reſpectiue
comportment of the exterior.

Beſides, al the Angels and the
                                  Celeſtial

Celestial Court do take particular contentment in the honour
and reuerence exhibited to their
foueraigne Queene; for if earthly Courtiers reioyce when any
new honour redounds vnto their
Prince, how much more reioycing may we imagine to be in
heauen, when they fee their
Princeffe fo honoured heere?
and of this reioycing the B. Tri-
nitie hath its part, when it beholds her reuerenced, in whom
they haue lodged al their fupreme and fingular delights; the
Father reioyces to fee his daughter fo honored, the Sonne his
Mother, and the holy Ghoft his
Spoufe.

Let al men then, of what eftate,
fexe, or condition they be, with
al diligence and folicitud procure

to

to honour the Glorious and euer
B. Virgin Mary, with al becoming reuerence; especially since
the honour due to her, redounds
vnto her B. Sonne, as the honour
done to Saints doth to God who
made them so. In honouring the
B. Virgin then, as the most excellent of creatures, we honour
God her Creatour, confessing al
those excellencyes we honour
her for, proceeding from his liberality vnto her, and thanking
and praysing him for making a
creature of our owne Condition
so worthy and excellent; besides,
the honour and seruices done
vnto the Mother for the Sonns
regard, the Sonne takes as done
to him, and proceeding from the
loue and respect we beare him,
nay, which is more, the deuotion
towards

towards the Mother encreafes the deuotion towards the fonne, in that she (as moft true vnto his honour (referrs al vnto it that is offered her , and leade them vnto him , who addreffe themfelues vnto her. Iuft fo then , as in honouring and glorifiing the B. Virgin , we do but honour and glorify God, fo we in placeing our Confidence in her , but place it in God himfelfe , for what is it to confide in him , but to confide in thofe meanes which he hath prouided vs for our faluation ; and amongft al the meanes one of the moft efficatious is to Commend our felues vnto her patronage, as we are inftructed by the holy Church in that her Antiphon : *Spes noftra falue : eia ergo aduocata noftra illos tuos mifericordes*

ricordes oculos ad nos conuerte: Haile
O our hope, and O our aduocate
Conuert your eyes of mercy towards vs. And that great light of the
Church S. Auguſtine. ſayes to the
ſame effect: *You are the only hope of
ſinners, & frō you, ô Glorious Virgin.*
We expect pardon of our ſinns, &
recompence for our good works.

Knowing then for certaine, that
in honouring the B. Virgin, we
do but honour God, we are often
to procure to honour her, and
both day and night offer vp vnto
her our reuerēces, eſpecially in
the night when the time is more
ſilent and more fitt for our deuotions. This how grateful it is vnto
her, she her ſelf declared to a certaine Capuchine of our order, one
moſt deuout vnto her. This good
Religious man had a laudable cuſtome profundly to incline vnto

L   her

her a hundred tymes a day, til hauing some special charge of the
Conuent, the performance of
which exacted much time of him,
not able to Comply with both,
he cutt-off one halfe of his deuotions, & diminished them vnto
fifty tymes : Now it happened
that one day whilst he was bu-
sily imployed in his pious exercises, the B. Virgin appeared vnto him, inuested with most glorious ornaments, wearing a riche
mantle ouer them, with only one
halfe of it embroydered with
starrs; and addressing her speech
vnto him she sayd, how comes
it, my sonne, thy loue is growne
so cold in thee ? that hauing begun to imbellish this mantle with
so many bright shiuing starrs,
thou hast giuen ouer and left the
rest

rest vndone ? it is a worke so grateful vnto me the performance
of it; as nothing can bee more vn-
gratefull vnto me then the neglect of it; wherefore as you respect my loue , finish your deuotions as you haue wel begun, and
so vanished away leaving the
good Religious man making his
profit of her so mild reproofe , &
renewing his ancient deuotions
agayne, he exercised them vnto
the end of his life , in that ful
number he began withal.

And let none imagine this a
deuotion only for women or the
simpler and vulgar sort , for al are
equally obliged to honour her, of
what sexe, estate , or condition
soeuer they be; the Patriarkes &
Prophets(as the Diuines affirme)
acknowledged her worth, and re-

uerenced

uerenced her for it thoufands and
thoufands of yeares , before she
was borne into the world : But
what do I talke of Patriarkes and
Prophets, when the Angels them
felues at the firft inftant of their
creation , beholding her in the
Eternal Word , humbly reuerenced and adored her , as one that
should one day be their Queene
in heauen , and be the mother of
their King on earth. And what
should we fay more ? euen
God himfelfe become man was
obedient vnto her commands,
and obferued her with al filial
loue and reuence.

To defcend now to the Chriftians of the Primitiue Church,
the Apoftles reuerenced her dedicated Temples to her feruice,
erected Altars to her , and according

ding to the opinions of some cõ-
fecrated to her the famous houfe
of Loretto. But omitting thefe,
let vs come to the Potentates of
the world ; how many Empe-
rours,Kings, and foueraigne Bishops haue there been , who haue
reuerently taken their Crownes
of their heads, and offered them
at her feete?

What titles of prayfe and honour by the Doctors of the
Church haue anciently been beftowed vpon her by S. Hierome,
S. Auguftine, S. Chryfoftom, and
innumerable others ? how Diuinely hath S. Thomas fpoken in
her prayfe ? how deuoutly S. Bonauenture ? and how affectionatly Albert the Great , in humble
acknowledgement of the learning which he receiued from her?

Let vs fixe vpon Alexander de Hales amongſt the reſt, as one ſingularly deuoted vnto her, and recount the motiue he had to leaue the world, and inrol himſelfe in the ſeruice of our Sauiour Chriſt vnder the banner of S. Francis of Aſſiſium.

This Alexander of Hales being English by nation, was of a ſublime ſpirit, and of ſingular erudition, the firſt profeſſor of Theologie in the Vniuerſitie of Paris, & one ſo affectionatly deuoted to the B. Virgin, as he made a vowe, neuer to refuſe any thing that should be asked him in her name; A certaine Gentle woman vnderſtanding this, perſuaded the Bernardines to make their vſe of it by winning him to their Order, and illuſtrating it by ſo great a

light

light of learning , which they reſolued to doe , and repairing to him they made their approaches a farr off , diſcourſing of learning and deuotion ; but God Alm. permitted not , that at that time they should come neerer to him ; the Gentle - woman vnderſtanding what was done , had recourſe vnto the Frier Preachers next , animating them and putting them in the way to make him one of their Order as she done the Bernardines before ; which was attempted alſo by them , & iuſt as they were putting him to his vowe , by chance two Frier Minors coming in , one of them diuinely inſpired thus ſayd vnto him ; Alexander , it is highe time for you to with draw your ſelfe from thoſe vanityes which haue abuſed you

L 4   ſo

so long; wherefore in the name of
God and his B. Mother I coniure
you to take the habit of S. Francis , for I know his Order hath
need of such as you are ; Alexander touched with these words as
by the finger of the holy Ghost,
and remembring the vow he had
made , answered him presently,
Goe you hence good fathers, and
I wil instantly follow to the ful
effecting of your desires ; and so
he did , taking on him the holy
habit , til being in his probation
he was greeuously tempted to
cast it off agayne , by reason of
some austerities he could not vndergoe so wel ; and iust as he was
vpon the point of doing it , behold S. Francis appeared vnto
him in his sleepe , bearing on his
shoulders a heauie Crosse, with
                            which

which he endeauoured to clime a
ftipe hil; at which he was fo moued with compaffion, as he offered him his feruice to helpe him
vp with it; wherupon the Saint
beholding him with an angrie
eye, goe offer thy feruice (fayd
he) to fuche weaklings as thy
felfe; for if thou canft not carry
thine that is fo light, how canft
thou help me to beare my hea-
uier one? the Nouice perceiuing
ftrait his mind from this his re-
prehenfion, refolued to continue
in the Order, not withftanding
al the difficulties thereof, and
concluded there was no other
waye to heauen, then by bearing
the Croffes which are offered vs.

L v   *That*

That the quality of Mother of God obliges both men and Angels to the adoring of her.

CHAP. III.

AMONG al dignities, graces, greatnesses, and prerogatiues, with which Alm. God hath honored the B. Virgin, there is none more highe and sublime, then that of being Mother of God, it surpassing al of which any creature can be capable; surmounts the heauens, and the celestial Hierarchies,

chies, comes neere to diuine, immense, and incomprehensible, & in fine goes beyond al that can be expreſſ't by words, or conceiued by any Angelical or humane thought. This S. Auguſtine in the beginning of his book of the B. Virgins Aſſumption, doth intimate, where he ſayes : *There is no hart that conceiue, or tongue that can expreſſe the effect of this grace and dignity.* And S. Bernard in diuers places and diuers manners aymes at the expreſsion of this great dignity. S. Anſelme in his Treatiſe of the B. Virgins magnituds ſayes; that next to the being God, there is no dignity in heauen or earth can equal hers : *To ſay only* (ſayes he) *of the B. Virgin, that she is Mother of God, is a thing that exceeds al ſublimity, which next to God can be said or imagined.* From hence the holy Fathers inferr, that the title of being Mother of God, is the foûtaine from whence do flow al her other graces and prerogatiues ; for so , say they, whence was it, that from al eternity she was in a particular māner predestinat ; because she was to be the Mother of God. Why was she sanctified by the holy Ghost in her Mothers wombe? to be the more worthy receptacle of the Sonne of God. Why in her Conception was she exempted from original sinne? that the eternal Word might from her body take immaculat flesh. Why was she exalted aboue al the Thrones & celestial Hierarchies? but because she was the Mother of God, who is the soueraine King of heauē & earth.

earth. Whence in fine, is it, that
the Princes of heauen and earth,
nay, euen of Hel it felfe, bow
downe and do reuerence at mention of her name, but only becaufe she is Mother to the fupreme Lord of al, to whom al do
homage, and in whofe prefence
al the great ones that are, fhrinke
vp to nothing, and not appeare
at al. O wonderful greatnes of
this highe and excellent dignity
beftowed vpon a fimple Virgin!
Who is not aftonifhed, who is
not alienated from his fenfes with
admiration? to be at once a mother, and a Virgin! to containe
in the narrow inclofure of her
wombe, him whom the heauens
with al their height & latitud can
not containe! to be Mother of
the moft deare delights of the
Eternal

Eternal Father, and the most glorious obiects of Angels, and finally (which is the most prodigious of al) to haue produced her Creatour, and brought her Father forth. These are things aboue al capacity, rauishing nature with astonishment and wonder, so as with good reason the holy Church sayes of her : *Nature admired, when you brought forth that holy one, who brought forth you.*

The B. Virgin then merits in being Mother of God, al imaginable honour from one creature to another, and in particular that which the Diuines intitle *Hyperdulia*, which also admits of a subdiuision, according to Suarez, into superiour & inferiour ; with the inferiour those are honored, who haue some particular excellence
lence

lence aboue the rest, as to S. Iohn
Baptist, & the Apostles, for their
eminency of place, to S. Francis
for the singular testimony of his
sanctity giuen by him. God in
the impression of the sacred Stig-
mats: but with the superiour, the
Mother of God alone, who only
had the honour to beare, bring
forth, nourish, & educat the only
Sonne of the only Eternal God.

And in regard of this high and
most eminent dignity of hers, al
Creatures in heauen and earth reuerence her, and acknowledge
her for their soueraigne Lady and
Queene, and at her name the
greatest Potentats on earth bow
downe their knees, and do humble reuerence; so al generations
of the world praise and honour
her, as she in her Canticle diuine-

ly

ly prefaged: *Behold from henceforth al generatiōs shal cal me bleſſed; & de facto*, what people, what nation is there on the earth, ſo irreligious and barbarous, who haue her not in honour and reuerence? Euen the Iewes, & their Rabbins haue written in her praiſe, and the moſt obſtinat of them haue experienced and acknowledged her moſt powerful aide in their neceſſities.

As witneſſeth this maruaylous ſtory recorded by the learned Pelbert in his Stellary of the B. Virgin; of a Iewiſh-woman, who being in the paines of childbirth, & neerer going out of the world, then bringing a child into it, ſome Chriſtians (who charitably came to viſit her) exhorted her to inuocat the B. Virgin for her deliuerance; the poore woman did

ſo

so and lifting vp her eyes & voice to heauen in a languishing manner; O most gracious Virgin (said she) I beseech you to haue pitty on me though I be of the vnhappy race of those who so crucified God your Sonne & consequently vnworthy of your fauours) yet notwithstāding if you shal vouchsafe me your assistance in this extremity, I do heere vow to relinquish the errour of my Religion, and together with the fruit of my wombe (as soone as it shal be borne to light) to receiue the holy Baptisme , and liue and die at your deuotion: she had no sooner pronounced this, but sodainly behold her safely deliuered of a sonne , which according to her vow within some few dayes (together with her self) she procured

to

to haue baptized; which her huſband (who then had vndertaken a Iourney) vnderſtanding at his returne , he was ſo mightily incēſed at it, and in ſo furious a rage, as he preſently in his mothers armes murthered the innocēt child; whereupon she out of feare of her owne death, and horrour of her childs , fled inſtantly crying al the way she went , in ſuch a vehemencye, and in ſuch affright, as the people flocking about her , & vnderſtanding the reaſon of her laments , rann al towards her home ſo violently bent againſt the Murtherer, as infaillibly they had torne him in peeces had they encountred him ; but he, (what with the horrour of his crime, and feare of punishment) preuented them, and fled towards the Citty gates

gates which finding shut, he was
forced to take sanctuary in a litle
Chappel of the B. Virgins then
open by chance, where hauing
leisure to looke about him, he es-
pyed an Image of our B. Lady in
Relieue, ouer the highe Altar, at
sight of which he was so strucken
with shame and repentance, as
casting him on his knees with a
dolorous accent; *Too great* (sayd
he) *too great, O sacred Virgin, is
your beingnity to me, who haue so
greeuously offended you, to Protect and
conceale me in this my flight; but I
see it is true what I haue often hard,
that your Clemency is the greatest
maruayle in the world, and that but
regard it, & it is vnmeasurable euery
way : I implore then that sweet clemency of yours not to saue my life,
for the horriblnes of my Crime, hath*
                              aswel

afwel taken from me the defire, as the deferuing of it, but to forget it, and to forgiue and washe it away in the foûtaine of my teares, & withal to accept his deed of guift of mine to your B. Sonne and you, of my hart and al I am, who now haue no other defire, then to be al, and wholly yours.

He had profecuted his fpeech, but the Officers entring the Chapel, interrupted him, and feazing on him, they carried him prifoner to the Prouoft of the place; where he was no fooner come, but falling on his knees before him, he fayd vnto him with a refolut countenance; I do not this to moue you to Compaffion of my crime, and faue my life, but only to begg this fauour of you, that I may haue the happines to be baptized before I dye.

The

The Prouost no lesse reioycing then wondring at his demand, gladly granted him his request, and hauing receiued him from the Font himselfe , that Ceremony, being ouer, he proceeding to the examination of his fact, not letting the pleasure of the one, hinder the displeasure of the other. But behold, while this was in agitation, the mother powring forth her affection in laments ouer the murthered carcasse of her Child , by degrees perceiued it stirr , and fixe its eyes vpon her with a gratious smile , and being in a transport of ioy and admiration therof , at the same instant was brought her the newes of her husbands Conuersion; whereupon she instantly tooke her child , and presented it aliue

before

before the Prouoſt, no marke
nor ſigne remayning that euer it
had been dead, but only a litle
ſtarr where he had giuen the
wound. The Prouoſt beholding
this ſupendious miracle, abſolued
the Criminal as one who already
was abſolued from heauen; who
being a learned man and a great
Rabby in the Iewiſh law, after-
wars wholy conuerted his tongue
and penne to the ſetting forth
the prayſes of the B. Virgin and
the Chriſtian law, which he ſtrő-
gly defended againſt the errours
of that ſort.

Nay, euen the Turkes themſelues, and impious Moores concurr in honouring the ſacred Virgin; and reuerencing her as Mother of God, as appeares by the
greeuous penaltyes impoſed by
their

their Alcoran, on any whofoeuer
shal blafpheme her name. But
what should we fay of the honour
exhibited to her amongft the
Chriftians, when fcarcely is any
fo poore a village or hamlett,
where she is not honoured; by
fome place of deuotion dedicated
vnto her? and her Images and pi-
ctures are in fuch veneration, as
who hath not part in the worship
of them?

A yong Scholler (as Vincentius in his hiftorial Mirrors recounteth it) being fo deuoted to
her, as he vfed on his knees, as
often as any Image of hers occu-
r'd, to falute her in this deuout
manner. *Haile Mary* &c. or this:
Bleffed is the facred Virgin; wombe
that bore the Eternal fathers fonne,
and bleffed the breafts that gaue him
                                    fuck

sucke, &c. But as God oftentimes
scourges those most , whom he
loues dearest, it hapned this yong
man fel into so violent a freinzie,
as he would teare and bite his
bookes and euery thing he could
lay his hands vpon ; One day
amongst the rest being in his furious fitts , beho d a yong man of
incomparable beauty , and shining with resplendant light (no
doubt but his good Angel) was
seen by his beds side , making for
him this pious prayer: O B. Lady,
see, see your poore seruant heere,
who so deuoutly and often hath
prayed vnto you ; and giuen a
thousand testimonies of his deuotion; behold him now in how pitious a state he is , so destitut of al
humane Comforts, as euen inhumanity it selfe would commise-

rat

rat his cafe; this is the mouth, thefe are the lippes that haue fo often pronounc't your praife; and is it not pitty to fee them now, the inftruments of rage & furye only, which were once only of deuotiõ and piety? O therfore haue mercy vpõ him, who of none with more right can expect it then of you, & reftor' him to that health he fo wel imploied in your honor hertofore; This faid, he dif-appeared, and the yong man felt inftantly the effect of his prayers by his recouery, which was fo fpeedy & miraculous, as acknowledging the B. Virgins particular fauour in it, he to grati-fie her for it, entred into an auftere Religiõ, where he liued & died as became one, who held his life on fuch a pious tenour of his good Angel, and his better Aduocate.

M   *How*

*Hovv we ought to reuerence
and adore the B Virgin,
in regard of the sublimity
of her glory aboue al other
Saints.*

CHAP. IV.

EEING the Saints
which are now in
heauen, in possession
of their eternity of
happines, are to be
honoured with that sort of reuerence which the Diuines cal *Dulia,* which is the lowest sort of reuerêce appropriated to any Saint, & the higher they are in dignity,
with

with the more high and particular reuerence are they to be honoured ; what supreme honour
may we imagine due, vnto our
soueraigne Lady and Queene of
heauen, who by so many degrees
of dignity is preferred before
them al, seated at the right hand
of her B. Sonne, so neere and
deare vnto him as she is , and
whom the rest of Saints, only a
farr off reuerence and admire?
And if it be true, that each ones
glory beares a proportion with
the grace they haue, & the more
their grace on earth the more
their glory in heauen ; how excellent in glory must she bee a-
boue them al , who was so farr
superiour to them in grace ? for
who knowes not, how from the
very instant of her Conception,

M 2   when

when she was sanctified in her Mothers wombe, God went heaping more and more graces vpon her stil, vntil her death when the accumulation was Complete, and how in al tymes she cooperated with him in al her actions, in al occureces, stil meditating how to add vnto it, accompanying al her exteriour workes with the interiour intention of the minde; Which Albert the great exemplifies very wel in that treatise of his, *de beata Virgine*; and S. Bernard more particularly where he sayes. This Virgin and mother of the highest, not only waking but euen sleeping had the fruition of heauenly things in Contemplation, no earthtlye affaire being so forcible, as to interrupt her Commerce of thought with heauen

uen, in so much as euen in her sleepe she was busyed more in Contemplation then the rest of the Saints when they were most perfectly awake. Who then, of what intelligent a spirit soeuer they bee, can comprehend the immensity of the grace and merits of the glorious Virgin, & consequently the infinit glorie she had in recompence, seeing as the same Doctours affirmes; *The more she excelled others in grace on earth, the more glory she obtained in heauen.* Let vs conclude then, that her glory there, is incomprehensible, and surpasses by infinite degrees that of al the Saints & Angels; Conformable to that saing of S. Iohn Chrysostome: *What is there more holy than the B. Virgin* (says he;) *neyther the Pro-*

3 M   *phets*

phets *Apostles, Martyrs, Patriarcks,
Angels, Trones, Dominations, Seraphins,* nor *Churubins*; *in fine, there is
no visible nor Created thing more
great or more excellent then she.*

And S. Anselme; *Ineffable* (says
he) *and euer-more admirable is the
grace and greatnes of this Virgin:*
And in prosecuting his discourse:
*And what, O B. Lady : is there more
to be sayd? when but Considering the
immensity of your grace , glory; and
félicity , I am destitut of forces; and
my Voice fayleth me.* And yet not
only from the abūdance of Grace
which was in her, but much more
from her humility may we argue
the greatnes and dignity which
she hath in heauen ; for it being
an approued verity to al the world
that the more we abase our selues
on earth, the more shal we be exalted

alted for it in heauen; as is testi-
fyed by verity it self: *Vvho humble
themselues, shalbe exalted*, &c. And
that great light of the Church S.
Ambrose sayes: *The more abiect we
are on earth, the more we shalbe exalted for it in heauen* : And he adds;
*That by so many degrees of humility
we descend on earth, by so many of
glory we shal ascend in heauen.* Since
no creature euer thought so humbly and abiectly of her selfe as
this B. Virgin did, we may wel
imagine, that by this pretious
vertue she so wonn the hart of
God, and gott such hold of his affections, that she euen obliged
him by it to descend from heauen
to earth into her wombe, and
choose her for his spouse and mother, which she in that Canticle
of hers Confesses of her selfe:

Because

Becauſe he hath regarded the humili-ty of his hand-maid, &c. Which ſhewes the excellency of her humility. And S. Bernard ſayes of it, that when the Angel ſaluted her, her anſwering him in that manner ſo humble, and reſigning her ſelfe entirely vnto the Wil of God : *Behold the hand-maid of our Lord*, &c. Was more grateful vnto God, and meritorious for her, then al the actions of men and Angels put together, and that by it alone, ſhe merited, the being Mother of our Sauiour Chriſt : *Neuer* (ſayes S. Bernard) *had ſhe been exalted aboue the Angels, if ſhe had not humbled her ſelfe before.*

And if ſome Saints, as namely S. Francis, haue merited by their humility, to be ranged amongſt the Seraphins the cheifeſt Order

of

of Angels and next to the Diuinity; to what immensitie of glory
are we to imagine the B. Virgin is
exalted, for the profoundnes of
her humility, which descended
lower then euer any Saints could
doe? In consideration of which,
we may wel imagine, that her
glorie and felicity as farr surpasseth that of al other Saints, as the
heaues do a litle point, the cleare
light of the Sunne a candle the
Ocean a smale drop of water, or al
the earth the least graine of sand.

With good reason then, since
she is exalted to such a height of
dignitie, we are to honour her, as
the soueraine Queene and Empresse of men and Angels; and as
eminent as she is in dignity so is
she in beautye and amability, a-
ble to obscure with the brightnes

M v   of

of its splendour, not only al humane eyes, but euen those of the Angels themselues, as appeares by this story recorded by Herod Religious of the Order of S. Dominick.

There was a yong scribe (sayes he) much deuoted to the B. Virgin, who being some-what conuersant in the holy Scriptures where her excellent beauty is commended with such Encomiums, he at last grew passionatly desirous to see her in that beauty she appeared with in heauen, & praying for the accomplishment of his desires, he heard a voyce reprehending him for it; in that he ask't a thing aboue his capacity & which his eyes were too weake to behold; nor could it cost him lesse then his sight the beholding it;

it; but he willing to put it to the venture, perſiſted ſtil in his Petition, yet at laſt vpon more mature reflexion, he reſolu'd, if the fauour were granted him, to reſerue on eye at leaſt whileſt only with the other he regarded it; And ſo it happened that she appearing vnto him in a moſt glorious and reſplendent manner, that one eye with which he regarded her, being ouercome with the excellency of the obiect, became wholy blind; but ſo farr was he from euer repenting it, as with iterated petition he beſought her, to appeare but vnto him in that glory once agayne, and he would be alſo willing to forgoe the other eye; the B. Virgin to content his deuotion, did as he deſired her, but was ſo farr from inflicting

that

that penalty vpon him which he
did expect , as she restored him
his other eye againe , wher with
we may imagine how contented
a man he was.

Neither doth she exceed al the
Angels and Saints in beauty and
splendour only , but also in ioy
and felicity , which with out
doubt she hath in as supermi-
nent degree aboue the rest, as her
glory aboue the rest is more high
and eminent ; And for that there
are diuers Doctours who affirme;
that she alone hath more glory
then al the Saints together ; this
being so , imagine of what ioy &
felicity she is possest the while;
the quality of which is so exceedingly rauishing , that S. Augustine doubts not to affirme of it,
that one dropp of heauenly felicity

city but falling into hel, would
sweeten al its torments. O strange
expression of the wôdrous sweetnes and deliciousnes thereof: if
one dropp of it could worke such
effects in hel, what must whole
torrents of it worke in the harts
of those who are possest of it? The
Apostles vpon an arid and barren
mountains topp, sawe but only a
litle glimpse of the glory of heauen in our Sauiours Transfigura-
tion, and tasted by it but a litle
superficial ioy, and yet you see
they could haue been content to
haue remained there al their liues. But that example which I
shal now declare, deserues yet
greater admiration.

A certaine Religious Monke
of holy life, exercised long in the
contemplation of the Ioyes of
Heauen, conceiued at last such

a feruent defire of it, that he in-
ceffantly befought Alm. God,
that (to comprehend it the better) if it were poffible he might
haue fome taft of it in this
mortal life; and continuing in
this deuotion many yeares, at
laft clofe by his Cell he heard a
bird fing fo wondrous delightful-
ly, as rauifhed with it, he prefently lyed him out to enioy more
freely its delicious melody, and
following it a flight or two, at
laft it ledd him into a wood therby; where it begann to fing; and
he rauifh't in hearing it, fatt
downe nighe the tree wheron it
was, where he might both fee &
heare it beft, nor did he know,
with whether he was delighted
moft; who when he beheld the
beauty of it, wifhed himfelf al
eyes

eyes, when he heard its diuine
notes wished himselfe al eares a-
gaine; In fine, feasting these two
senses so long he satt till the Bird
cea'st its melody, and flew quite
away; when he arising tooke his
way towards his Monastery, imagining he had been away only
some houre or two; but being returned back againe, he foūd it almost
al rebuilded a new againe, and
knocking at the gate, the Porter
and he were both so strange one
to another, as they admired at
either, the Porter that the Monke
should say he was Religious of
the house, the Monke that he
should say he had been Porter
there many yeares; In fine, the
Abbot came being informed thereof, whom he as litle knew as the
Porter, and vnto whom he was as
litle

litle knowne; who in fine exami-
ning him, foūd by the Records of
the Houſe that thoſe Religious
whom he named , to haue liued
in that Monaſtery with him, were
deceaſed ſo long before , as by
computation of time they found,
he had been abſent three hūdred
and ſixty yeares. If then ſo many
yeares ſeemed but a ſhort houre
to that Religious man charmed
with the ſweetnes of that Muſick
he liſtned vnto, perform'd perhaps by ſome Angel of heauen;
how delicious , ſweet , and rauiſh-
ing muſt the Ioyes of Heauen
needs bee, where al the Angels
ſing together inceſſantly praiſing
and glorifying their heauenly
King.

　And if this good Religious
man could remaine expos'd vnto
the

the iniuries of the time ſo many
yeares, rauiſhed with taſting but
one dropp as it were of the deliciouſnes of heauen; O God, who
can imagine the delight of thoſe,
who in al comfortable Eternity
ſhal bee feaſted with it to al ſa-
tiety; *They ſhal bee inebriated with*
the abundance of thy houſe, and drink
of the torrent of thy delights ; ſayes
the holy Scripture. Seeing then
the B. Virgin, next to God is
Miſtreſſe and Lady of this Pallace
of deliciouſnes, and as it were the
pipe that coueyes al its deliciouſnes from God the fountaine of it,
to al that participat of its Ioy in
heauen : Let vs honour, adore,
and reuerence her with al thoſe
due acknowledgments, of which
we haue already treated or ſhal
herafter treate.

That

*That we ought to adore the
B Virgin, for that she is
the soueraine Lady of all
Creatures both in earth,
and heauen.*

CHAP. V.

A PERSON which
is riche, noble, and
vertuous, deſerveth
honour, & the more
they excel in it, the
more honour they deſerue; as we
ſee by experiēce in perſons moſt
eminent in the world. The Bleſſed Virgin then, being ſo great a
paterne of ſanctity, a Compen-
dium

dium of al perfections, chosen by
God for his Mother, and elected
to a supreme height of dignity
aboue al the Quiers of Angels,
and finally being Empresse of al
superiour and inferiour Creatures; with good reason both Angels and men are to honour and
reuerence her, as the soueraigne Queene of the whole Vniuerse : neither should there be
any (me thinks) so impudent
to dispute her title to it, nor so
impious as to offer to defraude
her of those sublime honours due
to so sublime a title; she were a
Queene, if there were no other
reason but only because her sonne
is a King, *King of Kings*, & *Lord
of Lords*; and who knowes not
that the King and Queenes honours goes so conioyn'd in one,

as

as from the dishonouring the
one, redounds to the other a dishonour too? The B. Virgin, being
(as formerly we haue said) daughter to God the Father, Mother of
his Sonne, and Spouse of the holy Ghost, and consequently
daughter, mother, and spouse of
the holy Trinity, considering her
alliance and coniunction with
God, and namely with the hu-
manized Word of God the Sóne,
whom this great Al acknowledges for King; of her being Queen
can be no doubt al; and this S.
Athanasius affirmes where he
sayes: *He being King and Lord, his*
mother who engendred him, hath con-
sequently the reputation of Queene and
Mother. And S. Iohn Damascen:
She was vndoubtedly declared Queene
(sayes he) of al Created things when
she

she became Mother of the Creatour.

Let vs then conclude, that she being Queene of this Vniuerse, hath ouer it an absolut command, and that al are to obey her, and render her that honour and obeissance, which from Vassals is due to those who are ouer them; And in admiration of this power of hers, was that deuout exclamation of holy S. Bernard; *O blessed Mary* (sayes he) *al power is giuen you both in heauen and earth, do as you can do al that you desire.*

Among al the titles of Greatnes, which our Mother the holy Church honours her with, that of *Queene of heauen* she vses most frequently, & *Lady of Angels: Regina cæli,* & *Domina Angelorum,* &c. Now the greater the extent of ones Dominion is, the greater
 euer

euer is their power and magnificence; so as if one could attaine to the Dominion ouer al the world; how absolute and vnlimited should their power to be? and yet what is al this world to the Heauens amplitude which she is Lady of ? and where her subiects are perpetually honoring her, so as we may say of her: *The Heauens declare the glory of Mary* ; and the heauenly Courtyers take it for honour to obey her commands. To conclude, it is but litle we can say of her greatnes, how great soeuer that litle may seeme to be, and arriuing euen to admiration, which euer there takes vp , where humane knowledge leaues.

And so is it not an admirable thing, that the whole roundour of the earth in comparison of the
Heauens

Heauens should be but as the center point compared to a mightie Spheare? & who can imagine then the immenhty of that, when the earth which containes Empires, Kingdomes and Prouinces, is so meere a nothing in comparison thereof? Some are of opinion, that the element of water is ten times bigger then the land, the aire ten times bigger then the water, the fire then that, and so with proportion each heauen bigger then another, &c. And to giue you some dimme light of its magnitud, the Moone which in lesse then a moneth surrounds its Orbe, would be incircling the starry heauen according to the most expert of the Mathematiciens thirty sixe thousand yeares and more; which notwithstan-

ding

ding compared to the *Cœlum em-pyreum* or habitation of the Bles-sed, is but a poore litle Circle, & for magnitud not worthy the speaking of. For which reason some Authours are of opinion ci-ted by Philip Diez, that if a mil-stone were throwne from thence, it would be a thousand fiue hun-dred yeares in falling down. Who admires not in hearing this, and cries not out with him : *O Lord, I haue considered your workes, and remaine astonished and out of my self with wonder.*

One of the ancient Prophets in consideration of the greatnes of this glorious Pallace of Alm. God exclaime : *O Israel, how great is the house of God, how mighty great is the place of his possession ? he is great and hath no limits, he his high*

and

and cannot be meafured. And we may wel imagine it to bee great, fince euery Saint shal haue a habitation a part, and a place proportioned vnto its merits. And this we haue from our Sauiour Chrift himfelfe in comforting his afflicted Difciples for his departure, where he fayes : *Let not your harts be troubled for in my fathers houfe are many manfions.* And S. Vincent of S. Dominiks Order, fpeaking of thefe Manfions, fayes *that each of the Bleffed in heauen shal haue affigned them for their habitation a larger circuit them is betwixt the eaft and weft.* Now there being incomparably more Saints in heauen, then there be men on earth, I leaue it to you to imagine how infinit great the heauenly Kingdome is.

N   Now

Now the B. Virgin being Queen of this so immense dominion, hath al the Blessed there consequently for her subiects, & Courtiers, who being in due Order rankt about her Throne, alwayes make tender vnto her of their seruices and obsequiousnes, and if (as S. Iohn Chrisostome sayes) while she was yet on earth she was attended vpon by such an infinity of Angels to defend her against al the assaults of hel , and conserue vnto their king this faire tabernacle of his , Inuiolat ; how much more gloriously attended is she now in heauen , where she sits crown'd in possession of so highe a dignitie ? It is impossible to imagine the number that waytes vpon her there ; which the Prophet endeauouring to speake of
sayes

sayes. *Ten thousand serue thee, and a hundred times ten thousand assist before thee* : setting downe a finit number for an infinit. And S. *Denys* sayes, that the number of Angels by many parts exceeds the number of al Corporal and material things. And for those, we know, how the sublunary bodies yeild in greatnes to the celestial bodyes , and they vnto the tother, the more high they are; in so much as not a starr of the least magnitud, but is farr greater then al the globe of inferior things together. We know besides , that euery man from Adam to the Consummation of the world hath had and shal haue an Angel Guardian to attend vpon them, be they good or bad , al equally participating of this benefit; whence

N 2   it

it followes, (as we haue fayd before)that the number of Inferiour
Angels deputed to that charge,
exceedeth the number of al men
that euer were, are, and shal bee;
which being fo, how innumerous
muft the fuperiour bee, fince (as
we haue formerly deduced) they
increafe in proportion the more
fuperior they are. Certainly, more
eafy it were, to number al the
ftarrs in heauen, the drops of the
Sea, the leaues of trees, the plants
of the earth, and the Atomes of
the Sun, then the multitud of Angels knowne only to God himfelfe.

Let vs add moreouer, the better
to fett of the glory of our foueraigne Queene, a fecond wonder in
traine of this; to wit; That al the
Angels, as infinit as they are,
                              haue

haue each one yet a diuersity
among themselues ; and if it be
such a delightful sight, to see a
Garden al planted with variety
of flowers, how much more delightful must it bee, to see these
Angelical flowers adorning the
heauenly Garden with each one
their seueral species according to
their seueral dignity and merits?
And heere our Imagination hath
a spatious feild, to exercise it
selfe in deuout conceipts of the
B. Virgins perfections and excellence ; for if the Courtiers striue
with so much splédor, how much
more splendid must needes that
Maiestie bee, on whom they al
attend.

For so these B. Spirits are perpetually attending before her
Throne adoring her, and ready at

N 3   the

the least twinkling of her eye, to
execut her commands, which are
commonly for the good and saluation of man. This is the opinion of S. Augustine where he
sayes: *S. Michael and al the other*
Angels haue an eye in heauen vnto
the B. Virgin, to see where shee would
Command them any things for the
good of soules on earth. Let vs conclude then; that her Greatnesse
are vnspeakeable and incomprehensible not only by men but
euen by the Angels themselues,
and that next to God she hath
the most soueraigne command in
heauen , as being Queene of al
the celestial Hierarchies there,
and Mother of the supreme Mo-
narck and Creator of euery thing.

Neither-doth her dominion
terminate or end heere, but as
she

she is Queene of Angels, and of
Heauen, fo alfo is fhe of Earth &
the Inhabitants thereof; and for
this reafon the Diuines cal her frequently *Regina mundi*, the Queen
of earth. S. Gregory often intit-
les her to the name of *Lady of al
Chriſtians*; & fo with good reafon
may fhe bee, who was fo great a
part of our redemption, for God
had neuer been made man but for
her, and confequently had neuer
fuffered for vs, nor gone through
with the worke of our redemption; which ought to be a powerful Motiue to induce vs to honour
and reuerence her.

Nay, euen the very diuels themfelues do dread her power at the
fole inuocation of whofe name
they al are put to flight; When *I
pronounce but Aue Maria* (fayes the

deuout

deuout S. Bernard) *the Heauens do
smile, the Angels reioyce, the world
exults, hel trembles, and the diuels are
in difmay.* S. Bridgitt in the firſt
booke of her Reuelations ſayes,
that the B. Virgins rankes and dignity in heauen is ſo ſupreme,
as the diuels are conſtrained to
honour it; and ſhe addes : That
as often as any ſhalbe moleſted by
their temptations, let them but
inuocat her ſacred name, and preſently they al ſhal vaniſh and
be put to flight, of whoſe ſole
Command they more ſtand in
awe, then of al their torments;
ſo as whenſoeuer ſhe vndertakes
the cauſe of any ſoule, they dare
not withſtand her in it ; as witneſſeth this ſtory regiſtred in the
Promptuary of her Miracles, and
taken out from thence by *Pelbert*
iñ

in his *Stellary of the B. Virgin.*

There was a man (sayes he) of a nature so euil inclined and peruerse, as he neuer was exercised in any good, but only in some few reuerences and praiers which he daily offered vp to the B. Virgin. This man, though often inspired to leaue his wicked life, was yet so farr from it, as he persisted more obstinat in it euery day, vntil at last in drawing his latest breath, he imagined himself hurried by a crew of diuels, with horrible noyse and howlings vnto the tribunal of the Iudge; where they demaunding iustice, and the Iudge putting them to declaration of the cause, they clearly proued him a most wicked man, and as such desired sentence should be giuen on him; When

N v   the

the B. Virgin standing vp in his
defence , declared whatsoeuer
good she had knowne by him,
like a most faithful Aduocate;
but scarce had she finished her
speech, when in an insolent manner the diuels argued against her
thus; is this al you are able to say
for him ? vnlesse you defend his
cause better then so and bring
more proofes of goodnes in him,
what , for his bad, wil become of
him may be easily seen; & heere
he began to add vnto the list of
his offences thousands and thousands more , when the B. Virgin
seeing their number so great, as
by the way of Iustice there was
no hope for him , shee strait addrest her selfe by that of mercy,
and prostrating her selfe before
the Iudges feete, no sooner he had
raysed

raised her vp, but fhe began : if thefe pretenders to Iuftice (fayd fhee) were intereffed in the caufe more then out of malice, they fhould carry it and I would not fo much as difpute it with them, but to what end al this long re-capitulation of crimes what con-cernes it them whether your infpirations were obeyed or no ? or fince when haue they been foe iealous of your honour, that they fhould care fo much where you were difhonored? certainly, if there be any fault, it is cheifly theirs, and if there be any of-fence it is only yours; it is you only whom he hath offended,and to you alone he is ready to make fatisfaction,not with any boaft of merit, or that he ftands on iufti-fying his caufe, but with repen-

tance

tance in his heart, teares in his
eyes,& fighs in his mouth, to obtaine of your mercy, what of iuftice he cannot hope for. I côfeffe
the quantity & quality of his crimes are fo enormious great, that
they deferue nothing but death &
dānation; but if my prayers were
euer powerful with you now hear
my prayers for him, and by thefe
breafts which had the honour
once to giue you fucke, I coniure
you; for fo many drops of milke
you haue receiued from them, to
beftow one drop of bloud of the
aboundance you haue fhed for
finners, to wafhe this man from
his finnes; for his life hereafter
I wil vndertake, fo as you wil
pardon what is paft; for I fee al
fignes of a repentant finner in his
heart, his eyes, and al; and concluding heere with a profound re-

uerence, the Iudge remained a
while with his eyes fixt vpon the
ground in great suspence , now
weighing the mightines of his
crimes, now of her power that
interceded for him, whilst either
part was wauering betwixt hope
and feare; at last lifting vp his
eyes , & casting them on her with
a gracious regard : Though it be
exceeding much you aske,said he,
yet were it much more I could
not deny it such an intercession;
for your sake then I pardon him
this once, but neuer let him hope
for pardon againe , if he abuse it
now ; hauing sayd this, the diuels
confounded departed with horrible cryes saying; We knew wel
enough what would be the end of
it , shee euer hath the better of
vs , and 'tis our folly to contend
with

with her, she is too powerful an
Aduocate, and too gracious with
the Iudge: so they vanished away,
and the poore man returning to
himself againe, recounted to al
this horrible vision, and decei-
uing the Phisicians for his corporal health, and the diuels for his
spiritual, he recouered both, making of either such vse for the
time to come, that he entred into
Religion, and there to his dying
day ledd a most holy life.

By which we may see the pre-
ciousnes of the sacred bloud of
Christ our Lord, and how preua-
lent with him and powerful ouer
our aduersaries is his Glorious
Mother and our most faithful
Aduocate.

Of

Of the great honour we owe
to the B Virgin for her
being our most deare and
merciful Mother.

CHAP. VI.

THE Blessed Virgin standing at the foote of the Crosse on Mount Caluary accompanied with S. Iohn; Our Sauiour Christ beholding her with a pittiful and gracious eye, sayed vnto her; W*oman, behold thy sonne*; meaning S. Iohn, and then addressing his speech to him he sayd; *Behold thy Mother*; & from

from that time (fayes the holy
Scripture) he made account of
her as his owne, and to the end
of his life obferued her accor-
dingly.

From hence the learned gather this great myftery; how our
Sauiour in recommending her
vnto S. Iohn for his Mother commended al the faithful vnto her
for her children; for if S. Iohn
(fay they) reprefented them al
(as there is no doubt of it) the
B. Virgin being affigned him for
Mother, was likewife affigned
vnto al Chriftians. Whereupon
S. Bernard fals into this deuout
exclamation : *O worthy of al admiration! behold thy Mother, &c.
for know thou, if Mary be thy Mother, Iefus Chrift is thy brother, &
his Father : confequently thine then
embrace*

embrace thy happines in her ; And
so assuredly it is, God is our Father; *Our Father which art in heauen*:
We are brothers to our Sauiour
Christ : *Goe vnto my brothers, &c.*
sayes he to the holy Magdalen,
and for the B. Virgins being our
Mother, there can be no doubt
at al ; and heare S. Anselme pro-
ving it ; *Iesus Christ the sonne of*
Mary, is our brother, (sayes he) *&*
therfore consequently his Mother must
be ours. How much then ought
we to reioyce, and how excessiue
great our contentment ought to
be, hauing for our Mother the
Mother of God himselfe, Queen
both of heauen and earth.

And not only she is our Mother, but a most benigne and gracious Mother, sauouring of nothing but mercy and sweetnes, &
exer-

exercising nothing but the works of piety and pitty towards vs. So as her moſt ordinary title is *the Mother of grace and mercy* : *Maria mater gratiæ*, *mater miſericordiæ*, and ſo in that other Antiphon she is called *Mater miſericordiæ*, &c. where we, who lye ſighing and weeping in this miſerable vale of teares, implore her aide and gentle pittie of our calamities. And wherefore is it, that in euery publick place her Image occurr vnto our eyes holding her ſacred Infant in her armes, but only to ſignify she is alwayes in actual Tendring of him vnto vs for our good, as if she would ſaye, heer take my ſonne and the ſonne of the Eternal Father who for your ſakes deſcended from heauen to earth, and putt on the veſtment of.

of humanity in which he ſufferd
ſo many indignities euen at laſt to
vndergoe an ignominious death,
feare not but approach vnto him
heer with confidence, he is al gratious, al pittiful, and affable, and
if your ſinnes deterr you from
comming neare, remember how
to make you great, he is become
a litle infant, and their angers
are euer eaſily appeal'd; on my
word take him then, and enioy
him as a guift frō me, whoſe poſ-
ſeſſion can not but much aduantage you; and to render your ſelfe
more worthy of the intereſt in
him, wholly renounce al intereſt
in vice, and caſting your ſelfe
humbly at his feete, reſigne vnto
him your hart, and your beſt beloued deſires, and in recompence
thereof he wil beſtow on you a
laſting

lasting good and happines aboue
the iniury of death or time. O
happy, and a thousand times happy are those soules who harken to
these silent invitations of hers,
and hauing recourse vnto her in
al their afflictions know how to
prevayle themselues of her benignity; let them assure themselues they shal neuer finde the gates of her liberality shutt, nor sitt
downe with a repulse of what soeuer they lawfully desire. *God for-
bit* (sayes deuout S. Bernard)
*that I should thinke you can euer
abandon those, who haue placed theyr
Confidence in you.* And Theophilus
in the Booke intitled, *The mirrour
of the B. Virgin* , is introduced
saying: *I know, O soueraine Lady
your Care of vs how excessiue great it
is; for who euer hath hoped in you and
been*

been confounded ; who euer implored your aide, and been abandoned ? And to this purpose is that saying of Origen : *I hould for certainly true, that the B. Virgin being instantly beseeched for any thing, is neuer wanting to the necessities of him who beseeches her, for that she is al mercy, and so ful of grace, and therefore she cannot choose but haue Compassion of those who craue her helpe.* Excellent words, and able to animat the most desperat to a hope of his saluation, and allay the most outragious affliction which was euer in any breast. Being our Mother then, she cherished vs with a maternal loue, and hath more care of vs then euer any Mother had of her only child, neuer fayling vs with succour in our necessities, assistance in our dangers, comfort

in

in our afflictions, nor finally deliurance from any euil what soeuer, when soeuer with confidence and deuotion we importune her for it. So is she our aduocate in heauen with Alm. God, where she gladly vndertakes our protection, defends our cause, procures to assure vs the possession of Eternal blisse, and finally neglects no occasion of putting vs faire with her B. Sonne, and working vs into his grace. In consideration of the great prerogatiue we haue in heauen by such an Agent for vs, S. Bernard encourages man to present himselfe without feare before Alm. God : *Go, Go, with Confidence,* saies he, *before the throne of his diuine Maiestie where the sonne beholds the Mother; and the father the sonne; the sonne shews his father. his*

hands

hands and feete and side al wounded:
the mother vnto her sonne her sacred
breasts that gaue him suck, so as there
is no feare of a repulse where so many
signes of loue and charity are.

But yet this is not al, nor doth
this careful Lady and Mother of
ours only procure vs fauours, but
she assures them vs by appeasing
her Sonne when we haue offended him, and reconciling his loue
vnto vs againe; but for her, how
often had the world been thun-
dred by that iust Iudge aboue?
how often had the soules therein,
for their offences, been precipitated and cast downe head long into
Eternal hel? Of which a more
cleare example cannot bee, then
that memorable visiõ of S. Dominick, who praying one night, behold in vision our Sauiour Christ
feated

feated at the right hād of his Alm.
Father, al inflamed with wrath &
furie, holding three terrible thun-
derbolts in his hand, ready to dif-
charge on earth in punishment
of three finnes then frequently
raigning amongft men, Pride
Auarice, and Luxury; when the
Bleffed Virgin to mitigate his
wrath proftrating her felfe before his feete, and ftraitly embracing them ; I appeale, I appeale
(fayd she) from this your anger
how euer iuft it bee , vnto that
wonted clemency of yours , befeeching you by it , if not abfo-
lutly to reuoke your fentence,
yet at leaft to furceafe for a while
the execution of it; for, alas, what
wil you do? againft whom do you
prepare thefe armes ? and whofe
ruine haue you refolued vpon?
                                    wil

wil you annihilate your owne workmanſhip, and bee the perdition of thoſe whom you haue ſaued with ſo much coſt of paine and bloud? and would you) replied her ſonne, hauing rayſ'd her vp,& ſeated her by his ſide)would you haue ſuch crimes as theſe vnpuniſhed? who would not then in hope of impunity committ them hereafter in deſpight of me? no, it were but to proſtitute my Iuſtice to their abuſe not to exerciſe it heere; and now to pardon them were to make my pardon for euer more vile and contemptible? why alas deare ſonne (ſayd she) as they are apt to offend, ſo ar they to be ſorry for it, doubt not then but at your firſt ſummons of them to repentance, they wilbe obedient to it; and to this effect

O behold

behold heere ready two feruants
of yours (pointing out to S. Frã-
cis and S. Dominick) apt minifters to employ therein, and to
exhort them vnto penance, after
which if they perfift in their wickednes, do your iuftice what it
wil with them, I haue done with
them. Hereupon his diuine Maieftie let his thunder fal out of his
hands, his boyling anger coole,
and at his Mothers prayers was
for that once content to pardon
man.

Hauing then a Mother in heauen fo powerful as she, let vs haue
recourfe to her, and put vs in shel-
ter vnder her, as children do vnder
their Mothers when they fly their
Fathers wrath; and that efpecially
when wee finde our felues moft
preft with ill fortune or calami-
ty,

ty, and say vnto her : *Sub tuum præsidium,* &c. *O mother of God and of vs, wee put our selues vnder your paotection, refuse vs not in our necessities, nor abandon vs vnto the afflictions that threaten vs;* and haue a firme confidence that she wil succour you, and haue pitty of your miserable estate, who neuer refuses those who haue recourse to her. In so much as a holy Doctour sayes; If so great be the enormity of our crimes as we feare to appeare with them before Alm. God, our best course were to addresse our selues to her, and she infallibly wil succour vs. And S. Chrysostom in one of his Sermons sayes vnto her ; You haue been chosen from eternity (sayes he) Mother of God, to the end that those whom God in iustice

O 2   cannot

cannot faue, should arriue by your
pittiful interceſſion vnto faluation.

And with this accords wel that
Viſion which B. Leo had, one of
holy S. Francis companions, in
which he had a repreſentation of
the finall Iudgement day, where
he ſawe two ladders reared vpp,
the one a read one reaching from
earth to heauen, where our B. Sauiour al in terror ſate; the other
of white, iuſt of the ſame proportion extended to the B. Virgins
throne, where ſhe ſate in al ſweetnes and affability; and he obſerued that thoſe who mounted vp
by that read one, did fal to groūd
agayne ſome from the neather
rounds and ſo vpwards euen vnto
the very topp, vntil Saint Francis
called to them, and admoniſhed
them

them to clime by that white one,
and he would affure them of better fpeed; and he fawe that thofe
who followed his counfel were
gratioufly receiued by our Lady
& introduced into heauen. From
which vifion, and we haue before
deduced, refults an euidēt proofe
of her motherly Care of vs, and
how she loues vs euer to paffion
procuring with extraordinary folicitud al wee ftand in need of
both in heauen and earth. With
good reafon then ought we to reuerence her, and haue her in honour and veneration; with good
reafon are we to ferue her affe-
ctionately, and confecrat vnto
her the beft defires of our hart;
and this al lawes both diuine and
humane exact of vs, to witt, that
if she be our mother, we should

O 3　　loue

loue and honour her; and if a loue
and honour be due from vs to our
parents who engender vs into
this world, with how much more
reaſon is it due to her, who ſo carefully procures our regeneration
to a better life?

Let vs not ceaſe then to loue &
reuerence this ſoueraigne Lady
both of heauen and earth ſince
God himſelfe doth it as wel as
we, and (according to' *Methodius*)
hath a kind of obligation alſo to
doe it, ſhe being his Mother, and
conſequently the precept of honouring our parents hauing alſo
reference vnto him , yea and it
ſeemes in more particular manner vnto him then vs, ſince ſhe
was more particularly his parent
then any can be ours, both becauſe he had no other on earth
but,

but her , as also because she could
haue no other sonne. You haue
good reason to reioice (sayes the
sayd *Methodius*) since you haue
him in a manner on the score
with you , to whom al mortals are
indebted else. And so he went
still honouring her heer on earth,
as his deare Mother , and as such
was obedient to her ; *et erat subdi-
tus illis* , as the holy Scripture
sayes ; neither doth he lesse honour her now in heauen, but (as
some deuout Doctors sayd) after
his glorious resurrection first sa-
luting her with a *Salue sancta Pa-
rens* ; he iterated it at her Assumption into heauen , and there seating her at his owne right hand,
al the Court of heauen doing reuerence to her the while, he constituted her in absolut power and
O 4 authority

authority ouer the trine Empire
of the Vniuerſe ; where al bow
down before her, as to the daughter, mother and ſpouſe of the Al-
bleſſed Trinity, the Queene of
Angels, Empreſſe of the World,
and moſt faithful Mediatrix of al
Chriſtian ſoules vnto her Bleſſed
Sonne , who grants al things at
her requeſt.

How

Hovv to put these reueren-
ces in practise, wherby the
B. Virgin is to be honored.

Chap. VII.

IN the precedent cha-
pters we haue seen
of what excellency
and valour is the ex-
ercise of Reuerences
to the B. Virgin , and how acceptable vnto her it is , we haue
moreouer sufficiently informed
our selues of the reasons which
should moue vs vnto her reuerence, as that she is the mother of
the king of heauen , her surpassing
glory there , and that she is of

O v   higher

higher dignity then al the quiers
of heauen, that she hath al power
heer on death, and finally that
she is our Mother and soueraigne
Lady also. And yet much more
could alleage I alleage to moue
vs to deuotion, did not the feare
deterr me of ingulfing my self into so wide and profoūd an Ocean.
Wherfore now it remaines that I
treat of the Method we are to vse,
to put in practise this so laudable
deuotion.

First then I say, we are to endeauour by often genuflexions
and inclinations of the body to
honour her ; in which the better
to actuat our selues we are to banish from vs al tepidity and drow-
zynes ; and make choice of time
and place most conuenient for it:
and first ; touching the circum-
stance

stance of place, priuary is the cheifest thing we are to regard; of time, the night seemes fittest as that, which is freest from distraction, & best composeth the mind.

We reade in *Surius*, how S. Elizabeth daughter of the King of Hungary exercised herselfe with such affections in this so laudable deuotion, as she appointed one of her women euery night to awake her at a certaine houre by some secret way she had, when she would rise vnknowne to the Prince her husband, and spend most part of the insuing night in these adorations which the Roman Breuiary makes mention of; *shee rising in the nights* (says it) *from her husband, and the time in prayer and genuflections.* At which time, no doubt, but the Angels reioy-

reioyced to fee her vertuoufly imployed, being riche and noble by
birth, but far more by vertue and
her true deuotion, and finally her
performing that on earth, which
the Angels account themfelues
happy to do in heauen.

Now for the number of them,
I wil prefcribe none, but leaue it
to the deuotions of thofe who are
defirous to exercife themfelues
therin, nor the manner how it is
to be done, either of bowing one
knee to the ground, or both, of
lifting vp their hands or croffing
them before their breafts, but let
them choofe that pofture which
likes them beft, and which makes
moft for their deuotion.

Only I wil fpeake a word or
two in the commendations thereof in general, as firft, of the facility

cility wherewith it is don, there being none ſo much employed or infirme, who cannot with eaſe do ſomewhat in this kind, either in bending the knee, or bowing the head, actions which are compatible with al, in what eſtate or imployment ſoe'r they be. Then it is a kind of deuotion (this of adoration) of al others the moſt noble and acceptable to the Queene of Heauen, the office of Angels, and who then would not be ambitious of it? to doe the ſame on earth, which al the celeſtial Courtiers do in heauen? and I beſeech deuout perſons, that they would but conſider, how diligently and with what care your earthly Princes are ſerued and honoured by their followers and Courtyers; which whoſoeuer ſhal

but

but obſerue, muſt needs blush for
ſhame, if they be not as careful
and aſſiduous in ſeruing their
Queene of Heauen.

And to incite our deuotions
thereunto, it would do wcl to read
of the diligence of Saints in this
particular ; as namely in Surius
of *S. Albert* , how he bowed his
knees a hundred times a day, and
fifty times proſtrated himſelf on
the ground , ſaying each time an
Aue Maria in honour of the
Queene of Heauen ; And of S.
Catherine of Sucina daughter of
S. Brigit , how (according to the
ſame Authour) she was from her
tender infancy ſo exerciſed in
prayer , as beſides our Ladye Office which she recited euery day,
with the Penitential Pſalmes &
other ſuch deuotiõs, she imploy'd
                                    her

her selfe fower houres euery day
continually in this exercise of
genuflexions vnto the B. Virgins
honour, accompanying it with
many teares. As for that which
S. Iohn Damascen hath left written of *Simon Stilites*, it doth more
cause our wóder then imitation;
his standing on a pillar, exposed
vnto the rigors of winters and
scorching of sómers heate; thirty
sixe cubits highe, situated on an
eminent Mountaines topp; and
this continued for more then
thirty yeares, making a thousand
and a thousand genuflexions and
inclinations euery day; and one
of the seruants of B. Theodoret
Bishopp of Cyrene obseruing
him one day, counted aboue a
thousand two hundred and forty
inclinations of his, and that of
those

thofe more painful ones, he bowing (as it were) euen round in
performing them.

So of the glorious Apoftle S.Bar-
tholomew we reade, that, a hundred times a day and as many by
night, he vfed to bend his knees,
which was more in one who was
fo perpetually and affidually imployed in preaching and conuerting of the world, then a hundred
times fo much were in another
man. Wel did he vnderftand of
how highe price and value with
the B. Virgin thefe Reuerences
and adorations were,) vnderftanding things in fuch an illumina-
tiue manner as he did) or els he
had neuer been fo careful & pun-
ctual in performing them.

But no wonder that the holy
Saints and freinds of Alm. God
                              haue

haue produced such strãge effects
as these, & left to vs so litle hope
of imitating them, since the diuine grace that superabounded in
them, the ardent fire of the holy
Ghost that incessantly inflamed
their harts, and that height of
perfection they had attained vnto
al concurred vnto the rendring
them actiue vigours and diligent in this holie exercise. But
as for vs weaklings as we are,
destitut of those spiritual forces
which they had, and that mind to
apply those forces to the best; if
we cannot imitat them so nearly,
yet at least a farr off we may do
somewhat in their imitation; and
bitter is it so to do, & do it deuoutly, then weary our selues by en-
terprizing too much, and so become wholy dulled and dis-ani-
mat,

mat, and rather loofe fpirit then
gayne by the exceffe.

There is an Example concerning this, taken out of the Mirrour of examples which is this.
A certaine Religious woman had
a daily deuotion to fay an hundred and fifty *Aue Maries*, accompanying each one with a profound reuerence; but fhe growing cold in the performance of
them, by reafon the number feemed exceffiue great, was diuinely
admonifhed in vifion to diminish
them to a third part, vnder the
condition that she should fay
thofe with greater feruour & deuotion. And S. *Hierome* to this
purpofe fayes, it is farr better to
fay one Pfalme deuoutly and with
alacrity of fpirit, then the whole
Pfalter with negligence and tepi-
dity

dity. Notwithstandiug, supposing
al be equal, certainly much better it is, to do more then lesse, in
these or any other exercises of
piety, since good workes ar the
more meritorious stil with the
more difficulty, they ar perform'd
and the more gratefull is the doing
of it, to those vnto whose reue-
rencs it is exhibited.

How

Hovv the aptest time for the exercise of these deuotions, is the particular feasts of our B. Lady.

CHAP. VIII.

T H E Church euer guided by the holy Ghost, hath in al tymes erected Tēples, and consecrated Altars, in reuerence of the sacred Queene of Heauen, and hath honoured her with vowes, Hymnes, Canticles, and Laudes, and diuers other deuotions and seruices, which the feare of detayning

the

the Reader too long, makes me
forbeare the relation of; but a-
boue the rest, some feasts it hath
commaunded to be kept, wheron
she is more particularly honoured.

Those may be diuided into two
Classes, the greater & the lesser,
the greater include her Conception, Natiuity, Purification, An-
nunciation, and her Assumption
into heauen: The lesser (& which
are not of precept) her Præsenta-
tion, Visitation, & others; among
which we may add the Saturday.
To begin then from the lowest,
the Saturday is dedicated by the
holy Church vnto her honour, &
namely in the Councel of Trent,
where it is ordained, that Masses,
and Offices, should be sayd of
her, on those dayes, when they
concurr

concurr not with any other feaſt.
Moreouer it hath been an antient
cuſtome of deuout Chriſtians, to
faſt that day in her honour; which
kind of deuotion is moſt acceptable vnto her, as appeares by this
following ſtory.

S. Anſelme writes of a certaine Theefe, who entring once
into a poore widowes houſe, with
intent to deſpoile her of what she
had, and finding her ſo ſlenderly furnished as he imagined it not
worth his paines, he to decline
the ſuſpition of what he came for,
ask't her what victuals she had, &
whither she had broke her faſt that
day? God, forbid, replied ſhe,
that I should violat ſo my vow I
haue made to the B. Virgin, of
faſting in her honor euery ſatur-
day: why ſo? ſayd the theefe: becauſe

cause, (sayd she agayne,) I haue heard a certaine learned preacher say that whosoeuer did it, should neuer die without Confession: The theefe was so strucken at the report of this, as remayning a long time in consideration of his wicked life, at last he started out of that melancholy posture wherin he was, and setting one knee to the ground, and lifting his hands and eyes to heauen: Seeing, it is so, O B. Vigin, (sayd he,) and that each poore thing that is don for you is so richly rewarded. I heere promise and vow in imitation of this deuout seruant of yours, euery saturday to fast in your honour, as long as it shal please Alm. God to giue me life and health; which afterwards he inuiolatly obserued, but for the

rest

rest continuing stil his haunt of
robbing, it happened once that
being ouer matched by paffingers,
he had his head cut off, and they
thinking they had made him sure,
went on their way glorying in
what they had done, whē behold,
the head cried out, Confeffion, for
the loue of God, Côfeffion; when
imagine in what affright they
were, vnable a long while for a-
mazement to stirr or moue, vntil
at last they came vnto the next
village, and certified the Curat of
what had hapned; who running
thither accompanied with many
of his parifhioners brought thither by Curiofity, behold, rhey
hauing ioyned the head vnto the
body, he with a loue and audible
voice that al might heare ·him,
fayd : vnderstand al of you, that
I ne-

I neuer did any good in al my life, but only in honour of the B. Virgin fasting Saturdayes, for which reason when my soule was issuing forth of my body, as it was seperated from my head, and the diuels ready to intercept it, were al assembled, behold the B. Virgin hindred them, nor would she suffer it to issue forth of my body, vntil by Côfession it were expiated of its crimes; and therupon hauing confest himselfe, and desiring al the assistants to pray for him, he exchanged this life for a happier on.

This day then being particularly consecrated to the honour of the B. Virgin we should do wel; to add vnto our fasts this deuotion of lowly inclining and reuerencing her; It being of such

P   excellency

excellency as we haue declared
before, of which each one may
offer vp as many as his deuotion
shal suggeft, and time and place
permit. How euer for the more
certainty, might I prefcribe them
a taxed number, it should be the
number of the Beads, to wit fixty
three, in honour of thofe yeares,
which (according to fome Doctours) the B. Virgin liued vpon
earth, and fo it were beft to number them vpon their Beads, performing them the while with
that attention, as if the B. Virgin
were really prefent there ; and
while they do it, they may at earth
one pronounce thofe firft words
of the Angelical falutation *Aue
Maria*, which fome are of opinion
the Angel pronounc't in actually
bowing his knee and lowly reuerencing

rencing her, with bowing downe
his head; But of this we shal speak
more amply in the 11. chapter of
this booke, where we shal teache
an apt Method of putting in practise this exercise; and what I say
of the Saturday, may be obserued
when any of her lesser feasts occurr.

As for the Greater feasts, the
greater the solemnity is, with
the greater deuotion we are to
solemnize it; wherfore it were
wel if on such dayes as those, we
encreased to a hundred the number of those reuerences, it being
a number much celebrated in the
holy Scripture for perfect and mysterious; but I would not wishe
you to performe them al at once,
for feare of tædiousnes, but to di-
uide them so, as both morning,

noone, afternoone, euening, and night, may haue its parting, which in the former number of sixty three I would likewise haue obserued, that we may come to it with fresh deuotion, and renue the memory of our B. Lady more affectionatly and often; And if the feaft be celebrated with an Octaue, we may celebrat each day of the Octaue with this deuotion, when if we begin the vigil with a hundred and ten, and fo continue the Octaue out, we shal make compleatly vp, the number of a thoufand, a number perfect, facred, and myfterious.

This excellent deuotion was moft frequent with S. Margaret daughter of the king of Hungary Religious of the Order of Saint Dominick, who (as Doctor Que-
rin

rin of the same Order recounteth
in her life, was so affectionatly
deuoted to the Queene of heauen, as she no sooner sawe her I-
mage in any place, but she presently kneeled downe before it,
reciting in her honor the Angelical salutation, and on the Eues
of her most solemne feasts she
alwayes fasted with bread and
water ; from which day til the
conclusion of the Octaue she sayd
a thousand *Aue Marias* ; at each
one of which she humbly prostrated her selfe on the ground, making it her greatest delight next
to honouring Alm. God, to honour his B. Mother.

P 3   *of*

Of the Feasts of our Sa-
uiour Christ.

CHAP. IX.

PON occasion of treating of the feasts of our B. Lady, I am put in minde to speake a word of the feasts of our B. Sauiour which we are to honour aboue al the rest; and with good reason, for if the feasts of creatures (as we haue fayd) may be celebrated in their honour, how much is the Creatour on his feast to be honoured ? Al those deuotions we may exercise on his feast, which we

haue

haue taught to be exercised on the feasts of our B. Lady : alwayes prouided that we reuerence him in a higher straine of *Latria*, only proper to God himself : *Thou shalt honour & serue the Lord thy God*, &c

The principal feasts of our Sauiour Christ which are celebrated with their Octaues are fiue ; the Natiuity ; the three Kings adoration ; the Resurrection ; the Ascension ; & that of *Corpus Christi*. or the blessed Sacrament of the Eucharist ; amongst which I place in the highest ranke that of the Natiuity, because on that, al the Quires in heauen descended vnto the earth, to adore their King then an infant lying in the manger or in his mothers lap. And so the deuout soule that exerciseth theis deuotions on that day, is to

P 4   frame

frame a liuely imagination of the place imagining themselues in Bethleem, and adoring amongst the rest him, whom al both in heauen and earth adore.

The feast of the three *Kings* puts vs in minde of nothing but adorations, since on that day they al adored our Blessed Sauiour in his Mothers lapp, and in them al the nations of the world; and with how much deuotion it was accompained may be gathered from this pathetical expression of it by the Euangelist Saint Mathew : *And entring into the house* (sayd he) *they found the infant with Mary his Mother, and falling on the ground adored him.*

The glorious *Resurrection* ; to the dignity of which, al other
feasts

feaſts giue a kinde of pre-hemi-
nence, deſerueth Adoration likewiſe; becauſe on it our Sauiour
roſe againe al victorious and victory, charged with the ſpoyles
of hel, while the Angels adored
him reioycing at his triumph, and
ſinging in his prayſes their ſongs
of ioy.

And what should I ſay of his
moſt glorious *Aſcenſion*, on
which our Lord and Sauiour after
his victories, made his magnificent entrance into Heauen, and
there being ſeated at the right
hand of his Eternal Father, to
whom he was euery way equal
in power & vertue, al the heauēly
Hoſts the while humbly inclining before his Throne, did him
moſt profound honour and reuerence.

Now let vs come to the feast of *Corpus Christi* , or the B. Sacrament , in which al the others are comprised , and consequently more then al the others we are to reuerence it. And is not this continually celebrated each day , and in each place (almost) throughout the world? do we not behold a world of Masses sayd, and people dayly communicating throughout al Christendome ? do we not see in euery kingdome & almost euery litle village the B. Sacrament kept , and adored with vnspeakeable reuerence, where our Sauiour Christ is as really present as he is in heauen, where Angels and Saints are incessantly adoring him. Wherefore we are neuer to enter into any Church, or passe by any Altar where the

B.

B. Sacrament is kept, but we are humbly on our knees to reuerence it. And happy are thoſe, who performe this deuotion not perfunctoriouſly, or for cuſtome, as many do; but with guſt of deuotion and from their harts, reliſhing the ſweetnes of the exerciſe they do; perhaps they may deliuer ſome ſoule out of Purgatory by it; (with ſuch deuotion it may be done) : which arriuing vnto heauen, wil there become perpetual interceſſors for them to Alm. God; than which a greater benefitt cannot be imagined.

But alas, (I cannot ſpeake it without teares) we ſee Chriſtians the while ſcarce vouchſafe to vncouer their heade or bend a knee before this B. Sacrament, ſo vnreuerent and weak they are in

their

their faith of it; Impudent and irreligious as they are, not to know how this mystery surpasses al discourse and al humane capacity, and that faith heer is al the light we haue. *Let faith Commend to vs what we can neither see nor comprehend,* sayes the holy Church in one of its Hymnes, and in another place : *Ad firmandum Cor sincerum, sola fides sufficit* : *For to Confirme a hart sincere, only faith sufficient were.* And yet how many cleare testimonies haue we had of the verity of this by euident miracle: sometimes it hath appeared in the forme of a litle child in the Preists hands at the Eleuation : some times the very beasts themselues (lesse beasts then some men therein) haue acknowledged their Lord and Creatour

in

in it: as witnesse thofe Miracles
which I shal here recount.

Al Paris in the yeare. 1258. a
certaine Preift faying Maffe in a
Chappel adioyning to the Pallace, as he eleuated the facred
Hoft, a litle child of incredible
beauty appeared in the place of
it; Which Miracle being repor-
ted to S. Lewis King of France;
and fome foliciting him to goe
and fee it amongft the reft, he
made anfwer worthy of fo pious
a Prince; Let thofe goe who
doubt of the reality of his being
there (fays it); for my part I
behold him daily with the eyes
of faith.

The other Miracle happened
at Tholoufe in Fráce, recorded in
the Chronicles of the Minims,
as alfo by Surius and diuers o-
thers

others, and it is this: S. Anthony
of Padua being there, had a fearce
dispute one day with an obstinat
heretike, denying the reality of
our Sauiours body in the B. Sacrament, who being vanquish't
by the reasons of the Saints, Yet
not willing to Confesse it; sayd
vnto him; What need al these
words and disputations by which
although by Sophismes I Confesse I am ouercome, yet my reason remaines vn-conuinced: If
then you wil do any good with
me, let me see a miracle in confirmation of what you say, and I
promise you I wil turne to your
opinion; the Saint accepted of
the condition, and confident that
the Authour of the verity would
not be wanting to the confima-
tion thereof, he bid the Heretick
to

(to conuince him the more eui-
dently) name himselfe what miracle he desired should be done;
and he answered him, he had a
mule at home, which he would
keepe fasting three whole dayes,
and then procure him in the publick market place, where let one
of your Preists be (sayd he) with
your God in the Sacrament, and
if the mule refuse to eate of the
oates I shal offer him, to adore
him there, I wil promise you I
wil be ready to adore him also;
This was done, and at the fame
of this, there being a mighty con-
fluence of people from al parts to
behold what the issue of it would
bee; The day assigned being
come, & al things ordered as was
agreed vpon, the mule at sight of
the oates euen wild with famine
                              running

running towards them, and hauing taken some of them in his mouth, was in this manner coniured by the Saint with the Blessed Sacrament in his hand : *In the name of God (sayd he) whom I although vnworthy hold heer betwixt my hands , I command thee to leaue that prouinder , and come presently hither to adore and reuerence him* : When behold a most stupendious miracle , the beast not only forbore to eate any more., but euen let fal out of his mouth that prouinder it had, and ran presently bowing downe the head , and on his knees adored the holy and blessed Sacrament , to the vnspeakeable ioy and alacrity of al the Catholicks, the Hereticks confusion , and the conuersion of

the

the man.

Now *Friday* being the day dedicated to the memory of our
Sauiour in particular by reason
of his death and passion; I would
aduise the denout Christian, besides his ordinary deuotions in
honour of his fiue precious
wounds to make fiue reuerences, which can not but be very
meritorious and acceptable to
the Maiesty of Alm. God.

Of

Of the Feasts of Saints.

CHAP. X.

HAVING spoken of the adoration of our B. Sauiour, and his holy Mother, it wil not be out of the way of my purpose, to say somewhat also of the adoration of Saints, since the holy Church celebrates them for no other end but to incite vs vnto their reuerence. This article of faith is confirmed and ratified by many Councels, and lastly by the Councel of Trent in the 25. Section, where Angels and Saints are declared honourable

ble with the reuerence of *Dulia* proper and appropriated vnto them.

On the dayes then when any Saints are to be honoured ; especialy the more principally fort of them, we are to do it with the forefaid reuerĕces. On fimple feafts and thofe of leffer obligation , it may fuffice before we go to bed, to incline only once or twice in their reuerence;and when 'tis the feaft of thofe to whom we haue any particular deuotion,or whom we haue chofen for Patron or Aduocate, we ought with more particular Adoratiõs to honour them more or leffe according to the deuotion & affection of euery one.

Let al thofe then who defire with due reuerence to honour thofe Saints , to whom they are
deuoted

deuoted, accuftome themfelues
before they goe to bed, to make
profound reuerence vnto them,
imagining the while them really
prefent, and beholding what they
do; for fo, although corporally
they be not there, yet fpiritually
they are, and both wel know and
vnderftand what is done in their
honour there, and haue a particular care and protection of thofe
that are deuoted vnto them, perpetually procuring for them fauours and affiftances from Alm.
God; & this verity is Orthodox,
confirmed and approued by many
Councels, and holy Doctours.

Now for the Saints Founders
of Religious Orders, which by
excellence are called Patriarcks,
becaufe as Abraham (for exãple)
was ftiled by that name for that
fo

so many people descended from him; so from them so many Religious are propagated in the Church : Of this sort is S. Benet, S. Augustine, S. Francis, and S. Dominick, and of later-yeares S. Ignatius, &c. Al which are to be had in highest veneration by those of their holy Orders, not only on the particular dayes when their feasts are honoured; but euery day of the yeare besides ; and that Religious man who desires to augment in him the deuotion: he hath to the Founder of his Order, should do wel, to assigne a particular day of the week for honouring him, & that Wednesday in particular, as the most conuenient for this effect; when with some extraordinary deuotion of fasting, praying, reuerecing him,

and

and the like, he is to procure to honour him more particularly & referr vnto that end al which he doth that day, which finally hath reference al vnto the honour of our Sauiour Chriſt, and to imploy ſome houres of the day in the meditation of the particular vertues of that Bleſſed Saint.

It is the general doctrine of the learned, that the Founder of each Religious Order hath a particular care not only of the Order in general, but alſo of each Religious in particular (more or leſſe according as their merits are) and that they aſſidually defend them, ſtrengthening their forces , and weakening the enemies who oppugne and fight againſt them. Of which great priuiledge and prerogatiue Brother Leo in particular had

had an excellent reuelation, vision of holy S. Francis, which I
wil heer recount.

S. Francis being happily departed vnto rest, hauing rendred
his body to the earth and his soule
to heauen, Brother Leo one of
his most affectionat disciples bearing impatiently the absence of
one whom he loued so dearely
wel, prayed instantly vnto Alm.
God to make him so happy, that
once more in this life he might
enioy the happy aspect againe of
his beloued Maister, and iterating
his petition both earnestly & often; it pleased Alm. God; that
one day he being retired into a
solitary place, he beheld S. Francis appearing vnto him in a strãge
mysterious shape al shining with
glorious light, but for the rest
                                winged

winged with golden wings and tallonted both hands and feete with Eagles clawes; The Brother tranſported with ioy al ſight of him, was running to embrace and kiſſe his hands and feete, but eſpying in what ſtrange equipage they were, he al amazed demanded of the Saint, the reaſon why he appeared in that ſort: the Saint anſwered againe, vnderſtãd theſe are no other then markes of the affection I beare my Order and the Religious thereof; and theſe do ſignifie, that amongſt al the other riche prerogatiues his diuine Maieſty hath honoured me withal ſince my arriuing into heauen, one is the authority & power to vindicat my Religious from their neceſſities, and defend them from any aduerſity that preſſes them,

them, as often as with confidence
they invoke my aide ; and these
wings and tallons now I haue as-
sumed, to signify my readines and
promptitud in succouring mine,
and the force and violence with
which I oppugne al those who
iniure them.

Good reason then haue the
Children of this great Pattiarcke
to reioice on earth, for hauing
so powerful a protector of him in
heauen, so louing a father, and so
careful an Aduocate; I would aduise them to be assidual in honouring him with those reuerences
of which we haue spoken; and par-
ticulary to salute him euery day
with fiue times bowing their
knees vnto the ground in honour
of the fiue wouds so miraculously
imprest vpon him while he liued,

Q   reioycing

reioycing and congratulating
with him for ſo highe and ſo ſublime a dignity ; It being no
doubt one of the moſt acceptable
deuotions we can exhibit vnto
him now he is in heauen.

Of the *Adoration* of the Angels.

CHAP. XI.

 N D if we be obli-
ged to honour the B.
Saints with that due
reuerēce appropria-
ted their worſhip, as
we haue amply proued in the precedent Chapters; with farr more
reaſon are we to honour the holy
Angels,

Angels, as the nobleſt in ſubſtance of al created things, and
repreſenting moſt liuely their
Creatours vnlimited power and
magnificence. And although it
be true, that both men and Angels are both Creatures of Alm.
God, and workes of that ſoueraigne Artificer; that they are either framed according to his I-
mage, and by the faculties of
their memory, vnderſtanding, &
their wil, capable of his grace
and of being participant of his
glory and eternal felicity ; and
that many circumſtances there
are, which equal Man with Angels; yea and in conſideration of
the Hypoſtatical vnion, and the
Mother of our Sauiour Chriſt, it
may pretend ſome pre-eminence
aboue them alſo. Yet if we weigh

Q 2   their

their natures, and ballance them equally one againſt the other no doubt but we ſhal find the one farr exceeding the other; and as lead can neuer arriue to the excellency of ſiluer, nor ſiluer of gold : no more can a body any way equal in excellency a ſoule, nor the ſoule of man naturally ſpeaking, the moſt inferiour Angel that is in heauen. Vnto which our B. Sauiour infallibly alluded when he ſayd : *Verily I ſay vnto you, amongſt the ſonnes of men hath not been borne a greater then Iohn Baptiſt; neuertheleſſe the leaſt in the Kingdome of heauen is farr greater then he.*

But now before we wade any further into this matter, we are to vnderſtand, that the word *Adoration* is a notion general to good
Angels

Angels and men. In conformity,
to which we find it in holy Scripture indifferently vſed for either;
as where it is ſayd that the Iſrae-
lits *adored* both their king & God;
they bowed downe, ſayes he, *and adored God, and afterwards their King.*
So the Children of Iſrael adored
their brother Ioſeph then Gouer-
nour of Ægypt; *& after his brothers
had adored him*, &c. For which reaſon, the Doctours both ancient &
moderne haue diſtinguiſhed it
into three ſeueral ſpecies of Adoration; *Latria*, *Dulia*, and *Hyperdulia*; the *firſt* being exhibited only vnto God himſelfe, as a ſouue-
raine kinde of adoration, only
fitted to the ſoueraine power he
hath; with the *ſecond* we honour
Saints and Angels; And as for
the *third*, it appertaines to the

Q 3   B

B. Virgin alone , and vnto her
who surpasseth in excellence both
Angels and al rest of Saints besides ; and of this in the precedent
Chapters we haue discours't at
large.

In breefe then we establish this
conclusion : we are to adore Angels and men deseruing it ; and
this is an Article of faith (according to Suares) defined by Pope
Felix the first of that name in the
Councel at Rome , the 7. th. Synod; And S. Augustine speaking
of the B. Apostle S. Peter sayes:
*An infinit number of the beleeuers
adored the B. Fisher Peter.* And in
another place: *Men merit* (sayes
he) *to bee respected and honoured,
and to say more , adored.* Conformable vnto which verity we finde
in the holy scriptures many men
to

to haue adored the Angels ; as
Abraham in particular three, and
Lot his brother two. So *Iosua* the
famous Captaine of the Israelits
adored one, who appeared to him
in the likenes of a man ; *he'fel prostrate on the ground, and adored him.*

Seeing then we really owe
them this honour, let vs endeauour to discharge the debt, in honouring them with such frequent
genuflexions, as our owne deuotions shal incline vs to , as the
most excellent Creatures of heauen, ful of grace and glory and
participant of the diuine nature.

And amongst al the motiues
to incite vs to it, me thinkes one
of the most principal should bee,
the sublime priuiledges they are
endowed withal in heauen. For if
we consider their liues, we finde

Q 4   them

them to be incorruptible and immortal : of their nature and condition, they haue no body, and
consequently are aboue al its necessities, and are superiour to al
those miseries and afflictions to
which we are subiect heere. If we
cast our eyes on the agility and
promptitud with which they ope-
rat, we shal see nothing in this
vniuerse to equal them, and euen
the heauens themselues come
short of them, whose velocity
we so much admire. But what
should we say of the capacity excellency of their vnderstanding,
that comprehend perpetually
without discourse, and from the
first instant of their Creations
had a perfect knowledge of al natural things ? What of the con-
stancy and efficacy of their Wil,
　　　　　　　　　　wher-

wherwith they wil earneſtly, what
ſoeuer they deſire, and are irre-
uocable in al that they intend?
what of the tenacity of their memory, which neuer forgetts what
it hath ſtored once? laſtly what of
their ſo great and vnmeaſurable
power, that one Angel only in a
night ſlew one hundred eighty
fiue thouſand of the Aſſyrians?
and which is more, that one onely can turne with an incredible
facility the *primum Mobile*, in
compariſon of which al this great
machin of earth and water is but
like a litle point: and that with
ſo euen and regular a motion,
that in ſo many thouſand yeares
was neuer obſerued the leaſt di-
ſorder or deuiation. And to omitt
nothing that may conferr vnto
their honour, I wil heer declare

Q v   the

the feueral orders of them and numbers which they containe.

In the firſt Hierarchy then: which is that which receiues immediatly the ſplendors and illuſtrations from Alm. God, there are three Quiers or Orders, to witt, the Seraphins, Cherubins, and Thrones: of which the Seraphins in feruor of charity excel the reſt, the Cherubins in plenitud of knowledge, and the Thrones in ſeeing fartheſt into God the cauſes and origins of his diuine effects. In the ſecond Hierarchy are likewiſe three other Quiers or Orders to wit, Dominations, Vertues, and Powers; In the third, three others, to wit, Principalityes, Archangels, and Angels. For we muſt vnderſtand, though this name of Angel be com-

common to al, yet in a more particular manner, to thofe of the
third quire, it properly fignifying
a meffinger, and fo is rather a
name of Office then nature, which
becaufe they are more ordinarily
delegated to that function then
the reft, hath a more particular
reference vnto them.

Notwithftanding we muft obferue, that S.Paul fpeaking of the
fuperiour Quires of them fayes:
that they are minifters of God,
imployed for thofe who are to
participat of his inheritance:
which words of his S. Denis the
Areopagite his difciple, S. Gregory, S. Iohn Damafcene, and S.
Thomas interpret thus: not that
he meanes the firft Quire of them
are imploy'd immediatly with
men; but the fecond receiue their
intel-

intelligence from them; the third of them and of what they are to do. Yet S. Gregory Nazianzen, S. Cyprian S. Chryſoſtom, S. Auguſtine, and many other Doctors, are of opinion, that although ordinarily they are not imploy'd about the affaires of men, as the inferior are, Yet notwithſtãding when any important buſines concerning them is to be done, Alm. God ſometymes imployeth them: as a Seraphin to purity the Prophet Iſays lipps; the Archangel Raphael to accompany yong Tobias on his way; the Archangel Gabriel to Annuntiat to the B. Virgin the diuine myſtery of our Sauiours Conception; and laſtly, S. Michael in a particular manner to haue a care and protection of the Church.

Now

Now if the diuision of their quires and Orders be so admirable and great, farr more admirable and great is the number of them, which none can truely tel but Alm. God himselfe, although many haue giuen a guesse therat. Certaine it is, that if God for the Conueniency thereof hath furnished this inferiour world with such infinit diuersity of creatures corporal, much more aboundantly would he store the superiour world with creatures immaterial and spiritual, inuisible and incorruptible, such as the Angels are.

And for their Number, I leaue you to coniecture it, from this Consideration how this world in comparison of that, is no more than the Center point is in respect

pect of an infinit Circonference and consequently how many Inhabitants must goe more to that then this. And so Iob speaking of them sayes : *There is a multitud of his soldiers:* And if the Maiesty of a King on earth, is declared most in the number of those that serue and fight for him , as the Holy Ghost in expresse termes affirmes : *The dignity of a king Consists in the multitud of his people , and in the smal number of them the Princes shame.* We must needs conclude then to be infinit , in respect of the Maiesty of Alm. God. Touching their number in particular, I wil heer declare what Albertus Magnus amongst other Doctors hath left written of them. She sayes then , that there are nine Quires of Angels, and that euery

quire

quire hath its Legions , that each
Legion of them cōtaines. 6666.
and that there are , as many Legions in euery Quire as there are
Angels in a Legion. Others faye,
there are ten times more in the
fecond Quire then in the firſt in
the third then in the fecond , and
fo with proportion to the higheſt
Quire. So as there being, for example, in the Quire of Angels
fower and forty millions , foure
hundred thirty fiue thoufand,
fiue hundred fifty fixe Angels;
that of Archangels hath ten tymes
as many ; that of the Principalities as farr in number exceeds
them , &c. Who is not ready to
iſſue out of himfelfe , with admiration of fuch infinit multitud
exalted by Alm. God for his feruice and our benefit ? and who
                              entring

entring into himselfe againe, can comprehend with what profound reuerence they serue his diuine Maiesty of which Iob speaking sayes : *Those who moue the heauens, bow downe and lye prostrate before him, and the Pillars of heauen tremble at his sight.* So the Royal Prophet speaking of their readines & promptitud in executing his cōmands, sayes of them : And yee Angels praise our Lord, who are so powerful in performing of his wil, and obey so faithfully the voice of his commands. And this is the first reason, that should incite vs to render them seruice and reuerence.

The second yet is more forcible, and that is, our many obligations to them for their many good Offices don vs perpetually, which

which although it be at the appointment of Alm. God, and
they in their performance are
but his Minifters; yet they being
deriued vnto vs by them, from
the foueraigne fountaine from
whence al our good proceeds,
we are to receiue them from them
moft gratefully, & with a thank-
ful acknowledgement. I wil not
inlarge this Chapter to fumme
them vp, but remit the Reader
to the holy Scripture, where
they fhal find them recorded
both very particularly and frequently. Now let vs come to the
exercife of this deuotion. To
render them then that honour
which is due to the aboundance
and fublimity of Glory which
they haue, in being of fo neere
acceffe to God the fountaine of
it

it al, and participating by it of
his diuine nature; we are (to
do wel) for to retire our selues,
and there recollecting vs in the
interiour of our soule, (excluding al earthly cogitations) to
be the whilst the more in heauen, we are to imagine their
Orders and array, their beauty,
sublimity, riches, splendour, and
in fine their glory and admirable perfection, and thus discourse
within our selues : this Quire
then the rest, is more sublime,
this more specious, this fuller of
merit and luster, with a thousand
other considerations on a subiect
of such great worth and ampli-
tud. Then we are to salute them
troup after troup, with a comportment ful of reuerence and
respect, making the longer stay,
                              where

where our deuotions ſhal detaine
vs longeſt, either amongſt the
Seraphins, Cherubins, &c. Congratulating with them their greaɩ
ſplendours and prerogatiues;and
afterwards proſtrating our ſelues
before the throne of God, we are
to praiſe and render him humble
thankes for creating creatures ſo
perfect and excellent for his ſeruice and the honour of his Court.

The like manner of proceeding we may vſe in honouring
the Saints, as PatriarcksProphets,
Apoſtles, Martyrs, Confeſſours.
Virgins, and the like, eſpecially
thoſe which we are moſt deuoted
vnto, addreſſing vs to them, by
the foreſayd acts of congratulation, and adoring them, and taking delight to maintaine diſcourſe with them in our harts,
commu-

communicating with them our
affaires and necessities, and instantly commending our selues
to their prayers : seeing (according as the Doctours affirme)
they behold in God, and know
al our necessities, our most secret
wishes, and the affections of our
harts, and al the reuerences and
actions we doe in honouring
them.

Besides, I thinke it fitt, and
would counsel it to the zealous
Catholicke, who desires to go
on, in honouring these B. spirits;
to prescribe to himselfe a certaine number in reuerencing
them; as that of Nine in honour
of the nine Quires of them, &c.
But because the holy Church makes reuerent mention of three of
them in particular, S. Michael, S.
                                Gabriel,

Gabriel, and S. Raphael; I would
confel to begin with them: As
firft, with S. Michael, who is
Prince of al the reft, feeing as
Laurentius Iuftinianus fayes, although we are to honour al the
fouldiers of heauen, yet their General deferues more peculiar reuerence, for the greatnes & high-
nes of his qualityes and prerogatiues, his inuincible force, the
fingular loue which his foueraigne Emperour beares him, and
finally for his fidelity to his feruice and admirable valour ; of
which he gaue fo rare proofes in
that great battaile he fought a-
gainft the Infernal enemy and al
his followes. And certainly with
good caufe doth the holy Church
fo reuerence him, acknowledging him for her protectour, and
one

one that receaues into his patronage al departed foules that die
in grace and the fauour of God
almighty. Next S. Gabriel, as
he that had that happy embaf-
fage committed to his charge of
Annunciating to the B. Virgin
the Incarnation of the fonne of
God. Thirdly, S. Raphael the
guide & defender of Pilgrims in
this life, as he did by the yong
Tobias in al his pilgrimage.

If thou be then defirous to performe thefe deuotions, and haft
retired they felfe to performe
them the better, putting thy felf
in their prefence (as it were)
who really behold at al times
what we doe ; thou art twelue tymes to bow downe and do reuerence honouring by the firft Adoration S. Michael , General of
the

the hoſt of heauen; by the ſecond,
S. Gabriel, who brought the Embaſſage of our ſaluation; by the
third, S. Raphael, and by the reſt
in their ſeueral Orders the nine
Quires of Angels, &c.

For the better performance
thereof, I wil heer ſet downe a
moſt eaſy method (for al ſorts of
people,) of this deuotion.

The practising of honouring and reuerencing the Angels: saying as followeth.

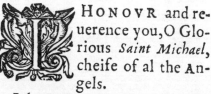 HONOVR and reuerence you, O Glorious *Saint Michael*, cheife of al the Angels.

I honour and reuerence you Blessed *S. Gabriel*, for deliuering that so grateful Embassage to the B. Virgin.

I honour and reuerence you, affable *S. Raphael*, for rendring to the yong Tobias so cleere a testimony of Alm. Gods ineffable goodnes to man.

I ho-

I honour and reuerence you moſt ardent *Seraphins*, who burne continually in the flames of the loue of God.

I honour and reuerence you moſt holy *Cherubins*, who in cleer knowledge and plenitud of the ſcience of God ſurpaſſe al other Angels.

I honour and reuerence you moſt happy *Thrones*, ſeing in you the eternal Maieſtie doth repoſe, and by you our ſoules are diſpoſed to peace and tranquillity.

I honour and reuerence you moſt noble *Dominations*, who by the great authority beſtowed on you by Alm. God, rule al other ſpirits of inferiour ranke.

I honour and reuerence you moſt powerful *Vertues*, who are deputed by the ſoueraigne King

R

of heauen to the regency and gouernement of al the souldiers in heauen.

I honour and reuerence you most valiant *Powers*, who by your might represse the insolency of the powres of hel, and oppose your selues to al the machinations & designes they haue vpon vs continually.

I honour and reuerence you invincible *Archangels*, to whom is giuen the protection and care of people, & Kingdomes, and to reueale vnto them for their good most sublime mysteries.

I honour and reuerence you likewise most humble *Angels*, who disdaine not to couerse with men, and vndertake their patronage and protection.

But if any be so defectiue of memory

mory, as not to be able to retayne
by hart what is before fett downe,
It wil fuffice only to faye : I honour and reuerence you O glorious S. Michael ; I honour and
reuerence you O glorious S. Gabriel ; and fo of al the reft, only
adding the fimple names of Seraphin, Cherubin, Thrones, Dominations, Vertues, Powers,
Principalityes, &c. So likewife
they may, more to facilitat the
memory, begin with the lower
Quires, and fo by degrees afcend
to thofe more highe. And if there
be any yet fo wanting memory
that they cannot remember this,
it may fuffice they make nine reuerences, with intention to honour each Quire of Angels by it,
without pronouncing any word
at al, but only imagining with
R 2   them-

themselues ; now I honour the first Quire, now the second, and now the third, &c.

Now it rests , that we assigne one day of the weeke for the exercise of this Deuotion ; and what more proper thē that the Church hath appointed to honour the B. Angels on ? to witt , the Tewsday : Let that then be it , and on that day let vs most particularly honour them, those that al Preists saying Masse of the Angels for them, those of the laity deuoutly hearing it, &c.

And because Psalmody is exceeding grateful to them , (: if it be accompanied with due attention of spirit;) those who are imployed in that laudable exercise, are to endeauour to comport themselues with al due reuerence
and

and deuotion; imagining themselues in presence of the Angels
while they are performing it : *I
wil sing Psalmes in the presence of
Angels, I wil adore in his holy Temple, and praise his holy name.* And to
this accords wel that which we
reade of S. Bernard in the hystory
of the illustrious men of the *Ci-
stercians*, how he sawe the B. Angels, while *Te deum* was sung, to
goe from one Quire to another,
encouraging the Religious to sing
it with feruour and deuotion:
Another tyme he sawe them bu-
sily writing downe what the Religious pronounced, those in
golden better which were pronounced with force of spirit and
from the hart, those in siluer
which were vttered with attention but not such feruour as the

former were; those in inke, which
proceeded from them with a litle
admixture of distraction ; and
those finally in puddle-water,
which were pronounced without
al sense of deuotion. Moued then,
by this example , and knowing
that the B. Angels are assistant at
our deuotions, let vs performe
them with such a spirit, not only
worthy of the Oratory that we
are in, but also of the Company
that is there. Happy and thrice
happy are they who shal so honour them, since they shalbe rewarded for it , not only by the
Angels intercessions in heauen
continually for them; but also by
their assidual assistance of them
heer , from al dangers both of
bodily and ghostly enemies, til
at last receiuing vs at the honour
of

of our deaths , they take vs out of this tranſitory and miſerable life , and tranſferr vs to a happy and eternal on.

Of the honour and reuerence We ovve vnto our Angel Guardian.

CHAP. XII.

ND who ſees not, how reaſonable it is, in lieu of ſo many benefits we receiue from them, to honour and reuerence the B. Angels for it ; and in particular our Angel Guardian, who hath the

R 4　　　care

care & protection of vs committed to his charge. For certaine it
is, & auerred by al learned men,
that (excepting our B. Sauiour)
each man hath his peculiar Angel attending ftil on him: whence
we may perceiue , how great is
the goodnes and charity of Alm.
God towards man; who (we being
fuch contemptible creatures as
we are) hath not only been contented to create the Elements for
our feruice , mixt bodies for our
vfe, and finally al corporal creatures els ; but alfo hath enchar-
ged the holy Angels with our
protection and defence , creatures fo excellent , fo fublime in
glory, wifdome, and power, to be
our inftructours in vertue , and
our guides to truth.

But if goodnes be to be admired

mired in beſtowing them vpon
vs;no leſſe admirable is his power
in creating them in ſuch innumerable multituds , that the very
loweſt Quire of them is ſufficient
to furniſh with Angels guardiãs,
not only al the men that are, but
al that haue been or ſhal be as
long as the world ſhal laſt : ſo
according to the probable coniecture of the learned, there being
a matter now of ſome million
million of ſoules in al the world,
not only euery one of them hath
an Angel guardian, but one ſo
particularly vnto himſelf, as he
was neuer Guardian to any one
before, nor euer ſhalbe to any
after him; God whenſoeuer he
creates a ſoule, appointing a pe-
cular Guardian that neuer in that
office was imployed before. And

R v   who

who can imagine then, how many millions of millions there
muſt be to ſerue for ſo many millions of men, that haue been &
ſhal be vntil the general Iudgement day? And this opinion is
the more probable, not only becauſe of Gods omnipotēce which
is more illuſtrated thereby, but
alſo of a certaine congruency on
the Angels part, who if they
ſhould not ſuffice in number to
afford each one a Guardian, it
would follow that the number of
men would exceed that of them,
which would argue a deficiencie
in them, and take from that proportion by which it is ſuppoſed,
that as the Archangels exceed the
Angels ten to one, &c. ſo there
ſhould be ten times more of Angels then of men.

The

The neceſſity we ſtand in of their cæleſtial aide, is great and vrgent; firſt becauſe our ſoules are ſpiritual, and conſequently ſpirits can beſt ſee their neceſſityes next becauſe we our ſelues are weake and ignorant of the force and imagination of the Enemy to enſnare and ouercome vs were it not for them; Who watching continually by vs obſerue al their wayes, and carefully meete them with preuention.

But heere ſome may obiect, how can they be continually by vs when our Sauiour ſayes, they continually behold the face of Alm. God, in whoſe viſion conſiſts their cheifeſt beatitud: *Angeli eorum ſemper vident faciem Patris mei qui in cælis eſt.* To this I anſwer

fwer, with S. Gregory, that it is
true the Angels are ftil in heauen, euen when corporally they
are employed elf-where; elfe we
could not reconcile that other
place of Scripture with this,
where it is fayed; that God im-
ployes them on his Embaffages
heer on earth; fo as while in contemplation of the heauenly ef-
fence they are ftil in heauen, we
muft grant them really the while
to be on earth.

And to incite in vs a greater
deuotion towards them, I wil endeauour to fumme vp the many
good offices they dayly do vs;
which although infinit in themfelues, may yet be reduced to
three heads. The firft is; they deliuer vs from many euident dangers, by their careful cuftody of
vs;

vs, which the holy Prophet testifies where he sayes : *He hath giuen his Angels charge of thee, to looke to thee in al thy wayes, and beare thee in their handes least thou shouldst dash thy foote against a stone.* And heer let each one Cal to minde, how many-fold dangers they haue escaped Heer, one the falling of a house vpon his head, which if he had not sodainly changed his mind, he had gone iust vnder it as it did fal; and to whom can he attribute this change of mind, but to his Angel Guardian: Another, being prepared to goe some voyage puts it off, he knowes not why, and afterwards vnderstands that if hee had gone, he had falne into the hands of Pirats or of theeues, and this was the worke of his good Angel also; with a
hundred

hundred others the like. Which
the Patriarke *Iacob* acknowledged to come from his Angel kee-
per, when bleffing the children
of his fonne Iofeph he fayd : *The
Angel who hath preferued me from
al euil, bleffe thefe children,* &c. And
fo did *Iudith* returning victorious
from Holofernes campe. *So it
hath feemed good vnto our Lord* (faid
fhe) *whofe Angel hath guarded me,
in going forth, in remayning there,
and in returning backe.*

And though the B. Angels care
extends it-felfe as wel vnto the
bad as to the good, yet notwithstanding they more fpecially impart their aide vnto the iuft; as
the Pfalmift teftifies where he
fayes : *Qui habitat in adiutorio Al-
tißimi*, &c. *Who dwelleth in the
aide of the Higheft, remaynes in the
                                    prote-*

protection of the God of heauen : And
there is no doubt , but God hath
a most particular care of the iust
and vertuous , and consequently
commends them in a most deare
manner vnto their Angels Guar-
dians; as may be gathered out of
that passage of holy Scripture :
*He hath giuen his Angels charge of
you,*&c. As if he would saye,those
who are Gods faithful seruants,
may goe securely in the midst of
dangers , for God hath giuen the
charge vnto his Angels to haue
especial care of them. Whether
they sleepe , or wake, they need
not feare; for being in this particular protection of God and their
Angel Guardian , it may be sayd
vnto them : *They may walke on the
Aspick and the Basiliske, and tread
the Lion & Dragon vnder their feet.*
What

What a wonderful priuiledge is this? to be able to contemne the Aspick and Basiliske, which euen kils with its sight, and the Lion and Dragon the most formidable of al other beasts? and who restraynes the killing lookes of the one, or cohibits the others fieccenes, but only our Angel Guardian?

The *second* benefit which we receiue from them, is the wholsome Counsel and aduice, which they are stil infusing into our minds. And of this we haue a cleere example in the Angel that accompanied Tobias on his way, and gaue him such wise and prudent instruction, in point of his mariage, how he should comport himselfe with his new spouse for to escape the fate

which

which had sent so many of her
husbands vnto death: as namely,
that he was to begin his mariage
(quite contrary to the custome
now a dayes) with watchings,
prayers , and deuotion. In the
like manner an Angel Guardian
is continually suggesting wholsome counsels vnto vs , now de-
terring vs from euil , now inci-
ting vs to good , which without
their incitement we should neuer doe : now proposing to vs the
example of our Sauiour Christ
before our eyes , now of some
other Saint, for to awake our Imitation ; then inflaming our wils
to embrace the occasion of imita-
tating them ; lastly, they go som-
tymes spurring vs on by the consideration of the mercy of Alm.
God ; & now refrayning vs againe
by

by that of his iuftice and feue-
rity; fo euer directing euen our
courfe betwixt heauen and hel,
that neyther the confideration of
the one extoll vs too much, nor
the other too much depreffe vs.

And tel me now, haue you neuer experienced, when you were
about to committ any greeuous
crime, a remorfe of Confcience,
and certaine shrinkings backe,
and bidding vs forbeare? and
what should this be; but our Angel Guardian, appointed to this
office by Alm. God? Befides,
how oftentymes may we imagine
God offended with our crimes,
to haue been in mind to haue
pluck't vs from the earth, like
vnfruitful trees, and throwne
into the fire of Eternal hel, had
it not been for their interceding
for

for vs ? like him who sayd vnto
the man in the parable, being
minded to pluck vpp his figg-
tree, which for three yeares he
had obserued never to haue borne
fruit that he should haue, pa-
tience with it another yeare, and
after he had cultiuated it, if it
bore not fruit he should doe his
pleasure with it; The Doctours in
explicating this passage saye:
We are these vnfruitful trees,
Alm. God the Lord of the Or-
chard, and our Angel Guardian
he that intercedes and vndertakes for vs : Imagine then how
much we contristat him if we be
wanting vnto his promises and to
the hopes which he conceiues
of vs

The third and last benefit for
which we are liable to our Angel

gel Guardian is, that he accompanies vs perpetually from the houre of our birth to the final period of our liues, and neuer abandons vs euen when we are abandoned by euery one besides; and such a freind we haue of him, as the world hath none; For behold a beautious Virgin in the flower of her yeares and pride of her beauty, how many, seruants she hath that make court to her, and with what obsequiousnes they obserue her, til that flower fading, and the winter of her yeares and decayes of age falne on her beauty once, they fal of as fast, and she is left only to solitud and neglect, who was before the only one frequented, and to whom al respects were payd. Whereas our good Angel is so constant a freind

of

of ours, as no change of fortune
qualifyes, or time makes vs goe
leſſe with him, but he is euer the
ſame, and neuer alters in loue
vnto vs, euen when he ſees vs ha-
ted of God and man; and the reaſon of this, is, becauſe he knowes
not as yet the final reprobation
of him whom he hath in charge,
otherwiſe he would not haue ſuch
care of wicked men, as moſt certaine it he hath.

Another benefit for which we
ſtand infinitely obliged vnto thē
is, that they carefully preſent our
Petitions vnto Alm. God our almes, watchings, and al our good
works we doe; which by thoſe
words of the Angel to Tobias is
rendred euidēt: *When thou prayedſt*
with teares, and buriedſt the dead,
when thou didſt leaue thy repaſt, and
didſt

didſt conceale the dead by day in thy houſe; and didſt bury them by night, I offred thy prayer vnto our Lord. And this by that myſtical ladder of Iacob was vnderſtood , where the Angels were ſeen aſcending and deſcending, betwixt heauen and earth , to ſignifie the continual commerce they haue with either for our avayle, not by local motion, but by a farr more ready way. Sometimes one Angel preſents to Alm. God the generous victory of this man ouer his temptations; another ſayes , behould, O Lord , the profitable vſe which this ſoule makes of that precious bloud you ſhed for it vpon Mount Caluary , and of al thoſe other graces which with ſo liberal a hand you haue beſtowed on *it*; A third cries out , Good Lord receiue

ceiue this charitable persons almes bestowed vpon you in the person of the poore, or these deuout teares shed only out of an affectionat loue of you; Another finally present the oblation of this good Religious person in wholy renouncing al worldly commodityes, or this Preists pietie and zeale, in offering vp the holy sacrifice of the Masse, or meditating our Sauiours Passion; and this the Canon of the Masse confirmes saying : *Iube hæc perferri per manus sancti Angeli tui in sublime Altare tuum in conspectu diuinæ maiestatis tuæ* : Command this to be carryed by the hand of your holy Angel to your sublime Altar in the sight of your diuine Maiestie, &c.

And as they are assistant to vs during

during our liues, so at our deaths
are they much more powerfully
defending vs from al the assaults
of the Infernal Enemy; as testifies B. Aloysius Gonzaga of the
Societie of Iesus, in that his deuout meditation of our Angel
Guardian where hee sayes, that
our Angel Custos at the time of
our death is most diligent in assi-
sting vs against the Enemy, pre-
seruing vs cheifly from those two
sinnes which are most incident to
men in that article of time, Infidelity and despaire, to the end
that making heer a happy end
they may repaire with them to
heauen, vnto their euerlasting
habitation; And in prosecuting
his discourse he sayes, that as
soone as the soule once is free
from the captiuity of the body,
its

its Angel presently conducts it to
the Tribunal of Alm. God, animating and encouraging it on
the way, to put its cheifest confidence in the merits of the sacred bloud of our Sauiour Christ;
and if it chance (the better to be
purified from its sinnes) to be
adiudged vnto the purging flames, he visits it often there, comforts it, brings it the suffrage and
succour of those prayers and merits which are offred for it in the
other world, and encourages in
middest of its suffrances, with the
hope it can not be long in suffe-
ring; and in fine when the time is
expired, he conducts it out, and
al bright and purified leades it
vnto heauen, and in the twinkling of an eye, presents it vnto
Alm: God to receaue from him

S   the

the Crowne of eternal beatitud, prepared from al eternitie for those, who heer fighe after it in this vale of teares. O happy and a thousand tymes happy is that foule, which hauing been faithful to its Creator, and pliant to his hand to be ledd whither foeuer his least motion carried it, in following his good Angel for guide leauing the world ful of the vertue of his example arriues at last vnto that Kingdome of eternal felicity, where with God and his Saints it shal for euer raigne.

But now touching the practife of this particular deuotion to our Angel Guardian; first being affured that we are committed to his Regencie, and that fo noble and excellent a creature, as al the eloquence of theworld rather diminifhes

minishes then add to its cōmen-
dations, vouchsafes to keep vs per-
petuall company, and defends vs
from al euil, with his careful watchings & his comfortable aduise,
we are on our parts to endeauour
a requital: Firit, by comporting
our selues with al deuotion and
due respect vnto his presence and
next honouring him with al com-
petent honour. Let vs then consider if we stood perpetually in the
sight of some earthly Prince or
Monarke; how careful we should
be so to compose our outward behauiour, as might render vs most
grateful in his sight; & with how
much more care and diligence
ought we in the presence of our
Angel Guardian to comport our
selues? Heare what S. Bernard
sayes in explication of these

S 2   words:

words : *For he hath giuen his Angels charge ouer thee to guard thee in al thy wayes,*&c. O mortal man, sayes he, what reuerence, what deuotion and confidence art thou to conceiue in thy breast from these comfortable words of the Royal Prophet; reuerence in standing in presence of thy Angel, deuotion for his loue of thee, & confidence for his care. Be therefore vigilant neuer to exceed the bonds of thy respect while these holy spirits are alwayes in thy sight by the appointment of Alm. God himselfe attending them thy preseruation in al thy wayes, and wheresoeuer thou art, either in priuat or publique, be alwayes careful neuer to commit that indecency before him, which before me thou wouldest not doe. Thus S. Bernard in
his

his deuout and pious manner.

Secondly, we are to honour them with thefe reuerences we haue formerly treated of, which may be beft performed when into priuat we haue retir'd our felues; efpecially before we retire our felues to reft with a profound inclination we are to fay, *Angele Dei, qni Cuftos es mei,* &c. befeeching him to keep vs in our fleepe from the affalts of the Enemy, that euer watches to harme and mifchiefe vs; fo when we awake, we are to commend our felues vnto them that day following, & whatfoeuer bufines we are to vndertake, that it may fort a wifhed conclufion; and we fhould do wel often to commend vnto them in fome vocal manner a deuout conception of our hart in our occur-

S 3   rant

rant neceffityes , befeeching them to affift vs in the mannage of this or that particular affaire.

This deuout cuftome had one Alexander Luzaqua an Italian Gentleman of a moft holy and vertuous life ; that as often as he faluted any man , he mentally intended that reuerence vnto his Angel Guardian whom he faluted; and an excellent confideration it was , to thinke a celeftial fpirit , more worthy the falutation then an earthly worme. Let vs imitate this deuotion , and in faluting any fay thus in our minds I offer this reuerence to the Angel Guardian that attends vpon him or her whom I falute. And moft happy it wil be for vs if we do fo, for by this meanes we shal indeare our felues in the loue and

care.

care of thofe B. fpirits, who can
do more for our real aduancement and good, then al the world
befides.

---

*Jn what manner we are to
proceed in the exercife of
thefe Adorations, worthi-
ly to honour the Mother
of Alm. God.*

C H A P. XIII.

VE being compofed
of two parts, the fu-
periour & inferiour,
of body and foule by
the fingular proui-
dence and goodnes of Alm. God,

S 4   that

that we might honour him with both, both heer and in the world to come; a great part of our corporal honour Consists in these fore sayd Adorations, which not only the Saints haue practised, but euen our B. Sauiour himself, we ofte reade how he bowed of whom his knees vnto his eternal father, and prostrated on the ground; as namely the night preceding his Passion, when according to the Euangelist S. Luke : *He kneeled and fel prostrated on his face.* And. SS. Matthew & Marke; *he prostrated on the ground* : by which words we may gather, how our Sauiour reuerenced his eternal Father *in spiritu & veritate*, in spirit and verity, with each part both of body and soule.

Let the deuout Christian then
desirous

defirous to render honour to the
B. Virgin, accompany his interiour deuotion of the foule, with
the exterior of the body; & firft,
when thou art retired in fecret,
for fo, *when thou wouldft Pray, enter
into thy chamber*, fayes the holy
Scripture; thou art to begin with
this Confideration, how excellent she is, whom thou art to
reuerence, and the excellency of
the reuerence thou exhibit'ft to
her, which the whole Court of
heauen take for higheft honour
to be imployed in. And touching
the exllency of her, thou art to
confider her large portion of
glorie aboue al the other Saints,
and reprefent her to the eies of
thy mind, Inthroned in a moft
glorious manner aboue al the reft,
as becomes the foueraine Em-

S v   preffe

preſſe of them al; al ful of glory
and of Maieſtie , encompaſſed
round about with innumerable
Saints and Angels perpetually
making Court to her, and honouring her with humble reuerences;
amongſt whom thou art to imagine they ſelfe, and making thy
firſt approches of adoring her,
without vttering any word , but
only fixing thy mind vpon her
excellent beauty and Maieſty,
procuring to begett in thy mind
the whilſt frequent acts of affectionat loue and complacency in
ſo much beauty and Maieſty as
thou conceiu'ſt to be in her, congratulating with her that her
high dignity of being Mother of
God , and conſequently Queene
of heauen and earth ; Acts which
if they be performed with due intention

tention and deuotion, it is impoſſible to imagine how grateful
they wil be to her, and how profitable for thoſe who are exerciſed therein.

We haue an example of a deuout Religious woman recounted
by F. Heroide Dominican) who
being afflicted with a greeuous
malady after much paine and ſuf-
ferance died thereof, whoſe ſoule
appearing ſome dayes after to the
ſub-Prioreſſe of the Conuent ſaid
amongſt other diſcourſes; Know,
Mother, that the reward which
Alm. God beſtowes vpon the leaſt
good work of ours, is ſo exceſſiue
great, as if it were putt to my
choice, I would returne euen
from the ioyes of heauen vnto
the earth againe, and ſuffer al my
former afflictions, only to recite
one

one *Aue Maria*, that returning thence againe, I might acquire a new merit by it in heauen, and this, although I were not certaine to say it without tepidity or distraction, so that I were but in grace the while, and free from al mortal sinne. And if this holy Religious woman would haue exposed her self to such cruel paine and sufferances, only for the merit of so smal an act, how great shal their merit be, who exercise themselues in this deuout exercise of reuerencing her, being one of the greatest & most excellent seruices which a Christian can render vnto the Mother of God.

Hitherto we haue treated of the interior coportment of the mind during this our actual reueencing
the

the B. Virgin; Now let vs come
to the exterior of the body. Firſt,
we are to bow the knee, in crof-
ſing our hands before our breaſt
with a litle inclination of the
head; and after hauing prayed in
that māner, we are to riſe agayne,
and iterat the ſame deuotion for
the ſecond time, and ſo forwards
as our deuotion ſhal inſtruct vs;
the which Adorations we likewiſe may performe only with bowing one knee to the ground,
ioyning of our hands, and fixing
of our thoughts on the Maieſtie
of the B. Virgin the while; and
if any through infirmity find difficulty in theſe inclinations, they
may helpe themſelues by leaning
or the like, or only bow downe
their body, or make ſome light
inclination with the head.

Alwayes

Alwayes remembring that this exteriour behauiour is not the cheifeſt thing we are to regard, but that which is proceeding from the interiour, as the words pronounc't , or by the hart or mouth the whilſt, now ſaying: I adore you ô ſacred Mother of God; & repeating it as ofté as we make our reueréces, or elſ pronouncing theſe two words only of *Aue Maria* , with which the Angel Gabriel ſaluted her , and in that reuerent manner (it is ſuppoſed) which we heer preſcribe to her deuout ſeruants to imitat : ſo doing we ſhal performe that Angelical office too , as wel as he, nay in a manner more excellent; for he ſaluted her but as a humble Virgin, we as the Mother of God, and daughter of the moſt

holy

holy Trinity ; he in the lowly house of Nazareth, and we in the highe Court of heauen, where she fitts maieftically enthroned and crowned Queene of the whole Vniuerfe; he finally while she was yet fubiect to mortality and the incommodities it goes annex't withal, but we now when she is aboue it, participant of eternal life glory and felicity. Great then is their prerogatiue who falute her fo, and great shal their merit bee, if they do it with that due deuotion and reuerence, as they ought.

Hov in the like manner we
are to reuerence God, as
also the Saints in Heauen.

C H A P. XIV.

HAVING spoken of
the Interiour & Ex-
teriour reuerences,
we are to honour the
Mother with al : Let
vs make application of them vnto
God himselfe with the soueraine
honour of *Latria* due to his most
diuine Maiestie. We must then
procure to reuerence him so, as
these exteriour deuotions may
proceed from the redundancy of
the

the Interiour; to which effect before we put in practise the fore-
said reuerences, we are to fixe our
interiour eyes on the Maiesty of
Alm. God , considering his immense greatnes & incomprehensible perfections in which we are
infinitly to take complacence; as
in his being what he is, so exceeding good, & so exceeding great;
and then we are to accompany
this Interiour act of ours with
most profound reuerences and inclinations, bowing euen vnto the
ground before that Maiesty , before whose glorious Throne the
Angels themselues, *adore in pro-*
sterning their faces on the ground.

And to acquit our selues the
better of this deuotion, we are especially euery morning when we
rise , as at night when we retire

to

to reſt, moſt profoundly to reuerence this our Alm. Lord , and
whilſt we remaine in that humble
poſture on our knees , we are to
caſt the eyes of our mind with an
affectionat regard on that high &
incomprehenſible Maieſtie, ſo to
begett interiour acts of Ioy and
complacency of the ſoueraine
power he hath , and ſoueraigne
goodnes accompanying it.

And this let vs do, as often as
we bow our knees in reuerencing
Alm. God , accompanying it ſtil
with ſome interiour act of the
loue of him , an act, which no
creature in heauen and earth can
truly imagine the excellency
of it ; being an operation which
God continually is exerciſing in
himſelfe , to wit of ioy and com-
placencie in his infinit goodnes,

nes, whence doth proceed the loue of it which must likewise be infinit; These acts of loue then let vs endeauour to stirr vp in our selues, and assure our selues that the least of them is sufficient to rayse a soule to a most highe degree of perfection.

As witnesseth this story extracted out of the second part of the Chronicles of the Friers Minors. A certaine Religious matron beheld in vision thirty Religious of the Conuent of Paris al departing this life at once, whereof fiue only were códemned to Purgatory, the rest went al immediatly to heauen; & one amongst the rest had his place assigned him amongst the Seraphins: She being returned from her vision and astonished thereat, had recourse

courſe to the Guardian of the
Friars where ſhe liued, and declared vnto him al that she had
ſeen ; who like a prudent man,
aduiſed her, to beſeech Alm. God
in continuation of his former
fauour to reveale vnto her the
name of him who was ſo highly
aduanced aboue the reſt ; therby
more particularly to know the
truth of the viſion : she did ſo, &
it was reuealed vnto her that his
name was *Venance* ; here-vpon
the Guardian diſpatcht an Expreſſe to Paris to informe him of
thoſe who were lately dead in
that Cóuent; whoſe nũber being
giuen him vpp, he found them
exactly to agree with that of the
Viſion ; and that this *Venance* was
only a ſimple lay Brother amõgſt
the reſt, whoſe Office was to haue
care

care of the Friars habits, and
mend them when they were
torne; which it seemes he had
executed with such charity, as he
had merited by it that highe place
in heauen.

Now if this good Religious
man, in exercising this slight and
manual Office could merit so
high a degree of glory, those
who are exercesed in this Angelical deuotion which we treat of,
if they do it with that attention
as they ought, how farr more
high an one must they needs merit by it? And for our encourage-
menr, it were good to consider,
how farr more profitably we may
be exercised in it, then the blessed Angels whose continual imployment it is: for they with al
that they can do, can never aduāce
higher

higher by it , an Angel can neuer become an Archangel, an Archãgel can never fitt equal with the Thrones, nor a Cherubin in fine be embraced with the fire of a Seraphin ; whereas we may not only accumulat merits fo;to rayfe vs from men to Angels, but euen furpaffe them themfelues , and being eleuated higher then Principalities and Thrones , become euen equal with the Seraphins: and by this only exercife may al this be effected.

So likewife may we app'y this deuotion to the honour of *Dulia* proper to the Saints , by the only turning of the minds intention, and this more particularly on the dayes wheron they are honoured, and their feafts are celebrated; when befides thefe external reuerences

rences we are to procure to honour them from our hearts, by
elicit acts from thence of congratulation for their felicities, and
thankſgiuing vnto Alm. God for
hauing predeſtinated thē from al
eternity to that high dignitie to
which he hath promoted them, &
to which they haue arriued, by ſo
many vertuous and meritorious
wayes, leauing to vs their Imitation, to trace their glorious foot
ſteps after them; That day likewiſe we are to aſcend in mind to
the particular actions of their liues, conſidering the ardent charity of this one, this others profound humility, and the like according as their liues ſhal giue
occaſion.

In concluſion, this aduertiſe-
ment I wil giue, out of that holy
Cardinal

Cardinal Bellarmine touching these exteriour reuereces, to wit, that they are only to be distinguished (whether don in the honour of Alm. God, of his B. Mother, of Angels, or of Saints) by the internal intetion of the mind, and the merit and excellency of those they are directed to. As for example, we adore and reuerence Alm. God for the immensenes of his gratnes and Maisty , for his infinit goodnes, and for being both our beginning and final end. We honour the Saints, as those who participat of his diuine grace and celestial glory ; and the B. Virgin, as Mother of Alm. God, and surpassing in excellency of title, al Creatures both, in heauen and earth. Conformable to this, we see in holy scripture, how

how Abraham with the same sort
of veneration , bowed downe
both to God , Angels , and men,
indifferently honouring them
according to their dignities ; and
in this manner we are to vnderstand the holy Scripture when it
occurrs to speake in any other
passage of these venerations.

---

*How these genuflexions may
deuoutly be exercised before
any Image of our B. Lady.*

CHAP. XV.

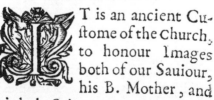 T is an ancient Cu-
stome of the Church,
to honour Images
both of our Sauiour,
his B. Mother , and
his holy Saints , nay an article of

T   faith

faith from Apostolical Tradition receiued, as we are taught by diuers Concels. This only is to be noted, that while we honour them, we direct not our reuerences vnto them, as they are materially what they are of wood or stone, &c. but as they represent them whose Images they are; it represents according to that ancient axiome; *the honour of the Image is referred to those whom it represents.* And this the Councel of *Trent* inferrs where it sayes: *In the Images, which we honour and fal downe before, we adore Iesus Christ, and reuerence his Saints.* And so the 7. Synod sayes; *Who adore the Images, adores the soueraigne king it represents*: the like we may say by the Image of the Queene of heauen; and it is confirmed by Origen

Origen where he fayes : *Who beholds any mans Image* , (fayes he)
*may be faid to behold him whom it re-
prefents.*

This verity then fo Catholike,
for the better performing this holy exercife we fhould do wel to
procure fom Picture both deuout
and faire, before which we are to
do our reuerences (although of
this there be no neceffity;) I fay
faire, for faire obiects do fooneft
ftirr vp the affections of the mind;
as appeares by that example of S.
Bernardine, who while he was but
very yong, was fo taken with deuotion to a certaine picture of
our B. Lady , more comly then
the reft, that he was neuer wel but
when he was on his knees before
it; and heer it was where he layd
the foundation of his fanctity,

T 2   which

which afterwards he built fo high
vpon, as it was an admiration to
the world.

Which manner of adoring the
B. Virgin in her Images, is a forcible remedy againft the temptations of our infernal Enemie; as
this following example doth declare, taken out of S. Iohn Damafcen by F. Suarez of the Socie-
ty of Iefus. There was a deuout
Religious man (fayes he) accuftomed to worfhip the Mother of
God in a certaine Image of hers;
who being one day fiercely affalted by the Enemy, with a greeuous temptation, as he was carefully imploying al his force for
the repelling it, the diuel appearing to him promifed him, if he
would forbeare to honour that
Image, he would not only free
                                him

him from that prefent temptation, but neuer moleft him with
the like againe. But the good Religious man in defiance of him,
fel a frefh to honour it before his
face, and the diuel and temptation both vanifhed away.

And a great help it would be to
this deuotion, to imagine the B.
Virgin the while beholding vs
from heauen (as without al doubt
fhe doth) & taking complacence
in our honouring her; & to make
the Imagination worke the liue-
lyer, let vs frame a conceipt, that
if an earthly Queene fhould take
fuch delight in being honoured in
picture, as she should place her
felfe where fhe might behold
with what alacrity and affection
it were done, and bountioufly reward thofe whom fhe fawe moft

forward in their honouring it;
what concourse would there be
by al who desired to ingratiat
themselues, and indeare their seruices to her Maiesty: and if this
for an earthly Queene would be
don with such forward & greedy
desire, how much more prompt
and ready ought we to be, to doe
it to please & gratify the Queen
of heauen? which while we doe,
deuoutly, we may suppose her
gratiously regarding vs, and taking notice of each particular
action, pointing vs out to the Angels about her, thus such one
doth, and thus such a one, therefore haue a particular care of them
to defend them from their enemies, and when their soules are
free from their mortal prisons,
be careful to conduct them higher
                                    vnto

vnto me. Which is cōſirmed from
this enſuing example recounted
by F. Razzi a Dominican, in his
Hortulus, of a certaine Shepheards
daughter axceedingly deuoted to
the Queen of Heauen, in ſo much
as ſeing her picture in an old rui-
nous Chappel (one day while ſhe
was tending her fathers ſheepe)
and much greeuing to ſee it ſo neglected, ſhe ſayd : O B. Virgin,
were it in my power, this your
Image ſhould be in greater veneration; but what it wants in exteriour ornament, I deſire my interiour deuotion may ſupply;
which deſire of hers was ſo grateful to the Queene of Heauen, as
minding to reward her for it and
her innocent life with an euerlaſting crowne of glory, ſhe ſent
her firſt a ſickneſ the fore-run-

ner

ner of her death, and iuſt as that
was ready to approach vnto her.
Two deuout Religious men, the
one in viſion, the other in prayer,
had eyther of them this reuelation. Concerning her; they firſt
ſaw a Proceſſion of Virgins richly
habited, al ſhining with glorious
light ; which paſſing by them,
another troupe followed them
more riche and glorious then the
former, al clothed in white, and
laſtly a third whoſe garmētsbeing
red, in ornament and beauty farr
ſurpaſſed and out-ſhined al thoſe
that went before; in the cloſing of
this laſt trayne, a Queene of incomparable Maieſty appeared, infinitly exceeding al that can be
imagined of venerable and amiable; at the feete of whom thoſe
Religious men proſtrating themſelues,

selues, desirous of her to be informed who she was, she thus answered them: I am the Mother of
God, and al those troupes, you see
marching before, are those who
haue conseru'd their virginities
al their life time; the first troupe,
not fully resolued of their course
of life, haue yet died Virgins, and
receiued the reward thereof, the
second is of those, who haue consecrated their virginities by vow
vnto their heauenly Spouse; and
the last, who to the Crowne of
virginity haue added the glorious
palme of Martyrdome; al which
are now attending me to a hamlet
heere to receiue the departing
soule of a poore sheapardesse;
whom for her deuotion to me in
mine Image, I meane to place a-
mongst these heauenly Quires,

T v   and

and reward her with the glory of
an euerlaſting Crowne. This Reuelation (it hapened) theſe two
Religious men cōmunicated each
to the other, when inquiring who
this poore Shepardeſſe ſhould be,
at laſt they were directed to a litle
cotage where lay this poore yong
Girle vpon a padd of ſtraw, euen
ready to breathe her laſt, When
ſeeing theſe Religious men entring in; Good Fathers (ſayd ſhe)
in reward of your charity I would
to God I could ſhew you what a
glorious Company is heer away-
ting to beare my ſoule to reſt; &
hauing ſayd this, ſhe rendred vp
her ſoule into their hands, who
willingly receaued it. By which
example we may ſee, how acceptable to the B. Virgin are our reuerencing her deuoutly in her
Images.   Now

Now to the end the frequent aspect of her Images may excite vs frequently to hononr her ; I would counsel euery deuout Catholicke to adorne their chambers with some Image of hers, or procure rather to haue some portable one, which they are neuer to depart withal; In imitation of S. Heduing a Dutchesse of Polonia, who to honour the glorious Mother of God more frequently, would neuer be without her Image in her hand ; the two first fingers & thumbe of whose right hand at the opening of her Tomb some fiue and twenty yeares after her decease were found whole & incorrupt, (al the rest of her body being wasted vnto to bone) holding betwixt them an Image of the B. Virgin so fast, as neither

when

when she dyed, nor then, could they take it thence.

So when in any place her sacred Image occurs vnto our fight, we are deuoutly to honour it, in vncouering the head, bowing the knee, &c. According as the ancient Chreftiãs were accuftomed: the like reuerence we are to do when we heare her name pronoūced; a deuotion fo punctually obferued by the ancient Chriftians, & Saints as S. Gerard Bifhop of Pannonia commanded it through al his Diocefe.

And that which we fayd of reuerencing her name, inuites me likewife to fay a word or two of the reuerence we owe to that of our Sauiour Chrift. Firft, for the name of the holy Trinity how venerable it is in the holy Church, witnefwitnesseth that verse in the conclusion of euery Psalme : *Gloria Patri*, &c. *Glory to the Father*, &c. in pronouncing of which, al rise vp and do reuerence, not only the Quires on earth, but also in heauen it-selfe; as is manifest by that wondrous example recounted by Petrus Damianus. There was a deuout man (sayes he) who one night, while they were singing Matins, rauished in extasy, beheld the B. Virgin accompanied with an infinity of Angels & Virgins entring the Church, and leading the Procession vp the high Altar, he saw thē al kneele down, and whilest each *Gloria Patri*, &c. was singing, they al fell prostrat on their face; who demanding the reason of his extraordinary reuerence, it was answered him,

that

that as often as thatverſe was ſung on earth, they in heauen were particularly touched with the reuerence exhibited vnto the holy Trinity, and reioyced that their ordinary exerciſe in heauen of adoring the Al Bleſſed Trinity, was in ſuch vogue on earth.

And how ſeuerely any irreuerence vnto this ſacred verſe, is puniſhed by Alm. God, we haue a cleare Example in the ſecōd part of the Fr. Minors Chronicles, of a Religious man, who for not inclining while this verſe was pronounc't out of a negligent cuſtome he had gott, was after death puniſhed in this manner ; ſhe was puniſhed placed on a moſt highe and narrow pillar, inuironed about with ſea, where a hundred tymes a day and as oft by

night,

night , he was condemned , to most profound inclination vntil he had satisfied for his neglect of them , in the other world. Which punishment being expired , he reuealed vnto one of his fellow Religious , that at euery inclination he felt such a horrible feare, as if at the instant he had ben falling into hel.

As forthe B. name of Iesus, there needs no other testimony, nor incitement to honour it, then those words of holy Scripture where it is sayd : *That at the name of Iesus, al knees should bow both in heauen, Earth, and the Infernal deepes below.* So likewise do we reuerēce those words of S. Iohns Gospel *Et Verbum Caro factum est* : *and the worde was made flesh* : and that other particle of the Nicen Creed : *Et incarnatus*

carnatus eſt , *&c.* by which we are reduced to memory of the ſweet goodnes of Alm. God, and his infinit loue; which cauſed him for our ſakes to vndergo ſo many tormēts, & afflictions in this mortal life; and that man were a very monſter of Ingratitud, should he refuſe to honour him for it.

Admirable truely, and worthy the notice of al the world is that hiſtory which Ceſarius an author worthy of credit recounts. There was (ſayes he) a yong Gentleman of a proud and hauty nature, who being preſent once at Maſſe ſung in the Cathedral Church, whilſt al at pronouncing theſe words, *Incarnatus eſt*, *&c.* bowed downe their knees in humble reuerence , he neuer offered to ſtirr or moue him from his ſeate;

In

In punishment of which irreuerence, it pleased Alm. God to
permit the diuel presently to appeare vnto him in a most horrible
and frightful shape , who giuing him a furious blow on the
face , sayd vnto him; Poore impious man, dost thou not know
that the Eternal God became
man for thee? and art thou not as-
hamed then to Sitt while others
kneele , & beare thy selfe so high,
for whom God stoop't so lowe?
and what art thou more then
others or what priuiledge hast
thou aboue the rest? vngrateful as
thou art; if he whom thou neglect'st so much, had done but a
hundred part so much, for me,
as he hath done for thee , I
would not only bow downe vnto
the earth vnto him, but euen vnto
hel

hel it selfe.

For the honour which appertaines to Images, hauing by the
way spoken of it before, I wil
heer omit it, and passe vnto.

The Reuerences We are to make in saying our Beads.

CHAP. XVI.

AVING spoken of diuers sorts of Adorations, that which we intend to speak of
now, humbly to in-
cline our selues at euery *Aue Ma-ria* in saying of our Beads, of al
others is the most excellent, we may gather from the excellency

lency it selfe of Rosary and the Angelical salutation.

And first for the Beads or Rosary, its excellency Consists in this, that it is a deuotion wholy composed of our Lords Prayer & the Archangels wordes, with and addition of Saint Elizabeths, out of the holy Ghospel, &c. vnto which the holy Church hath no deuotion comparable. Then for the number, it consisting of. 63. *Aue Marias*, being the number of yeares the B. Virgin liued on earth, it is both deuout and mysterious; wherefore it were good, that in saying ouer the Beads, we inclined at euery *Aue Maria* in memory of each yeare of her B. life, and each vertue in which she was exercised the while; which if it be duely per-

performed, what an excellent deuotion muſt it neceſſarily bee; whilſt we commemorat, how she liued an infant, how in womans ſtate, and how al her life in euery age thereof, according to the ſeueral decades of our Beads' vpon euery one, whilſt we make deuout and humble reuerence me thinkes we exceed in deuotion, euen the Angel whom we imitat, for he only once ſaluted her, but we as often as there are Beads in the Roſary, and as oft as we shal ſay them ouer.

And whilſt we are exerciſed in this deuotion, what do we elſe but compoſe a Garland for our ſelues of the Roſes and lillyes of immortal life, with which after this mortal life we shalbe Crowned, or rather she doth it for vs, to whom

whom we offer vp this our deuotion; as whilſt a certaine deuout
Virgin ſaye her Beads, an Angel
was obſerued on a goulden thread
for each *Aue Maria* to thread a
Roſe, for each *Pater noſter* a lilly,
which the following Miracle giues worthy credit vnto, taken out
of the third part of the Fr. Minors Chronicles, and it is this : A
certaine Guardian had commanded a Nouice of his called Lewis
Albanois, to ſay euery day his
Beads ouer before he eate or
drunke. This deuotion the good
Nouice once by chance (hindred
by other buſines) did omitt,
which the Guardian vnderſtanding inſtantly commanded him to
performe, it (iuſt when they were
then ſitting downe to eate,) ſe-
uearely reprehending him for his
negli-

negligence, the Nouice obeyed,
and repayred vnto the Church,
where after he had for some
good space remained, the Guardian sent one of the Religious to
seeke him out: who going, found
the Nouice on his knees before
the highe Altar deuoutly saying
his Beads, and saw an Angel close
by him threading of roses and lillyes on a golden thread) as we
haue sayd before) : wherupon he
remaining astonished at the thing
the Guardian dispatch't another
in search of him, who hauing
found him out, ioyn'd with him
in astonishment at so rare a spectacle; In fine, one in traine of a-
nother, being sent, and none returning thence, the Guardian at
last with the rest arose, and al re-
payring to the Church, were al
wit-

witnesses of the Miracle; In testimony of which, afte the Angel disappeared, (which was not til the Nouice had finished his take) the place remaind', for a long while as freshly sauouring of roses and lillyes, as if they had growne there.

For diuers reasons is this deuotiõ of the Beads to be exceedingly esteem'd, First for that the Angelical salutation cõsists of words inuented first in the consistory of the sacred Trinity, and afterwards pronounced by the Archangel Gabriel one of the chiefest in heauen; for which reason *Albertus magnus* sayes on these words *Missus est*, &c. that the Angel saluted the B. Virgin with these words *Aue gratia plena* : *hayle ful of grace*; not in his person, but

of

of the B. Trinity, Secondly, be
cauſe they are words pronounced
firſt by one of the higheſt Seraphins, according to S. Gregory
the great and diuers others; and
certainly there was a congruency
in it he ſhould be one of the higheſt in the Court of heauen, who
should be imployed from Alm.
God in a buſines of the higheſt
Conſequence on earth.

Thirdly, by reaſon of the obiects
dignity, which is the B. Virgin,
whoſe ſoueraine greatnes and
perfections are farr tranſcending
al other Saints.

Fourthly, becauſe of the magnificence and reſpectful manner this heauenly Embaſſage was
deliuered her by the Angel Gabriel, who accompanied with
multituds of Angels apparailed
in

in a white vestment sett of with
shining beames of light , with
countenance full of cheere and
humble demeanour saluted the
B. Virgin with the glorious titles
of ful of grace, & our Lord being
with her, *Aue gratia plena, Dominus tecum : &c.* so as with good
reason the holy Scripture sayes,
she was troubled at the aspect of
so great Maiesty and magnificence , and especially at so vnac-
customed a salutation, attributing
so much honour to her , and dignity; for (as Lyra wel obserues)
it was that , and not the Angels
presence she was so amazed at,
for they had often been present
with her before; but *Aue gratia
plena, Dominus tecum* , she had neuer heard before; and so the scripture sayes , she stood musing at
Y   that

that falutation , comparing the
dignity of it with her owne vn-
worthines (as she imagined)and
that high fauour with her low
eftate. The excellency finally of
this Angelical Salutation confifts
likewife in this , that it containes al the vertues, graces prerogatiues , dignities, and greatneffes , which God hath aduantaged his Bleffed Mother with al,
it comprehending the higheft
and deepeft myfteries of our redemption , and there shining
brightly in it the infinit loue and
immenfe goodnes of the foueraigne wifdome and incompre-
henfible omnipotency , of God.
Which being fo, with how much
deuotion and reuerence ought
the deuout feruant, of the B. Virgin to pronounce it , and how
                              high

high esteeme are they to conceiue the whilst of so mysterious
a prayer? what sweet resentments
and gusts of Ioy are they to conceiue, while they pronunce these
words so ful of sweetnes and consolation? But what should I
speake of the dignity thereof, of
which the Angels can neuer
speake enough.

Those then, who would deuoutly indeed performe this exercise,
are before they begin their
Beads, to imagin the B. Virgin
seated in a highe Maiestik throne
inuironed about with innumerable Angels and Saints, honouring and reuerencing her; which
Imagination being framed (as
soone as we haue been speaking
it) they are to begin their beads,
making at each a profound reue-

rence

rence in bowing either the head
or knee , and let the meditation
of their heart accompany their
words of the high titles of honour and dignity attributed vnto
her therein , and although they
reach not fully the fenfe of the
words, yet it wil fuffice that they
keepe the eyes of their Imagination fixt vpon the B. Virgin imagining they fpeake in perfon to
her ; which wil much auayle to
ftirr vp in them, a liuely deuotion ; and this is the aduife which
Nauarr giues vs in his Commen-
taryes , to recite with attention
the *Pater nofter*, and *Aue Maria.*

Befides we muft obferue , that
we are to make our reuerence at
pronouncing of thefe words *Aue
Maria* , &c. natural reafon tea-
ching vs that in pronouncing of
the

the name of those we honour, &
giuing them *Al hayle*, we are to
make the greatest demonstration
of Reuerence. And how grateful
vnto the B. Virgin this deuotion
is, if deuoutly indeed performed,
and how it Crownes her as it
were with celestial honour; we
may learne from this Example
recounted by the B. Bernardin of
Felthe at Verona in publik Sermon. There was (says he) a deuout Religious man, who one
day saying his beads before the
high Altar of the Church, another who secretly obserued it beheld the Angels at euery *Aue*
Maria he sayd crowning the B.
Virgin with a crown of sparkling
diamonds, which action they iterated at euery bead which he let
fal, whilst others presented her

the whils with seueral flowers of
lillyes roses and the like. Which
deuout vision ought to be al of
great consolation to those who
are piously exercised in this deuotion.

---

*Remarkable Instructiõs how
to say the beads, extracted
out of the second Tome of
Nauarrs Commentaries,
and other Authours.*

CHAP. XVII.

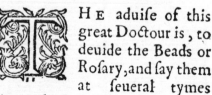THE aduise of this
great Doctour is, to
deuide the Beads or
Rosary, and say them
at seueral tymes
(euen those we are to say of obligation)

gation) now one or two decads, and as many another tyme, more or lesse as our commodity shal serue; so as there passe no houre of the day that may not haue part of our deuotions; and he instances in the Canonical Houres, al which although they integrat one Office, yet the Church deuides them into seueral houres, and assignes seueral parts of the day for the reciting them; so says he, although the Rosary be but one prayer, as it were, yet may it be deuided into seueral parts to be sayd at seueral tymes.

And what on excellent commodity is this, for al sorts of persons, euen in the midst of the presse of their affaires, to be able to comply with their deuotions, to her, who of al other creatures

V 4 can

can beſt proper them; the mar-
chant or citizen may ſay his beads,
one part as he goes in the ſtreets,
the other at his rerurning home,
the lawryer in going to the Hal,
the Courtier to the Court, without any danger of diſtraction, or
interruption of their deuotions
on the way; the Sodaliſts of our
Lady whilſt the Sodality is aſſem-
bling, the deuout perſons whilſt
they await the beginning of a
Maſſe, or returne homewards after it is done.

And by this deuotion of the
Roſary, or any other particular
prayer, the pious Catholike rea-
pes a world of good: For firſt he
often entertaines diſcourſe with
Alm. God and his B. Mother, by
their ſeueral prayers, and that in
a manner moſt ſuccinct & breife;
which

which is the best, if as the saying
is; *short prayers do soonest penetrat
the heauens*; For which reason S.
Chrysostome in one of this Ho-
milies, counsels the people of
Antioch, rather to the exercise of
Iaculatory prayers, that is short
and often repeated, then to seldome and long prayers, for this
(sayes he) soonest begets tedious-
nes; and he confirmes it from the
doctrine of S. Paul, and of our B.
Sauiour himselfe ; and this (according to Cassian) was much in
vse with the ancient Fathers of
the Desart. The secod good which
we reape from it is , that the more
short and breefe it is , with the
more feruour and attention it is
said; for we see by daily experiece
that when we haue much to recite,
we make more hast with it, then
V v   when

when we haue but litle; which
hafte takes much away from our
feruour and attention.

The third Good is, that it puts
vs more often in memory of the
B. Virgin, and confequently awa-
kes our loue of her, more often
too.

And laftly, it actuats vs more
frequently in thefe Adorations
and Reuerences of our foueraine
Queene & Emprefle of Heauen.

Now if by bufines any one be
hindered from faying their
whole Rofary in a day, they may
do it in a weeke (in this manner)
faying each day a feueral decad of
it, &c. which is fo facile and eafy
to performe, as none in reafon
can excufe themfelues from it.

How

Hovv alternatim, or by turnes, vv: may say our Beads.

HIs learned person also teaches vs, how in maner of Quire, we are likewise to say our beads, one answering the other; which Responsory Custome was very frequent in the Primitiue Church, and we read in the Ecclesiastical History of S. Ignatius the Martyr who liued in the Apostles time, that he rauish't one day in extasy, beheld two Quires before the Throne of God, one answering the other in this manner; and so the

the ancient Hymne of Angels
sayes : *Alternantes concrepando,
melos damus vocibus* : which confirmes the receiued opinion to
bee, that the Angels in that manner sing in magnifying God and
his B. Mother , whom men to
their no smal ioy and comfort
ought to imitat.

The manner then to say the
Beads alternatly, or by turnes, is
this ; Two, or more , are with
their beads in hand to say a *Pater-
noster* first vnto themselues , and
then with an audible voyce recite
the *Aue Maria gratia plena , Dominus tecum;* the other answers ; *be-
nedicta tu in mulieribus , et benedi-
ctus fructus ventris tui Iesus*; when
the first resumes agayne , or both
may ioyne together and say : *Sancta Maria* &c. and so forth vnto
the

the end. And this may be done
eyther walking in the feilds, or
visiting the stations in the streets,
or the maisters or mistresses of
families convocating them together may distribut the in Quires,
& do it with much profit & deuotion; which if it be done with
due attention, it is impossible to
imagine how grateful it wilbevn-
tothe Queen of heauen. To conclude this Chapter then, I wil only recount a certaine Miracle in
confirmation thereof.

What tyme the B. Brother Bernardin of Felthe preached at Pa-
uy, a certaine noble Matron had
this deuotion to teach al her children daily before they went to
schoole, to say their beads before
a certaine Image of the Queene
of heauen which she had in her
Cham-

Chamber; now it happened that one of the leaſt of them, one day fel into the Riuer in paſſing ouer a bridge; of which accident the Mother being aduertiſed, ſhe preſently caſting her ſelf vpon her knees before the Image of our Lady in lifting vp her eyes to heauen, al bedeawed with teares; O mother of God, ſayd ſhe the, vſual hope of the afflicted, if it be your bleſſed wil, ſaue my poore child, if not, your B. wil be done; and concluding with the Angelical ſalutation deuoutly ſayd, ſhe ran to the place where many people were aſſembled to ſaue the child, and was no ſooner arriued at the bridge, but behold ſhe ſaw her child floting vpon the water and calling her by her name; at which much reioicing ſhe cried out, take

ſtrong

strong cheere my child, cal vpon the B. Virgin, and my life for yours; when presently the child was taken vp safe, and brought vnto its mother, when embracing it; the child, said vnto her its is not to men I owe my deliurāce, but to our B. Lady, before whose Image you so often instructed me to pray; and therupon it recounted vnto her, how being falne in, she had receiued it in her armes, and bore it aboue the waters; At this, al the Assembly moued to deuotion towards the B. Virgin, did render praise and thankes to Alm. God, and his B. Mother, for being so fauourable and succourable to those who deuoutly inuoke her in their necessities.

of

Of the moſt excellent deuotion of the Roſary.

CHAP. XVIII.

HOSE who are diligent in seruing of great Princes, are ſtil inuenting ſome new way of honouring them; and ſo we Chriſtians being ſeruants of Alm. God and of his B. Mother, are to do the like. Now amongſt al the Inuentions of which deuotion hath ben moſt fertil, none hath been comparable to the Inuention of the Roſary.

And to ſay nothing of the
name

name, or whether it were ſo called to ſignifie, that as the Roſe
holdes the firſt ranke amongſt al
flowers ſo the Roſary amongſt al
deuotions; or that the contexture of it ſeemes to be as a Garland of roſes, for to crowne the
head of her whom we honour in
it. Finally there is none more
vniuerſally exerciſed then this
deuotion of the Roſary, whoſe
Invention the whole Chriſtian
world owes to that great Patriarke S. Dominike; as the propa-
gation thereof vnto the Religious
of this Order, who take care to
celebrate it euery where on earth.

Neither is it celebrated on
earth alone, but the very Angels
in heauen do exerciſe it too, as is
confirmed by this viſion, recorded
by two graue & learned Authors
Lanſper-

Lanspergius the Carthusian, and
Blosius the famous Abbot in his
spiritual Mirrour, as followeth:
The Prior of the Carthusians at
Treuers a very holy man, and one
much exercised in this deuotion
of the Rosary, one day rauished
in vision, (as he was frequently)
beheld the glorious Cittizens of
heauen, praising and blessing with
ineffable ioy our Lord Iesus-
Christ and his B. Mother by commemorating the mysteries of the
Rosary, and recommendation of
al those who deuoutly exercised
it heere on earth; besides he obserued that singing in their praise
as often as they repeated the glorious names of *Iesus* and *Maria*,
they made humble obeissance to
it; and lastly it was reuealed to
him that those who deuoutly e-
xerci-

xerciſed this deuotion on earth,
ſhould obtaine by our Ladyes interceſſion a plenary Indulgence
of al their faults, with diuers priuiledges in this life , and more
then can be imagined in the next.
From whence we may gather the
excellency of the Roſary, & how
acceptable it is to our Lord and
Sauiour Chriſt, to his B. Mother,
& al the Court of Heauen. Wherfore we are to endeauour to performe it with al due reuerence &
attention , if we deſire to be grateful vnto them, and to haue them
propitious vnto vs.

The whole Roſary conſiſts of
fifteene Decads of *Aue Matias*
and fifteene *Pater noſter* , that is, a
hundred and fiftie *Aue Marias*
which admitting of a triple di-
uiſion , your beads of fiue decads
are

are thofe , moft ordinarily in vfe.
Now the manner of Meditating
on them , the feueral myfteries of
our Sauiours and B. Ladyes life,
is this. On the firft fiue decads
they vfe to meditat the fiue Ioyful myfteries , to witt , vpon the
firft , the Angelical falutation;
when the Eternal Word by the
holy Ghofts cooperation, was conceiued : Vpon the fecond decad,
the Vifitation of S. Elizabeth:
On the third , the Natiuity of our
Sauiour Chrift : On the fourth,
the Prefentation in the Temple
of our Sauiour Chrift, where holy
Simeon and Anna the Prophe-
teffe foretold to his glad mother
his future greatnes and miracles.
And on the fifth , our B. Ladyes
finding her B. Sonne in the Temple difputing with the Doctors.
&c.

&c. On the fiue next decads, we
are to meditat the fiue Dolorous
myfteries ; The firft of which is,
our B. Sauiours prayer in the
Garden, where he fel into that
bloudy Agony : The fecond, the
cruel Flagellation, or his whip-
ping at the Pillar, til he was al
goary bloud: The third, the crowning him with thornes, their fpit-
tings in his face, buffeting, re-
uiling him, and the like : The
fourth, the Carrying of the croffe
on his B. fhoulders to Mount Caluary, when his body fo enfeebled
as before, muft needes finke often
vnder the heauy waight : The
fifth, his Crucifixion, or nayling
vpon the Croffe, with vnfpea-
kable cruelty, and indignity.

On the laft 5. Decads we are
to Meditat, firft our Bleffed Lord
and

and sauiours glorious Resurrection, next his Ascension into
heauen; Thirdly the happy departure of the B. Virgin hence;
Fourthly, her Assumption into
Heauen: Fiftly and lastly her glorious Coronation there, where
she is declared Queene ouer the
vniuersal Kingdomes of heauen
and earth.

Where is to be noted, that for
the obtaining of the Indulgences
granted to the sodality of the Rosary (then which I do not knowe
any more ample) it is not requisit to meditat al these mysteries in
order as we haue sett them down;
but it may suffice to entertaine
ones mind the while, with meditating any one or two of them in
which we shal find the greatest
deuotion, nay only to say our
                              beads

beads ouer vocally (according to
Nauarrs opinion) is sufficient, so
it be don with due attention and
deuotion.

Now for the more ignorant,
that they may participat likewise
of the fruit of deuotion, before
they begin their beads I would
counsel them, to frame an Imagination of the B. Virgin, in one of
these three manners, as vulgarly
they are accustomed to delineat
her: Either with the Angel salu-
ting her, or holding her B. Sonne
betwixt her armes, or finally al
glorious in heauen, ready to heare
and grant our Petition; and this
there is none but may make benefit of, for the stirring them vp
vnto deuotion; And that learned
man Nauarr when he was fower-
score yeares of age, not only
made

made vſe of this Imagination in reciting of the Roſary, but alſo in al his other deuotions, and prayers, ſtill Imagined the dignity of the perſon to whom he directed them. Whicn manner of ſtirring vpp attention is both eaſy, recreatiue, and deuout, maintayning the ſpirit in attention and recollecting the memory the whilſt, & opening a way to great familiarity with Alm. God and his B. Mother; which if (as we ought) we practiſe and eſteeme according vnto its dignity, we shal in short time make wondrous progreſſe in the way of ſpirit, and shal heape vp in heauen riches enough to make vs happy for al eternity. There only reſts, that I add to this, a moſt ſtupendious accident, by which we may ſee

the

the great importance of this deuotion, & the great benefit those
of the Confraternity of the Rosary enioy thereby, & it is extracted out of a litle booke intitled,
The Rosary of our Lady.

At what time S. Dominik preached in the Kingdome of Aragon,
a certaine yong Virgin of good
account called Alexandria made
instance vnto him as he came
downe, from out of the Pulpit
(where he had omitted nothing
might make for the commendations of the Rosary) to be admitted into the Sodality thereof,
which she obtained although for
the rest, her life was no wayes ac-
cordingly, she being one who
spent much more time in adorning her body, then to haue her
foule wel adorned. Now it hap-
X ned,

ned, that two Gentlemen at once
making suite vnto her, it was sufficient ground of quarrel (as they
in their madnes thought) one to
challenge the other into the feild,
where they both remayned dead
vpon the place. The freinds of either hearing of this sad accident,
and imagining her (as it was true)
the cause to be revenged on her,
they rushed into her house, and
notwithstanding she desired at
least, but so much respit as to confesse her selfe, they would not al-
low it her, but presently cutt of
her head, and threw it into a pitt.
But our B. Lady, who has euer a
special care of her deuoted seruãts, (though neuer so defectiue)
reuealed the fact vnto S. Dominick, who in order to her merciful commands, went to the pit, &
cal-

called on Alexãdria by her name,
when behold (a wondrous accident) the Angels visibly in sight
of al the people, brought vp the
head from the bottom of the pit,
which ioyned vnto the body, she
besought the Saint to heare her
Confession ; which being done,
she declared three things worthy
of particular note, arriued vnto
her both before and after she was
dead: The first, that by vertue of
her being of the Confraternity of
the Rosary, she had a perfect act
of Contrition at the instant of her
death, without which infallibly
she had died eternally : The second, that assoone as she was dead,
the diuels putting her to great affright, she was maruelously secu-
red & comforted by the glorious
Queene of Heauen : The third,
X 2   that

that for Penance and satisfaction
of the death of those two Gentleman, she was condemned to Purgatory for two hundred yeares, &
for fiue hundred more, for her vanity in attire the cause of, that
so lamentable effect. But that she
hoped by the merits of the same
Confraternity, to be soone deliuered from that punishment, and
hauing sayd this, after she had remained a liue two whole dayes,
for the confirmation of the miracle, and to augment the deuotion
of the Sodality : she left this life
againe, whose body was honora-
bly interred by the sodalists there.
When fifteen dayes after, she appeared againe vnto S. Dominick
al in glory clothed in resplendant
beames of light, declaring vnto
him after a world of thankes for
the

the inestimable benefits she had receiued of him, two things of especial note concerning this deuotion of the Rosary; the one was, that she was delegated to him from the soules in Purgatory with a Petition to be likewise inrold in the Sodality, to receiue the benefit of it amongst the rest; The other, that the Angels much reioyced at the erection of his Sodality, and that God instiled himselfe the Father of it, the B. Virgin the Mother, &c. And hauing sayd this, shee flew away to heauen.

This example ought to be a great incitement vnto euery one to make themselues of this Sodality, and the better to become participant thereof to recite euery weeke the whole Rosary, at

X 3   least

least a payre of beads cannot be burthensome vnto any one of what imployment soeuer they be ; at the end of euery decad thereof they are to make a profound inclination, saying with hart and mouth : O most holy Mother of God, I adore you, and wishe the Saints and Angels may reuerence and adore you a thousand and a thousand times together, with whom I haue firme confidence through the grace of Almighty God, and your fauourable assistance, to blesse, praise, and adore you hereafter for euer and euermore,

Twelue

Twelue most notable Adorations to be made, in the honour & memory of twelue dignities and priuiledges bestowed on the B. Virgin by Alm. God, answerable to the twelue Starrs, which go to the composing of a Crowne for her most sacred head.

CHAP. XIX.

THE B. Euangelist S. Iohn in his sublimes Reuelations of the Apocalypse beheld a woman of incomparable beauty, euironed with Sun

X 4   beames

beames, the Moone vnder her
feete, and on her head a crowne
of twelue brighter ftarrs : by
which according to the expofi-
tion of the holy Doctors and In-
terpreters , our B. Lady is vnderftood, by the Sun , the glory and
Maieftie which she shines withal
in heauen; by the Moone which
she treads vnder foote , is figni-
fied how al that is vnder God,
fuch as are fublunary and earthly
things she is Superiour too, and
for the twelue ftarrs which adorn
her head, are prefigured twelue
fingular priuiledges and prerogatiues , which Alm. God hath endowed her with al , aboue al the
Monarks in this world, and higheft Angels and Seraphins in heauen; and thefe her words haue a
relation vnto it, in that fo excellent

lent Canticle of hers, where after she professes her soule doth magnifie our Lord, she adds the reason why, *quia fecit mihi magna qui potens est*, because he hath don great things for me (sayes shee) which, in that she specifies not what they are, we may imagine to bee aboue al expression. These then how infinit and vnspeakable they are, we shal endeauour to speake a word or two of, reducing them vnto the number of twelue, answerable to the twelue Starrs, which go to the composing of her Crowne.

X v   *The*

The declaration of the first Starr.

THE firſt ſtarr, or rather prerogatiues ; which our heauenly Lady is adorned with al, is
her Eternal and particular *Prede-*
ſtination, who before the Creation either of heauen or earth , &
before al times was diuinely ele-
ſted and predeſtinated vnto ſan-
ſtification, the plenitud of Grace,
and the accumulation of al heauenly guifts, to the end that she
adorned therwith , might be the
better diſpoſed to the Côception
of the Eternal Word. The holy
Church makes mention of her diuine predeſtination in theſe
words

words of the holy Scripture attributed vnto her : *Dominus posse-*
dit me ab initio viarum suarum : the
Lord hath had the possession of
me from the beginning of his
wayes. And this other : *Ab initio*
& ante sæcula Creata sum, &c.
from the beginning I was created
& before al times. So S.Bernard
discoursing with the B. Virgin
vpon this point , *You haue ben pre-*
destinated (sayes he) in the Spirit
of God , before al creatures , to the
end you should ingender God himselfe,
This then is the first starr which
crownes the B. Virgin. Where
we may obserue , that , what is future and to come to vs, is present,
and as it were past vnto Alm.
God. So S. Paul speaking of the
predestination of Alm. God,
speaks of things to come, as if
they

they were already paſt : *Thoſe whom ſhe hath prædeſtinated* (ſayes he) *he hath called, and iuſtified, and glorified.* This B. Virgin then hauing euer been preſent to the eyes of Alm. God as the moſt endeared obiect of his loue , may wel ſay of her ſelfe ; *ab initio & ante ſæcula creata ſum* : And ſo at the firſt inſtant of the Angels creation amongſt the Idæas which they beheld as in a Chriſtal mirrour preſented vnto their eyes one of the moſt beautiful of al next to the humanity of our Sauiour Chriſt , was this celeſtial Virgin; when with what delight and delectation may we imagine them to haue contemplated her, and in her the myſtery of her redemption , and the reſtauration of humane kind : *Where were you* ſfayes

(sayes the Wifeman) when the morning starrs did prayse me, *and al the children of God ioyfully cried out?*

Hauing been then in so particular a manner of predestination elected before al creatures ; by consequence in excellency she was to excel them al, for so vndoubtedly being honoured with the greatest dignity which a creature could be capable of, she likewise had as great grace and sanctity as in any Creature possibly could bee, with al the other endowments requisit, for one who was to be Mother of Alm. God, who in preparing her vnto that dignity, hath heaped vpon her more perfections, and shewed greater proofes of his Omnipotence, wisdome, and infinit good-

nes

nes in creating her, then in creating the whole Vniuerfe befides;
and fo whofoeuer had an eye fo
cleare and piercing to penetrat
God Alm. work in her, would
admire it more then his worke
manship in al other things befide,
in perfectioning of whom he hath
been more exact, then in whatfoeuer elfe.

The fecond Starr declared.

THE fecond Starr which a-
dornes and imbellifhes our
deareft Lady is, the prerogatiue
of her fanctification or *Conception;*
in which, her moft pure foule
when it was vnited to her body,
receiued no ftaine of original
finne at al, it being endowed
euen

euen at that inſtant with more
aboundant grace then any celeſtial or terreſtrial creature elſe,
euen at their greateſt height of
ſanctity; for which it neceſſarily
followes, that in the wombe of
her holy Mother, she should haue
more perfect vſe of reaſon, then
any other at the ripeſt yeares; by
which she both knew, loued, and
contemplated her God and Creatour in a more perfect manner,
then al the Congregation of Saints
and Angels could together. Naturally ſpeaking it is true indeed,
as deſcendant of Adam she should
haue been ſubiect to original
ſinne, as alſo al other miſeries
which follow in trayne thereof,
had not God with his ſuperabon-
dant Grace preuented her, as one
whom he had choſen to be his
Mother,

Mother, from al eternity, and so by an especial Priuiledge exempted from the common condition, which al the rest are generally borne vnto, through our first Fathers disobedience, and so it was most conuenient, if we consider the excellency and dignity of the Sonne of God, and his B. Mother; Now the manner by which was don was this.

At the same instant as Alm. God created the soule of the B. Virgin, and infused it into her body, the newly receiuing forme in S. Anne her mothers wombe, it pleased Alm. God to enriche it with his grace; so as to free it from the contagion of al sinne, which else naturally it had been infected with, in such manner as the diuel neuer had any interest

in

in it ; but to ſay , in what aboundance it was, not only exceeds my
capacity and expreſſion , but that
of al other creatures beſides. For
God at that inſtant did not conſider her , as iſſuing from Adam a
ſinner and his enemy , but as his
Mother choſen out for the reparation of our ſinnes, and to bruze
the head and trample on the pride
of the Infernal Enemy. Which
being ſo, if (as they ſay) the Em-
pyreal Heauen be compoſed of
ſo noble a ſubſtance , and ſhine
with ſo pure and rarified a light,
only becauſe it is the medium,
wherein the obiect of Alm. God
is ſeene ; how pure and noble
muſt the B. Virgin haue been,
who was choſen to be the tabernacle , where he was to inhabite,
and in which the eternal Word
was

was to vnit himselfe to his holy Humanity.

And what a glory is this for humane one of their owne linage, not only thus exempte from al original and actual sinne, but also from the very instant of her natiuity, to begin to lead a life ful of grace, celestial, and diuine? What a consolation is this for poore sinners, who desire to conuert them from their sinnes, to haue one to ayde them, who hath so gloriously triūphed ouer them? what comfort to those who fight against them, to haue her assistāce in the fight, who formerly hath ouercome them? But yet, not only men, but Angels themselues, reioyce and glory in it, to see their Queene, and the mother of their king, graced with so ritch

so

so ritch endowmēt, with so many graces adorned, and accumulated with so many priuiledges, al deriued from this her immaculat Cōception. For which reason S. Vincent Ferrerius saies, that at what instāt the B. Virgin was cōceiued, there was vniuersal Ioy throughout the court of Heauen.

The declaration of the third Starr.

THE third Starr, or prerogatiue, that goes to composing the Crowne of our B. Lady, is her Virginal *purity*, with which shee was endowed by the holy Ghost, at the first instant of her Immaculat Conception; and if, before her birth shee was so pure and holy, how pure and holy must she necessarily

cessarily haue been afterwards? finally, so pure shee was, as S. Anselme sayes of her, that next to God there was not to be imagined the like; & Theodoret sayes, shee surpast in purity al the Angels in heauen, treating of these words of the Canticle; *There are sixtie Queenes amongst the saued soules of men,* (sayes he) *shee who had the honour to bring forth Iesus Christ, the Virgin Mary his mother, no doubt surmounts both the Cherubins and Seraphins in purity*; And so holy, so pure, was this B. Virgin stil, as shee held that strict guard ouer her affections, that neuer any disordinat action came neere them, neuer any vnlawful desire, or repugnant to her deuoir had neuer any accesse vnto her, finally neuer had she cōmitted any venial sinne

as

as the sacred Councel of Trent
obliges vs to beleeue, seconded
by the opinion of al the most famous Doctours of the Church;
And the exceeding affection she
bore to this Angelical vertue (as
S. Anselme sayes) was it, which
made her consecrat to God her
virginity from her most tender
yeares, so as shee was the first In-
uentrix of this rare and excellent
vertue, which equals men with
Angels, and the first who by perpetual vow hath offered vp her
virginity to God, and led the way
which so many since haue followed, so as with good reason she is
stiled *Virgo virginum*, the Virgin
of virgins; besides we must beleeue, a rare purity was requisit
in her, who was to be the habitation of the holy Ghost, Mother
of

of the Eternal father fonne, the
light of Heauens, and mirrour of
al purity and perfection. Befides,
fuch an affectionat loue she had
to this pretious flower of Virgi-
ginity; as in her tender yeares
she left parents freinds and al
worldly delights; to retire her
felfe within the inclofure of the
Temple amongft other Virgins
there, where she remained til
the fourteenth yeare of her age,
the great fortunes which acerued
vnto her by her father and mothers death, (which hapned
about the eleuenth yeare thereof) not being able to diuert
her from her holy refolution;
meane while she refufed al offers
of mariage, being at marigeable
eftate, profeffing that she had
confecrated her virginity to God,
                              and

and that she had rather suffer a thousand deaths , then once in the least thought violat her vow.

Wherupon the Priests of the Temple suspended at the strange nes and nouelty of the thing , betooke themselues to prayer , and consulting the diuine Oracle how they were to comport themselues in this affayre , it was reuealed vnto them , they should assemble al the men of the Image of Dauid , and he to whose lott she fel , should haue her for his wife ; which , being don , (she hauing a reuelation on the other side that such was the wil of heauen) it was S. Iosephs lott to marry her , who had the happines by it to be the Foster-father of Alm. God.

The

The fourth Starr declared.

THe fourth ſtarr, which in ſplendor and beauty ſurpaſ- ſes al the reſt, is her being the *Mother of Alm. God* ; ſo great a prerogatiue (according to S. Au- guſtin) that no mortal greatnes can equal it, and nothing can goe beyond it but God himſelfe, ſo much it hath in it of the Infinit (as S. Thomas ſayes) being ſo neerly conioyn'd with the infinit perſon of the Sonne of God ; and this dignity of hers it is (ſayes he) that implyes in vs an obli- gation, to adore her with a more excellent ſort of Adoration, then any other Saint.

But is it not a wondrous thing, that

that a Virgin in the closet of her wombe, should containe him whom heauen and earth and sea cannot containe, who hath appointed to the Sun and Moone, and starrs, their seueral orders and stations; which maruayles are sufficiently exprest in these three verses: *Quem terra, pontus, æthera,* &c. *Cui luna, sol, & omnia,* &c. *Beata mater munere,* &c. Is it not a wondrous thing, the same woman should be both mother and a mayde, that one should conceiue and bring forth a child, without any detriment of her Virginity? that she should haue a mothers fæcundity ioyned with the purity of a Virgin, that she should haue a sonne both in heauen in his fathers bosome, and on earth in his mothers wombe to-

Y   gether

gether which fonne in heauen
should be ingendred without mother, and without father on earth?
Thefe are the exclamations of
the great and learned Origen on
thefe words ; *Cum effet defponfata,*
&c. O grace (fayes he) to bee
admir'd ! O incredible fweetnes!
O Sacrament eneffable! the fame
is both mother and Virgin, the
fame both mother and feruant
too, and engendred one at once
both God & Man! who hath heard
of fuch wondrous things as thefe:
fo farr Origen.

And fo great and incompre-
henfible is this diuine myftery,
as the B. Virgin her felfe, although she were moft extraordinarily illuminated by the holy
Ghoft, yet could she not comprehend, when the Angels tould it
                                    her

her how it could be, that she
who was a Virgin could conceiue
a child without any detriment of
her virginity, as appeareth by
her ; *Quomodo fiet hoc , quoniam
virum non cognosco? &c.* neither
could the Angel too informe her
how ? but he remitted her to the
holy Ghoft; *Spiritus fanctus fuper-
ueniet in vos* ; for the vnderftanding of the myftery. O myftery
of myfteries ; & maternal dignity
to be admir'd both of Angels and
men', and neuer fufficiently to be
vnderftood ! but let vs yet proceed to delineat her prayfes more
vnto the life.

When God out of the ribbs of
Adam had framed *Eue* , he waking out of his fleep, fayd to himfelfe ; *this now is bone of my bone,
flesh of my flesh* ; *wherfore a man is*

to leaue both father and mother , and ioyning himself to his wife , to become one flesh with her. Let vs apply this mystery now to our Sauiour Christ and say, that in like manner the humanity of our Sauiour Christ , by its vnion with God vnited humane nature so straitly with the diuinity, that the B. Virgin might as properly say of our Sauiour Christ ; this is flesh of my flesh , bone of my bone, &c. seeing , as S. Augustin sayes , the flesh of Christ, was the B. Virgin flesh.

From whence S. Peter Damian inferrs , that God not only was present to her by his vnlimited being as he is vniuersally with al, nor by his grace as he is only with the Iust, but in a farr more excellent manner of Identity , in that

that

that the ſonne of God, is her
ſonne alſo, and (as we haue ſayd)
fleſh of her fleſh, &c. hauing taken from her the ſubſtance whereof his ſacred body was compoſed, a dignity in her ſo great, as
admiration muſt there take vp,
where humane diſcourſe layes
downe, and with its tongue of ſilence only celebrat it.

This ſo ſtreit vnion or Identity
betwixt Alm. God and the B.
Virgin, is by the Angelical Doctor S. Thomas ſtyled *Parentela,*
or affinity betwixt God and her,
which can be ſayd of no other
creature liuing beſydes her ſelfe,
neither of man nor Angel, to be
naturally allyed, with God like
her, hauing the natural ſonne of
God for her ſonne. In conſideration of which, S. Anſelme ſayes;

Y 3 *The*

The Eternal father had not the hart to suffer, that his only beloued sonn, should be only his sonn, but would withal he should be truly the only and natural sonne of the B. Virgin also; and this not as of two seueral persons but the person of the sonn of God, was likewise the person of the sonn of the Virgin also; and so the contrary. By which we see, that she was truely the Spouse of the holy Ghost, who wrought in her womb the Conception of the sonn of God, and by this she becomes euery way allyed vnto al the persons of the B. Trinity. To conclude then, this dignity and prerogatiue we say (as we haue sayd before) is the greatest in a creature, as can possibly be imagined.

The

The declaration of the fifth Starr.

THe fifth ſtarr brightly ſhining and adorning this celeſtial Princeſſe, is the *Illuſtration* of her ſpirit, by the holy Ghoſts ouer-ſhadowing her, conformable to that which the Angel ſayed in her ſalutation : *Spiritus ſanctus ſuperueniet in te, & virtus Altiſſimi obumbrabit tibi* : which diuine obumbration was then, when the Sonne of God was incarnat in her wombe, the diſpoſition to ſo miraculous a conception ; and ouer-ſhadowing her with its diuine vertue, the better to enable her to endure thoſe celeſtial ardours which inflamed her breaſt the while, and which doubtleſly but

Y 4   for

for it, had wholy confumed her, the flames of diuine loue were fo vehement the while.

Neither (according to S. Auguftin and S. Iohn Damafcen) did the holy Ghoft obumbrat her body only, but her foule likewife; which obumbration is no other then its light and grace, which was conferr'd vpon to her moft abundantly, when the Sonne of God was Incarnat in her womb, at which tyme her fpirit was enlightened, & the darknes of ignorance wholy expeld from thence by which diuine light was clearly reuealed vnto her the profound myftery of the Incarnation, and diuers other myftical fecrets of heauen; as alfo the vnderftanding of the holy Scriptures, and the fpirit of Prophecy was communicated

nicated to her thereby, in a more ample manner then it euer was before to any other of the Prophets.

And it is the opinion of diuers Saints and learned men, as namely of S. Antonin, S. Bernard, S. Cyprian, Vrſin, and Caſſal, &c. that what tyme the Sonn of God was Incarnat in the B. Virgins womb, ſhe was often rauiſh't vp to the Third heauen, where she beheld the cleere viſion of Alm. God, more face to face, then eyther Moſes or S. Paul. And Rupertus on theſe words of the Canticles : *Oculi tui columbarum* : thy eyes, are the eyes of Doues, clearly ſayes that *shee was rauish't vp to the third heauen, where shee beheld in a more excellent manner then S. Paul did, thoſe ſecrets which it is not law-*

Y v　　*ful*

ful for me to know. This if it were granted to any, (as moſt certaine it is, it hath) no doubt but it was to the B. Virgin; who as farr excels al Saints and Angels, as the Sunn in ſplendour and brightnes a litle Starr. But what tongue can worthily expreſſe the ſacred motions of her hart, while the Sonn of God was Incarnat in her wób? the light and ſplendour which illuſtrated her mind and vnderſtanding? the fire and ardour which embrac't her wil? the Ioy finally, which her bleſſed ſoule poſſeſt, when the Word eternal taking fleſh from her, ennobled her with the high title of his *Mother.*

What beames and rayes of light, may we ſuppoſe, reflected from her countenance, while the Diuine ſpirit illuſtrated her ſoule,
in

in whose eyes were two continual fires burning with Diuine
loue, al who beheld her, and yet
in an admirable manner quench-
ing al carnal loue the whilst; And
if Moses issuing forth from con-
uersation with an Angel, had his
face shining with such maiestick
beames, as struck an awful reuerence in the children of Israels
harts; what may we imagine of
the B. virgin, who was perpetually accompanyed with Angels,
who tooke it for honour, euer to
be seruing her.

In the meane while, her vnderstanding was so cleerly illuminated as she had perfect knowledge of the Creator and al his
creatures, and how much loue she
was to bestow on euery particular
thing; and so she burned in the
loue

Ioue of God, as she loued him
not only aboue al earthly things,
but aboue her very foule, aboue
her life both fpiritual and temporal, aboue al glory, and finally
aboue al defired felicity and beatitud in heauen. So fhe enioyed
fuch a tranquillity of mind, and
had al her apprehenfiue and con-
cupifcible powers fo wholy at her
Command, that the inferiour part
of her foule neuer rebeld againft
the fuperiour, but was alwayes in
fubiection & fubordination to it.
Whence it was, that fhe breathed
forth in al places where she came,
fo excellent and fweet an odour
of fanctity, which increafed in
her daily more and more, the
longer she went with our B. Sauiour in her wombe; which fanctity of hers we cannot better
praife

praise nor speake of, then by silent admiration; notwithstanding
euery one is to make some reflexion on it in his mind, and seeke
to draw forth from thence some
spiritual profit by it.

The sixt Starr declared.

THE sixt starr of the B. Virgins Crowne, & which was
one of the cheifest motiues the
Omnipotent God had to choose
her for his Spouse; Was her *plenitud of diuine grace*, and of euery
vertue else. Of this there needs
no other testimony then the Angels words vnto her : *Hayle ful of
grace*, &c. Which plenitud of grace
in her (sayes S. Augustin) was a
disposition no lesse then necessary

ry for conceiuing the Sonne of
God. And although many Saints
haue ben fayd to be ful of grace,
and of the holy Ghoſt, as Zacha-
rias and Elizabeth, with S. Iohn
Baptiſt their ſonne; the Apoſtles,
the ſeauen Deacons, and many
more; Yet none of them al in that
plenitud as ſhe, the word admitting a ſuperlatiue; one B. Sauiour
as the fountaine of al grace deri-
ving it vnto others from himſelfe according to their ſeueral
capacities now the B. Virgin
being the moſt, capacious of al,
no wonder ſhe had more in her
then al the reſt. But yet it was a
greater plenitud the Angel meant by ſaluting her ſo, and the
greateſt indeed that poſſibly
could bee in any Creature; a plenitud which (as S. Bernard ſaies)

deriuing

deriuing it felfe to others, giues liberty to the captiue, comfort to the afflicted, to finners pardon, grace to the Iuft; to the Angels Ioy, glory to the holy Trinity, and to the Eternal Word the fubftance of her proper flesh. Befides, as S. Hierom fayes, Grace was giuen vnto others by parcells only, but to her, fully and in its intire perfection, in that the fulnes of al was included in her; and confequently by this fulnes of grace, she muft be ful of al other vertues elfe, which euer yet any Saint was endowed with al; Nay, the holy Fathers, and in particular S. Cyril and S. Hierom fay, she was not only ful of grace, but had al other vertues, diuine guifts and endowments congregated in her alone, which

in

in scattered peeces were disper-
sed amongst al the other Saints.
There is nothing (sayes S. Herom)
*if we consider it wel , of pure, splen-
dious, or of vertuous , which shinnes
not in the glorious Virgin* most
particularly.

Now if so large a portion of
vertues fel vnto her share, before
she was Mother of God, how must
they afterwards be augmented ,
when shed was indeed? assuredly,
no tongue is able to expresse,
how infinit & incomprehensible
they were, (sayes S. Bernard) the
greatnesses & perfections of God
being infinit and incomprehensible , his Mothers who conceiued
him in her wombe , must needs
participat of the incomprehensi-
bility & infinitnes of them also.

Besides, there was also congregated

gated in her al moral vertues in greater meafure then euer was in any one, nay had an Angel come to the earth inuefted in humane flesh, it could not haue been more perfectly accomplifhed then fhe; for proofe of which affertion, I wil fumm vp in a catalogue thofe moft excellent parts of hers, which are recorded to haue been in her by diuers holy men; the admirablenes &perfection of whofe life, was propof'd as a paterne for virgins to imitat by S. Ambrofe in thefe words: Neuer did she offend any (fayes he) though she had neuer fo iuft a caufe; but fhe both wifhed and willed wel vnto euery one, and did wel them too; she was reuerent towards her fuperiours, and no way moleftful to her equals; she shun'd al boaft, al

al her actions were conformable
to reafon ; and she loued al vertues with her heart ; she neuer
contriftated her parents, and neuer with freind or acquaintance
entred into conteft : she difdained
not the humble, derided not the
fimple, nor thought it shame to
accompany the poore; there was
no affectation in her behauiour,
nor diffolution in her gate, and
her words were fo tēpered, as the
modefty which shined in them
and her actions sufficiently declared her interiour fanctity, and in
ward vertue & perfectiō of mind;
no otherwife then a fumptuous
Portal doth the magnificence of
the Pallace that is within. Neuer
but to the Temple did she ftirr
abrode, and then neuer but accōpanied with her father, Mother,
                                   kinsfol-

kinsfolkes, or the like : & within
doores she was delighted with solitud , and imployed her thought
alwayes in somewhat of good and
profitable for her soule. This
much S. Ambrose, who hath much
more besides.

And S. Hierom describing her
Heroick vertues & celestial māner
of life in the Temple amongst the
sacred Virgins, sayes: She alwaies
endeauoured to be the first at Vi-
gils of the night , to be best instructed in the law of God the
most humble in her demeane, the
most eagre in the workes of Charity, the purest in purity and most
perfect in al sorts of vertues and
perfections , she was assidual in
prayer, & (as the Prophet sayes)
meditated night and day in the
law of God, she was iealous of the
honours

honours of thofe she conuerfed
with, and that without any dif-
guft or molestation of theirs;
Deo gratias was her anfwer to al
falutations; and in fine, her whole
life was fuch as for prayer, humility, modefty, folitud, filence,
virginal bashfulnes, and the like
noble vertues of her fexe, she was
a paterne and model for al to
imitat.

The feauenth Starr declared.

THe feauenth Starr nothing
inferior in brightnes to the
reft, is her neere *Communication* of
truft and fecrecy with Alm. God,
fo as no earthly Prince was euer
more confident with Secretary or
chamberlaine, then he with her,
nor none euer more fecret and
faithful then she to him. When
he

he was an Infant, she with incredible care and diligence attended
him, made him ready and vn-
ready, gaue him milke from her
sacred breasts, and with her virginal lipps tenderly kissed him;
Al which she did with such deuotion and respect, as (according
to Albertus Magnus) she never
layed him to rest nor tooke him
vpp, but she adored him first with
profound reuerence, and entred
so farr on the consideration of
his infinit loue, that made him
doe what he did for vs, as for the
most part she fel into extasy. Afterwards for the space of 30.
yeares, in al times, in al occasions
she was present to his necessityes,
in al his trauails, miseryes, and
calamities both winter and sum-
mer, in cold and heat, raine or
snow,

snow, she euer willingly would accompany him; neyther was he wanting on his part to correspond vnto the dearenes of her affection communicating with her the greatest secrets of his diuinity; so as she neuer desired him to vnfould any hidden mystery as of the Trinity the Quires of Angels, the vocation of the Gentils, the vnion of the faithful with his holy Church, but he did it presently; & if he reuealed to his disciples with such candour and promptitud, the secrets of his heaue̅ly Father *I cal you no longer seruãts but freinds* (says he) *for what I haue heard frommy Father, I haue declared to you*: much more would he do to his B. Mother, we suppose; And if in frequ̅eting of his co̅pany & hearing of his doctrine only, during his
last

laft three yeares he could render them fo learned & expert in the diuine myfteries, how much more learned & expert muft she needs be, who both frequented & heard him for more then 30. yeares? whilft he reuealed vnto her thofe myfteries heere on earth, which the very Angels of heauen were ignorant of. As Princes then vfe to ennoble thofe with great titles of honours and dignityes, whom they entruft with their perfons and fecrecies ; fo not only did our Sauiour heere on earth aduance the B. Virgin to eminent dignity, but much more now in heauen doth he intitle her to the higheft degree of glory and excellence, not ranking her with the quires of Virgins, Cõfeffours, Martyrs, Apoftles, Prophets, nor

Patriarks

Patriarks, but to a high fublimity aboue them, and aboue al the heauenly Hierarchies he hath ad-uāced her, feating her at his owne right hand, where she fits inftaled Queene of heauen : *The Queene is at thy right hand*, (fayes the Pro-phet Dauid) *adorned with al va-rieties*; whilft al the Bleffed grant her the precedencie willingly, and deferr it vnto her as their fo-ueraine Queen. Finally she rules ouer the whole Vniuerfe; and al the moft important affaires of the B. Trinity, in a manner, do paffe through her hands, so as al the heauenly Cittizens, the inhabi-tants of the earth, the foules in Purgatory, nay euen hel it felfe acknowledge he power and reue-rence her for it with al humility.

The

The eighth Starr declared.

THE eight ſtarr is the high Priuiledge ſhe had of *Contemplation* and enioyed al her life; ſo as from the very firſt inſtant of her ſanctification in her mothers wombe, (according to Suarez) ſhe had the vſe of reaſon, & conuerted it to the knowledge, loue, and contemplation of Alm. God, from which nothing could diuert, her euer after ; and he confirmes it, for if this guift (ſayes he) was beſtowed on the Angels at their firſt Creation, with greater reaſon may we imagine it beſtowed vpon the Mother of Alm. God, and Queen of them. Whileſt ſhe

was

was resident in the Temple with those other consecrated Virgins, she was still in highest contemplatiõ, supplicating the diuine Maiesty with the feruorous prayer oftē interrupted with amorous sighes for the Incarnation of the Messias that was to come the whilst there are graue Authours who report, that the Angels daily administred her her food, still entertayning her with some heauenly newes, or some diuine rapts she had during those nine moneths the Incarnat Word lay couched in her sacred wombe. Some times she being wholly transported from her selfe, and absorpt in God, at other times her soule making such sallyes forth, *per modum transeuntis* (according to some) as cleerly to behold God face to face; and no won-

wonder, she hauing so spacious a
feild for her Contemplation to
walke in euen to the third heauen,
and farther if it were possible as
her B. sonne then actually present
with her, his heauenly ffathers
delight and Mothers ioy; who
can say, or so much as imagine
her sweet transports through the
consideration of the maruaylous
excesse of that loue of his, that
had inclosed him in womb whom
the Heauens cannot containe ,
and held him in the restraint of a
litle body; who in his hand held
al that is comprised in this great
vniuerse? ffor my part I am of
opinion with SS, Bernard, Bonauenture, and the learned Cani-
sius, that she continued whole
nights rauished in contemplation
of these diuine and wondrous my-

Z 2   steries

fteries; for we may beleeue, fhe
was of a complexion and temper
fo excellent, as she required but
litle fleepe, and during that litle
time she flept, F. Suares is of opinion, that fhe was fo inflamed
with the loue of God, that fhe
often ftarted out of her fleepe, (as
loue is a reftleffe thing) and was
tranfported by the force of loue
to God the only obiect of her affections; and S. Bernardin affirmes, that fhe enioyed fo fuper-
natural a contemplation, that
fhe had the vfe of it in fleepe, in
a farr more excellent manner,
then euer any Saint in waking
had. Howfoeuer, whether waking or fleeping, or howfoeuer
imployed, we may wel affirme
with the learned Canifius, that
fhe neuer interrupted her medi-
tations

tations, but thad al her life was but a continual exercise of exta-fy and contemplation ; whilft euery thing miniftred matter to meditation ; she read with incre-dible affection the holy fcripture, which fhe vnderftood exactly wel, both by her owne cleere vnderftanding, as alfo by the light communicated vnto her from Alm. God ; and to her me-ditations a great helpe was the moderatnes and temperature of her diet, which together with her folitud and filence difpofed her fpirit to meditation and vnion with Alm. God, with whom she was fo perpetually vnited, as fhe rather feemed diuine them mor-tal. For which reafon perhaps it was, that God would haue no mention made in holy Scripture, neither of her father nor mother; to witt, that we might confider her rather a celeftial creature coming from heauen, then a terreftrial, borne on earth. Meane while, the Angels, that fhe might the more wholy attend to contemplation, did dayly bring her food; a miracle, which we are the leffe to admire, fince we reade of S. Paul fome what to the like effect, who was one by infinit degrees inferior in fanctity and perfection vnto her.

And what wonder is it, that fhe fhould feeme more diuine then humane, when fhe was arriued to fuch a high degree of innocencye, that fhe neuer fett into the leaft defect, nor was euer tranfported fo much as with the firft motion of any difordination; which

which were no wonder, if (as a graue Authour affirmes) ſhe were borne impeccable, a quality, ſayes he, but, in a manner, neceſſary for her, who was deſtinat to the high honour of being the Mother of Alm. God. Neither was it poſſible for her to be other wiſe, conſidering how Alm. God tooke vpp al the lodging with in her for himſelfe; while she conſidering her owne humility on the one ſide, and the high honour on the other, to which God had aduanced her, was ſo ſtudious how to comply with her obligation to him for ſo great a benefitt, as her thoughts had neuer leaſure to thinke of any thing beſides; To ſay nothing of the abſolut mortification of her body and exterior ſenſes, and the continual watch

the

the Angels kept ouer her by turnes, that no euil should approch
her, as one who was the liuing
Tabernacle of the liuing God. As
for the diuels, they fled her more
then they follow others, as we
may wel imagine if S. Antony,
S. Bernard, and other Saints were
so formidable to them as they
durst not approche their sight;
And for her, she fled synne more
then any wicked person followed
it, as knowing that whosoeuer
sinned, *ipso facto* felt into the disgrace of Alm. God, a thing which
of al other she dreaded most so as
al her delight was in the exercise
of vertue and sanctity of life. To
conclude, she despised al honours
of the world, as knowing she was
shortly to go to the possession of
that supreme honour of being
                                    Queene

Queene of Heauen hauing nothing then to diuert her from it;
and al helps and incitements to
it, how could she choose but be
perpetually in contemplation?

The Declaration of the Ninth Starr.

THe Ninth Starr of our B.
Ladyes crowne, is the *Di-*
gnity she is exalted to, aboue al
creatures both in Heauen and
earth , which by proper name,
we may cal her *Exaltation* ; since
by it she is exalted aboue the highest heauens , aboue al the Orders of Saints, and Hierarchies of
Angels , as the holy Church sings
of her prayse : *Exaltata es sancta*
Z v *Dei*

Dei genitrix super choros Angelo-
rum ad Cælestia regna. Neither can
we admire, that next vnto himfelf, the foueraine king of glory
fhould aduance her to the greateft he had, for fhe being his Mother there was a kind of obligation on his part to honour her
and do her al good he could, fince
the honour which Children are
bound to giue to their parents,
Confifts not only in words and
ceremonious refpect, but much
more in effect and really doing
for them. Wherfore (fayes Hip-
polytus) he who hath commanded this : *Honora patrem & ma-*
trem : honour thy father and thy
mother, to fulfil the law which
he himfelfe prefcribes to others,
would not (we muft fuppofe)
be wanting to his Mother, in
what

foeuer honour grace and glory he could beftow vpon her. Now al the priuiledges and aduantages aboue others which the B. virgin hath, are founded vpon thefe two principalls; the firft, the infinit power of her B. fonn; in confideration of which S. Auguftin fpeaking of her Affumption both in foule and body. fayes, that God could do it and why he did it not, thofe who denied it were to giue him a reafon for it, The like argument we may vfe in point of the B. Virgins glory,

The feconc is her dignity in being the *Mother of God*, who is infinit, wherefore as the title of *Sonn of God* is the foundation on which we ground the excellency of the humanity of Chrift; fo the title of *Mother of God*, is that, on
which

which we ground al her prerogatiues, her singular graces, and her supreme glory; for natural reason teacheth vs that the mother is more nigh to her sonne, (excepting the Father) then any other kynn. Wherefore the B. Virgin being the Mother of Iesus Christ, who was Incarnat in her sacred flesh, must needs be nigher her sonne, in grace and glory, too, then any elle besids.

Soe he would not ranke her amongst the Hierarchies of Angels, for then there had been others higher aduanced then she amongst the Powers and Thrones; nor amongst them, because the Cherubins and Seraphins surpast them in dignity; but next vnto himselfe, as was most fitt, that his Mother might not

be

be inferiour vnto his seruants, nor the Queene vnto her subjects, where she sitts enthroned with incredible pompe and Maiesty, making a Hierarchie more high and excellent by her selfe, then any of them al.

But what vnderstanding can comprehend, or what tongue expresse the Glory she is possessed of? For if the eye hath neuer seen, the eare neuer heard, nor the hart of man euer conceiued, what God Alm.hath prepared for those who loue him; how can one conceiue, what he hath prepared for her, who not only loued him, but brought him forth, nourished, educated, and serued him with such affection & diligence? Only this we may imagine and say of it, that glory and felicity next to Alm.

Alm. Gods, is the greateſt that
is in heauen, and that in compariſon of creatures ſhe is holy a-
boue al holyes, happy aboue the
happieſt, hath more grace then
thoſe who haue moſt beſides, and
hath more glory then the moſt
glorious.

The holy Doctors ſpeake mar-
vayles of this Exaltation of hers,
and amongſt the reſt, S. Bernard
ſayes, that the glory ſhe enioyes
in heauen, beares a proportion
to the plenitud of grace ſhe had
on earth aboue al creatures els;
and adds, that as on earth there
was not a more ſanctified place
then the ſacred Temple of the
Virgins wombe, which contained God himſelfe, ſo in heauen
there is not a more glorious then
her Throne, where ſhe ſitts exalted

ted at the right hand of God. In another place he sayes, the vnder-standing of man cannot conceiue her glory, nor his tongue declare it, which puts the Inhabitants of heauen it selfe to their admiration in beholding it. Andræas Cretensis sayes, that her glory can not be comprehended, for that it exceeds the glory of al the Saints and Angels putt together. S. Iohn Damascen, that there is a mighty difference betwixt the seruants and the Mother of God. S. Iohn Chrisostom, that the B. Virgin is more glorious incomparably then the Seraphins. B. Laurentius Iustinianus, that al the glory and felicity which in scattered peeces is distributed amongst the Saints, is found vnited in the B. Virgin And the

Sera-

Seraphike S. Bonauenture fayes,
that the greatnes and goodnes of
God doth more manifeftly appeare in the B. Virgin only, then
in al the reft of creatures, and that
al their perfections are in a more
excellent manner to be found in
her then them; and he concludes,
that as in grace and merits she
furpaffeth al other Saints, fo likewife doth fhe in felicity and
glory. This and much to this effect is fayd by them of the B. Virgins high exaltation anfwerable
to the height of her other merits
and prerogatiues, who being Mother of God, the fupremeft dignity which any creature could be
aduanced vnto, on earth. Corref-
pondent to it is this ninth Starr,
and one of the brighteft in her
glorious Crowne of being aduanc't

uanc't to fo fupreme a dignity in
heauen.

The tenth Starr declared.

THe tenth, and that a moft
refplendant one, is the Empire and foueraine command she
hath ouer the whole Vniuerfe, al
creatures both in heauen & earth
and in the deapes below, acknowledging her fuperiority in
reuerencing her for it, and adoring her; there being a congruency, fayes S. Iohn Damafcen,
that the mother should partake of
the fonnes dignity; And fince
he (fays S. Athanafius) who was
borne of her, is King and foueraine Lord of al, confequently
she who bore him, is to beheld
for

for foueraine Lady and Queene; fo fays S. Bernard; who can deny her a legitimat claime to be Lady ouer al, of which her fonne is Lord. Let vs then acknowledge her authority ouer al, to be as great and vnlimited as her wil. In confideration of whofe greatnes S. Bernard breakes forth into this exclamation : *Al power, O foueraigne Lady, in heauen and earth, is giuen you to do what you wil withal.* S. Brigitt in one of her Reuelations fayes, that at the inftant of her folemne entry into heauen, God aduanc't her aboue al the heauens, gaue her the Empire of al the Vniuerfe, aud conftituted her Lady and Miftres of the Angels; and fhe confirmes it in thefe wordes dictated vnto her by the holy Ghoft : *The principality of al people*

people and nations she had (says she)
and by her vertue she treads vpon the
harts of the Proudest and highest there.
And truely a wonderful dignity it
is, which equals her (in a manner)
with the Lord of al ; but a more
wonderful and stupendious it is,
that she should haue an authority
euen ouer him; which that it may
seeme lesse strange vnto the eares
of flesh and bloud, let vs remember only, that she is his Mother
and our admiration wil cease, for
that filial obedience he owed her
heere on earth, he stands not so
quitt of in heauen, but it induces
a kind of obligation in him to
grant her whatsoeuer she desires;
whom there we may Imagine
speaking vnto her thus : *Demand*
of me, deare Mother, whatsoeuer you
please, it is not lawful for me to turne
away my face. This

This our triumphant Empreſſe, to expreſſe vnto vs more vnto the life the greatnes of her dignity, declares vnto vs in theſe remarkable words fower things: *I alone haue incircled the round of heauen, and haue penetrated the depth of the Abiſſe, and haue walked on the waues of the ſea, and haue the principality of al nations*: ſignifying by the firſt part of the text the dominion she hath in heauen, by the ſecond, that which she hath in hel; by the third, the benefit the ſoules in Purgatory receiue by her; and by the fourth, her dominion ouer al the world, and what can be more ſayd of her dignity? Vnleſſe what a deuout ſeruant of hers in a certaine prayer vnto her hath ſayd; O moſt pure (ſayes he) and ſingularly happy Virgin , al ful of grace

grace and glory, the moſt bleſſed
amongſt al women, who ſurmoū-
teſt the Angels in purity, and all
the Saints in benignity next to
your B. Sonne, you only cōmand
ouer this world in cheife, exten-
ding your fauourable hand to al
who lye and craue your ayde; and
there is no houre nor moment
equally amiable and admired. who
haue conceiued the Sonne of the
Higheſt, and brought for the Sauiour of the world; O Mother of
ſaluation, & fountaine of mercy,
we miſerable ſinners in rendring
of them vp, without laſt breaths
ſighe and grone to you, praying,
ſaluting, and acknowledging you
Queen of this world, reioycing
at your greatnes, congratulating
your glory, your ſouerainty and
the place you hold at the right
hand

hand of you B. Sonne, where becoming wholy in a manner diuine, and hauing nothing of mortal in you, you gouerne the heauens at pleasure, illuminat the
Sunn, rule the world, trample
vnder foote the pride of hel, and
haue dominion ouer the starrs, the
elements serue you, the seasons
obey you, the Angels adore you,
the diuels stand in awe of you,
whole nations and Kings bow
their knees before you, and doe
you honour and reuerence: O
Lady of heauen and earth & hel,
your Maiesty and Empire is so
great a thousand tongues cannot
speake it to the ful; and euen the
foules of the aire, the beasts of
the land, and the fishes of the sea
do al acknowledge it at your beck,
the flowers spring vp, plāts grow,
and

and seeds sprout forth, the earth
is fertilized, riuers flow, & winds
do blow, the left wil of yours can
incline the destinies, and order
second causes, whilest the first is
wholy at your dispose. Cast a gratious & pittiful eye vpon vs poor
sinners heere, & declare the greatnes of your power, by helping vs
to ouercome our selues, and to obtaine remission of our sinns, grace
heere, & glory in the life to come
by your prayers and merits, vnto
which is nothing impossible; that
after this miserable life, we may
come to enioy that happy life,
where we shal see our soueraine
Lord, in whose sight consists al
our felicity.

The

The declaration of the eleuenth Starr.

THE eleuenth ſtarr, whoſe ſplendour not only adornes her head, but the rayes of it théce do likewiſe reflect on vs, & crown vs with a ſupreme felicity, is her *Mediation* betwixt God and man; one of the cheif reaſós according to the holy Doctours, why God from eternity choſe her for Mother, that as a moſt powerful mediatrix her maternal prayers for ſinners might moderat the rigour of the diuine iuſtice, and occaſion a reconcilement.

Ieſus Chriſt (ſays S. Bernard) was ſufficient) it is true) for our
repa-

reparation, from whom proceeds
al that ſuffiſeth thereunto; but it
was wel for vs he ioyned with him
ſuch an one as ſhe; for although,
as he is man, he be our moſt
faithful and powerful Aduocat,
Yet ſuch dayeling beames break
through his humane nature
from his diuinity that we cannot
looke vpon him with that confidence; and though he be infinitly gratious, yet being Iudge with
al, offenders haue ſmal hart to approch vnto him; for which reaſon the B. Virgin was choſen for
Aduocat, and meditatrix betwixt
God and man, to whom there is
none can feare to approch, she
hauing nothing in her of formidable or auſtere; but rather being
al ſweetnes and benignity and
abounding in al goodnes and

A a   mercy

mercy. Thus S. Bernard.

None then, how great sinners soeuer they be, but may be confident of their saluation, if they haue but recourse to this our sweet and pitiful Lady, who being constituted the mediatrix betwixt Sinners and Almightie God, most faithful performes the charge, and like a true Mother of mercy stands alwayes with open armes ready to embrace those sinners who haue their refuge vnto her; & it is impossible they should perish, if they haue but recourse vnto her as they ought, if you wil beleeue S. Anselme in his Booke of the miracles of the B. Virgin: *O happy Mary* (sayes he) *as the sinner whom you forsake and detest cannot but perish: so who conuerts him vnto you, and you receiue,*

and

and our *Sauiour*, *cannot but be ſaued.*
To which concords theſe excellent words of S. Bernard ſo frequent with preachers to giue
hope vnto the deſperat ſinner : *O
man* (ſaye this great Doctor)*thou
haſt a ſure acceſſe to God, where the
ſonne, beholds, the mother, and the
father beholds the Sonne, whilſt the
Mother shews her ſonne the breaſts
that gaue him ſuck and her chaſt
wombe ; the ſonne to his father his
wounds & pierced ſide; where ſo many
louing ſignes concurr to the entertayning thee, thou canſt not be repelled.*

And this cannot but be a great
comfort to poore ſinners, that
they know they haue with the
Eternal Iudge ſuch an Aduocat
ſtil preſent, or rather a mother
indeed who is his mother alſo.
For ſo in the perſon of S. Iohn,

our Sauiour on the Croſſe by theſe words, *Woman behold thy ſonne*, commended her for mother vnto vs al; at which time ſhe had two ſonnes on Mount Caluary both dead, the one in body, the other in ſoule, one by the torments of the croſſe, the other by languiſhing of ſpirit; of which one was her natural ſonne, the other only by adoption, the one innocent the other culpable. This in theſe words S. Anſelme would ſay: *O ſhure refuge that we haue,* (ſayes he) *the Mother of God is our mother alſo, and either of her children ſuffred death, in his paſſion, the one vpon the croſſe, the other by Infidelity; Iudge you in what bitternes of mind the while was the B. Virgin, &c.*

And ſo there is no Mother would

would more reioyce, to see her
only sonne reuiued from death to
life againe, then the B. Virgin
doth when a sinner repents and
hath recourse to her; and for me
I am of opinion, that she glories
in no title more (excepting that
of Mother of God) then of being
Mother of sinners, and conse-
quétly is most glad when she may
shew it most: *Maria mater gratiæ,
mater misericordiæ*; sayes the holy
church; the very sound of whose
name, me thinks, hath a certaine
sweetnes in it, that promiseth al
grace and clemency: In confidence of which, S. Ignatius the
martyr who liued in the Apostles
tymes, thus supplicats vnto her:
Receiue me then, sayes he, *in the bosome of your maternal piety, you who
are the mother of the soueraine Deity,*

Aa 3   *true*

true Mother of our Sauiour and of sinners by Adoption. She is painted in a long vestment, vnder which many are protected, to signify the maternal care she hath ouer them; & amongst the rest, the Fathers of S. Dominicks Order, are pictured so, vpon this occasion, (as S. Brigit receiued it by Reuelation); S. Dominick neare his happy end, thus with teares in his eyes conuerted himselfe vnto the B. Virgin and sayd; Receiue, O soueraine Queene, receiue my brothers, whom with such care I haue nourished and educated vnder the spreadig vaile of your great mercy; gouerne them, and giue them such force and courage, as their ancient Enemy may neuer preuayle against them; To whom she answered

swered; I promise you, my beloued Dominick for that you haue
loued me better then your selfe,
to take a tender care and protection of yours; & to receiue both
them and al those who shal embrace your Rule vnder the couert
of my veyle, which is my mercy,
the benefit of which and but demand it, I refuse to none. From
whence we may perceiue, how
great her mercy is to her deuoted
seruants, to sinners who haue recourse vnto her; and finally to al,
in that she is the Mother of God,
the Mother of grace and mercy,
the mediatrix betwixt God and
man, one, of the greatest dignityes she hath in heauen.

The Twelfth Starr declared.

THe twelfth and laſt Starr, which diffuſes ouer the world its brighter rayes, is the Vniuerſal *honour*, exhibited to our B. Lady, both from the Angels in heauen, and men on earth, al calling her *Bleſſed*, in fulfilling that prophetie of hers : *Behold, al nations shal cal me bleſſed*; and she giues the reaſon ; *Becauſe the Almighty hath done great things for me*. Thus this diuine Oracle of verity hath preſaged of her ſelfe. that for her gratious priuiledges, and ſublime dignityes heretofore declared, she should be called *Bleſſed* by al the nations of the Vniuerſe.

And

And so it is, for there is no cli-
mat so remote, no nation so barbarous no people so vncultiuat,
where the mother of God is not
blessed and adored, and her name
celebrated by the tilte of the
Queene of Heauen and earth,
The first Christian consecrated
Temples and erected Altars to
her honour those now make solemne vowes, and institut Soda-
lities in her name, so as there is
no countrey great or litle, fertile
or barren, where some Church or
Oratory is not dedicated to her
name, nor any man so impious
and wicked, who hath not some
particular deuotion to her; yea
the Iewes themselues, according
to Iosephus in his Antiquityes,
though mortal enemyes to the
name of Christan, are yet effused

in her prayse ; and S. Bonauentur
sayes, this they affirme of her,
that though on the one side she
was exceeding beautiful, yet on
the other she neuer stirred vpp in
her beholders other then chast desires, her modest and maiestick
presence repelling al vnchaste
thoughts, and purifying their
mindes with whom she was present. Neyther do the Nations
more Infidel & Barbarous render
her lesse reuerence; since according to S. Antonin in the third
part of his Summe, the very Turkes and Moores in their Mosquees
prayse and honour her, and haue
her name in such veneration, as
whosoeuer blaspheme or speake
irreuerently of it, they punish
them most rigorously. Whence
we may see, how vniuersally honoured

noured she is, which is the dignity reprefented by the Twelfth Starr, with which we conclude the contexture of her glorious Crowne.

The faithful Chriftian then, who would cal to memory thefe twelue prerogatiues of the B. Virgin, or rather would crowne her with thefe 12. bright ftarrs, muft euery day in memory of them make twelue reuerences or inclinations ; which while he doth) in profound filence) he is to cal to mind the immenfity of her greatnes in them, and endeauour to produce as many Acts of complacence and congratulation with her for them, according to the inftructions we haue giuen heretofore. There are many fpiritual perfons, who in memory

of

of thofe 12. ftarrs, vfe to recite
twelue times the *Aue Maria*, faluting her as often in that manner as the B. Archangel S. Gabriel did.

I would counfel alfo, to do
thefe reuerences with more deuotion, and to ftirr vp our affection more to the feruice of the B.
Virgin, that at euery reuerence
they would expreffe by word of
mouth, her feueral dignities and
prerogatiues, which for that purpofe I haue breifly heere expref-
fed.

1. I reuerence and adore you, O
   bleffed Mary, the moft illu-
   ftrious Daughter of the foueraine and eternal Emperour.

2. I reuerence and adore you,
   the celeftial Spoufe of the holy Ghoft,

3. I

3. I reuerence and adore you, the glorious Mother of the Incarnat Word.

4. I reuerence and adore you, Mother of the Omnipotent God.

5. I reuerence and adore you, both Daughter, Spouse, and Mother of the holy Trinity.

6. I reuerence and adore you, who are highly seated in a Throne of glory aboue al the Hierarchies of Heauen.

7. I reuerence and adore you, Treasurer of al the riches and graces of the Diuinity.

8. I reuerence and adore you, most glorious Queen of Heauen.

9. I reuerence and adore you, most worthy Lady of the Angels.

10. I

10. I reuerence and adore you, Empreſſe of al the Vniuerſe.

11. I reuerence and adore you, our moſt pittiful Mother and faithful Aduocat.

12. I reuerence and adore you, whom al Kings and Monarkes of the earth do reuerence, and whom al heauenly Courtiers adore.

Another ſort of Adoration, which for the greater variety of the deuout ſeruants of the B Virgin, I haue heere annext.

1. I Reuerence and adore you, O B. Virgin Mary, with al the Angels of heauen.

2. I reuerence and adore you, with

with al the Archangels.

3. I reuerence and adore you, with al the Vertues.

4. I reuerence and adore you, with al the Principalities.

5. I reuerence and adore you, with al the Powers.

6. I reuerence and adore you, with al the Dominations.

7. I reuerence and adore you, with al the Thrones.

8. I reuerence and adore you, with al the Cherubins.

9. I reuerence and adore you, with al the Seraphins.

10. I reuerence and adore you, O B. Virgin Mary, with al the Nations of the world.

11. I reuerence and adore you, with al the faithful departed foules.

12. I reuerence and adore you, with

with al Creatures of Heauen, earth, and depts below.

These 12. reuerences the zealous honourer of the B. Virgin is to make with great resentment and reflexion of mind, becaufe of the profound mysteries contained in them; And by so doing, he shal adorne the head of the B. Virgin, a more grateful Crowne of these 12. Starrs, then if it were al composed of 12. of the richest Iewels in the world, nay of 12. of the most radiant Starrs in heauen.

Touching the acts of complacence, which we formerly mentioned, I haue heere sett downe a forme of them, which each one may exercise according to their deuotion.

Twelue

---

*Twelue Reuerences corręſpondent
to the Bleſſed Virgins
12. prerogatiues.*

1. **O** Bleſſed Virgin, I hartily
congratulat and reioyce
with you, for your being pre-
deſtinat from al eternity to be
Mother of our Sauiour Chriſt,
and the liuing Sanctuary of
the holy Ghoſt.

2 O B. Virgin, I hartily congratulat and reioyce with you,
for being conceiued without
al ſpott of original ſinne, in
ſuch manner as you out-shine
in purity & ſplendor the very
Angels themſelues.

3. O B. Virgin I hartily congratulat

tulat and reioyce with you, for
your being the firſt in conſe-
crating your Virginity to God,
which ſo many Virgins haue
imitated ſince.

4. O B. Virgin , I hartily congratulat and reioyce with you,
for being Mother of the Omnipotent , the higheſt honour
which you haue in heauen, and
on which al your dignity depends.

5. O B. Vigin , &c. for the holy
Ghoſts illuminating you, in ſo
excellent a manner , at the holy Incarnation of the Sonne of
God.

6. O B. Virgin, I hartily congratulat and reioyce with you, for
your being ſo repleniſhed with
diuine grace, & endowed with
al rare vertue and perfection.

7. O

7. O B. Virgin, &c. for your dignity of being of neareſt truſt and ſecrecy with the ſoueraine Monarke both of heauen and earth.

8. O B. Virgin, &c. for that high priuiledge of yours, to haue perpetual fruition of the wiſdome of Alm. God.

9. O B. Virgin, &c. for your being ſo highly ſeated in an eminent Throne aboue al the Quires of Angels.

10. O B. Virgin, I hartily congratulat and reioyce with you, for the great power and authority you haue ouer al the Vniuerſe, and for that both heauen earth & the depts below, obey your Commendements.

11. O B. Virgin, &c. and with our ſelues, for your being our care-

reful & affectionat Mother, and
like a faithful Aduocat procuring euery way our greater
good and aduancement.

12. O B. Virgin: &c. finally for
that al the world honours and
adores your name, celebrats
your prayses, and prayses your
graces, merits, & perfections.

And this deuotion of taking
complacence in the B. Virgins
perfections and dignityes, is fo-
uerainly grateful vnto her; as was
manifeft to S. Brigit in her Reuelations vpon this occafion. Her
fonne being a braue and noble
fpirit, dying in the holy warrs,
she anxious for his foule, befought the B. Virgin to reueale
vnto her, in what eftate it was;
when

when behold, when she was in the greatest feruour of her deuotion, the B. Virgin appeared vnto her, and comforted her in this sort; my deare daughter, sayd she, be no longer solicitous for your sonne, for I haue taken care of his saluation, in visiting him before his decease, and rendring his hart inaccessible to al sorts of temptations, and so as no doubt of faith could bow it from the rectitud it was in, nay more, I made the passage of death both sweet and easy for him, to the end the feare and terrour of it might not transport him either to impatience or despaire. So, I cleared his chamber of those diuels assembled there, to lay snares for his soule, and intrapp it at its departure thence, and at the instant of his soule and bodyes se-

para-

paration, I took it, in myne ary-
ues, vnder the protectió of which,
I caryed it safe away from its infernal enemyes.

And the reason of this tédernes
of hers she declared in another
reuelation , when one day the
holy Saint making her prayers at
the Sepulcher of Chrift , was rauisht in extasy into a sumptuous
Pallace , where she beheld our
Sauiour Chrift on an Imperial
Throne, and his B. Mother seated by his side, with an infinity of
Angels incircling them about;
Presently after , she beheld her
sonne present, al trembling & in
great difmay before this Throne to receiue his Iudgement
there , his Angel Guardian on
his right hand, and the diuel on
his left , who with a horrible
voice

voyce thus cryed out : most omnipotent Iudge , I appeale to you
for Iustice , and right of the greatest iniury that was euer offered
me; your Mother against al equity
hath rauisht that wicked soule out
of my hands , entring his chamber at the houre of his death , and
excluding me and my company,
hath debarred me of that priuiledge which you haue granted
me , to tempt euery soule at the
article of tyme , when it wil best
be testified whether they belong
to me or you , then which greater iniustice can there be imagined ? To this , the B. Virgin answered , though thou art the father of lyes, yet in this thou hast
but declared the truth, I haue don
al this indeed , and my reason for
it was this : This soule , while it

was

was conuerfant in the world, was
fo deuoted to me, as it reioyced
and tooke complacency in my dignity of being Mother of Alm.
God, and at my exaltation aboue
al the quires of heauen, the pleafure of which it would not haue
exchanged for al the contentments and pleafures of the world;
Iudge then if I had not iuft reafon to do what I did : O but (replyed the diuel), al this cannot
excufe it from an Iniury to me,
your debarring me acceffe to
tempt him, as alfo your receiuing
his departing foule, and conue-
ying it hither which cheifly be-
longs to me ; when conuerting
himfelf vnto the Iudge he fayed,
of you then I demand iuftice(who
ought to be as equitable, as you
are powerful) againft this wicked

cked soule heer, who being arriued vnto the yeares of diſcretion,
in ſteed of taking the right hand
way of your commandements,
went on the left, in his tranſgreſ-
ſing them; wherefore I demand
but Iuſtice that he be condemned;
and heer he inſiſted in particula-
riſing his mortal and venial ſins;
at this, his good Angel inter-
poſed himſelſe ſaying; thou wicked feind, al this is but true, I
grant what thou haſt ſayd; but
knoweſt thou not, that his holy
Mothers prayers inceſſantly offered vp vnto Alm. God for him,
haue cancelled theſe, and obtay-
ned for him a true contrition, and
ſacramental abſolution for them
before he dyed; beſides her, and
his many other holy workes don
in ſatisfaction of them, how then

B b   canſt

canſt thou haue the impudence to vrge them any more? goe home, and keepe company with damned ſoules, looke not after him, for he is a ſaued one. At this, the diuel vaniſhed away.

And by this we may ſee, the benefit of being deuoted to the B. Virgin, of the prayers of others for them, and of dying in a good eſtate, prepared vnto it by true contrition and Confeſſion.

---

*An excellent way of adoring the
B. Virgin, in remembring the
ioyes vvhich she had heere.*

CHAP.   XX.

T HE common opinion
is, that the B. Virgin
had in this world, ſea-
uen ioyful times in
particular.

The firſt was, at her Annuncia-
tion.

The ſecond, the Viſitation of S.
Elizabeth.

The third, the glorious Natiuity of our Sauiour Chriſt.

The fourth, the Adoration of
the three Kings.

The fifth, at the finding of her
B. sonne in the Temple.

The sixth, at our B. Sauiours
apparition to her after his most
glorious Resurrection.

The seuenth, her happy decease,
and glorious Assumption into
Heauen.

Now her deuout seruants may
dayly administer her matter of
fresh Ioy, by calling these vnto
remembrance, and occasion to
themselues a great increase of merit and glory. The Angel Ga-
briels salutation to her of *Aue*,
&c. was no other then an Inuita-
tion to reioyce, according to the
interpretation of Origen; so the
holy Church sings her Antiphon:
Gaude virgo gloriosa, *&c.* and in
other: *Regina cæli lætare &c.* and
bids her reioice and be glad; and
in

in a third; *Gaude & lætare Virgo Maria.*

Let vs then announce vnto her Ioy by commemorating thoſe her ſeauen Ioyful myſteries , in this following Method , making at each one of them a low reuerence.

1. Reioyce, O B. Mary , for that vpon the ſalutation of the heauenly meſſinger , you conceiued in your ſacred wombe your ſonne,to the incredible conſolation of your ſoule.

2. Reioyce, O B. Mary, for that you burning with diuine loue, and incited by the holy Ghoſt, ouercome the toyle and labour of paſſing ouer the high mountaines of Iury,and viſited your coſen Elizabeth , where you heard her vttering your celeſtial

Bb 3

ftial praifes, and magnifyed in
fpirit your Lord and Sauiour.

3. Reioyce, O B. Mary, for that
at the end of nine moneths, you
brought forth into the world,
the fo long expected Meffias,
bright as the fun of heauen,
while al the celeftial Angels
played in the beames of him,
to your vnfpeakeable comfort.

4. Reioyce, O B. Mary, for that
you faw the three Kings adoring your B. Sonne, and conceiued a fortunat prefage from
thence, of the Gentils conuer-
fion.

5. Reioyce, O B. Mary, for that
after three dayes fearch, you
found your B. Sonne, to your
exceffiue gladnes, amongft the
Doctours in the Téple, where
you were aftonifht amógft the
reft,

rest, to heare him expound the deepest mysteries of the holy Scripture, foe clearly, and with such admirable perspicacity.

6. Reioyce, O B. Virgin, for that after three dayes deluge of teares, by the appearing of your glorious Sonne in his Resurrection, they were al dryed vp, and you exceedingly reioyc't and comforted.

7. Reioyce, O B. Mary, for that al the Apostles being assembled together at the happy houre of your departure out of this mortal life, the third day after you were glorioufly Asfumpted into heauen, where now you fitt crowned and instated by the holy Trinity Queene of Angels and of all the Vniuerfe.

Bb 4   S. Ai-

S. Anſelme, amongſt our B. Ladyes miracles, records this for one ; that a certaine deuout Religious man, whoſe cuſtome it was, dayly in his deuotiõs, to remember the 7. Ioyes of our B. Lady, being now neere his end, and exceeding fearful of that laſt Agonie , our B. Lady appeared vnto him, and comforting him ſayd, my ſonne why should you feare? you who haue ſo often reioyced me with the remembrance of the greateſt Ioyes I had in my mortal life ? take courage ; and aſſure your ſelfe no euil shal happen vnto you , but you shal ſoone be partaker of thoſe Ioyes which you haue ſo often announced to me: with whoſe celeſtial preſence he was ſo comforted, that forgetting his ſicknes while he endeauoured

to

to rife, and through ioy to caft himfelf at her feet, his foule pre-uented his body, and went out before to the fruition of thofe Ioyes which she had promifed him.

The forefayd Ioyful myfteries may be diftributed to each Houre of the Office of the B. Virgin, The firft, at Mattins; the fecond, at Prime; the third, at the Third Houre; The fourth, at the Sixt; The fifth, at the Ninth; the fixt, at Vefpers; and the feauenth, at Complin; On each one of which we way deuoutly meditat the while, and fo in the like manner we may meditat then on our Beads; a deuotion moft accepta-ble to our B. Lady, as from this Example we may perceiue, re-counted by Pelbert in the Stellary of the B. Virgin.

There was, fayes he, a yong
man, who making himfelfe Religious of S. Francis, his Order,
was accuftomed before he entred
into Religion, to crowne a certaine Image of our Lady with a
wreath of flowers which he dayly
gathered for that intent, but
being once become Religious,
wanting the commodity of flowers, he intermitted this deuotion, though fo vnwillingly as
the leauing that, made him refolue at laft, to leaue being Religious alfo, and being vpon the
point of departing the Conuent,
behold our B. Lady appeared vnto
him faying; leaue off that your fo
pernicious refolue vpon fo triuial
an occafion, and if you defire to
vndertake a deuotion grateful
vnto.

vnto me, in steed of making me a
material crowne of flowers , offer me vp a spiritual one of salu-
tations , and I shal be farre more
delighted with it , and the forme
of it shalbe this: you shal first say
a *Pater noster* , in memory of the
Ioy I conceiued when the Angel
saluted me and the Eternal word
was Incarnat in my wombe , and
say. 10. *Aue Marias* in consequence thereof. Secondly , you
shal do as much ; in memory of
the Ioy I had in visiting my co-
sen Elizabeth : and so forth, vnto
the seauenth Ioy I had ; which
you shal conclude with the last
three *Aue Marias* of your Beades , so the whole number wil
amount to 7. *Paters* and 63. *Aue
Marias*; which deuotion if you
shal dayly performe in mine honour

nour, know you shal much more
pleafe me, then in that other deuotion which you had; and hauing fayd this, she vanifhed
away, leauing him exceedingly
comforted and ftrengthened in
his vocation. Now it hapned that
whilft one day he was performing this deuotion, a certaine
Religious beholding him by
chance, fawe an Angel ftanding
by him, threading on a golden
thread, as many rofes as the Nouice fayd *Aue Marias*, and for
each *Pater nofter* a golden lilly : al
which when the Nouice had done
he ioined them together, and
crowned his head with them; the
Religious man aftonifhed at this
vifion, charged him by vertue of
holy obedience, to declare vnto
him what deuotiōs he vfed; which
he

he doing with great sincerity, the Religious man encouraged him to persist therin, assuring him it was a deuotion the B. Virgin was delighted with.

And S. Bernard exercising this deuotion our B. Lady appeared vnto him once, saying vnto him; **my sonne,** this deuotion of thine, is exceeding grateful to me, and that thou mayst perceiue so much, I haue obtained of my sonne for thee in reward thereof, the grace of preaching, and of working miracles ; besides, I promise you, one day to make you participant of those Ioyes which you dayly cal to remembrance ; and *de facto* soone after, the holy Saint began to be famous indeed for miracles, and to abound in innumerable graces, and conuerted a world of
soules

foules by his learned preachings
and force of his miracles.

―――――――――――

*Of the Interiour Reuerences we
are to exhibit to the Glorious
Queene of Heauen, and of the
place, time, & occasion of exercising them.*

CHAP. XXI.

ITHERTO we haue
ſpoken of the Ado-
rations we are to
make, the exteriour
accompanying the
interiour, with relation to mans
compoſition conſiſting both of
body and ſoule; Now becauſe
thoſe exteriour are not alwayes
to be performed, neither are all
places

places and times accomodate for them, we wilonly speak of such interiour Adorations as we may be exercising, they being only acts of adoration produced by the Wil; which according to S.Thomas, are those which the Blessed in heauen only exhibit vnto Alm. God. These then, there is none but may performe, when in the performance of the others, they are hindred either for want of commodity of place or time, and these indeed are the most excellent of al, and most acceptable to Alm.God, as those without which the others were nothing worth.

And it being our principal scope, to treat of reuerencing the Mother of God, we wil only exemplifye in that, and instruct her votaries in the place, and Time, when

when and where they are principally to be exercised. In al times
and places they may comodiously
be produced, but cheifly when
for the company of others we
cannot exercise any other deuotion, as also when we ride, walke,
eate, or take repose; at al which
times it is but lifting vp our mind
to heauen, and to say with our
hart: I humbly adore you, O B.
mother of my Sauiour Christ; I
adore you O Queene of Angels,
or the like; in only doing of
which, we sanctify al we do, making euery one of those indiffe-
rent actions, æquiualent to prayer: happy the ground they goe
on, happy the bread they eate, &
the rest they take, who are so exercised the while; So when the
Clock strikes, it were a good deuotion

uotion in this ſort to eleuat our
mind, as alſo before each Houre
of our B. Ladyes Office, producing an act of interiour complacence, ſaying with our heart : *I*
exceedingly reioice O B. Virgin,
for your high honor of being Mother of God, of being Queene of
heauen, &c. which cannot but be
moſt acceptable and gratefull vnto
her. In the meane time this deuotion were beſt perfomed on
their knees, it being a poſture
moſt repugnant to ſlouth and tepidity.

Beſides, for thoſe who are troubled with infirmity, age, or any
other weaknes, this deuotion
were beſt, as that which without
any difficulty they may performe,
ſince there is none but haue their
ſpirit free, or at leaſt ſo free, as
for

for a glance or so they may reflect
it vpon heauen, how euer other-
wise they are incumbreds, And
a great consolation this ought to
be to euery one, that without any
other paynes, then the only lifting vp the mind to God, so it be
don with spirit and viuacity, one
may merit so much, as to arriue
to most high perfection. When
one then, is sitting by the fire, or
reposing on the bed, let them but
exercise their mindes in these Interior acts of deuotion, and euen
when they seeme to men most
idle, they shal appeare vnto God
most vertuously imployed. O
most happy imployment, that a
man in a manner doing nothing,
may do as the very Angels in
heauen, And while some, to finde
out solitud and deuotion, retire
them

them to the Desarts, and liue Ere-
mites liues, he that exerciseth
but these adorations, hath al that
within himself, which they seeke
abrode, and may assoone arriue
to the height of perfection by
this easy way, as by the most fa-
tigable they can go. Besides, these
acts of Adoration haue yet another benefit, that they expose vs
not to vainglory, which others
perhaps may do, as being only betwixt God and our selues performed in the interiour of our soule,
which by so much the more in-
nobles them aboue the other, as
the soule exceeds the body in nobility; and therfore of the bodyes
operations we are to haue no regard at al, further then they go
accōpanied with the attention of
the mind, cōformable to that saying

of the Apoſtle : *Corporalis exerci-*
tatio ad modicum vtilis eſt.

But to returne to our purpoſe,
the ſeruant of the Queene of
heauen is to the vttermoſt bent
of ſpirit and induſtry to imploy
himſelfe in theſe interiour Adorations, as farr forth as the circumſtances of time place, & occaſion
ſhal giue him leaue. Notwith-
ſtanding he is to haue regard the
while to accompany them (if he
can) with exterior reuerence both
becauſe the one much aydes the
other, as alſo becauſe the neglect
of them alwayes implyes an inex-
cuſable negligence ; which that
Example which Pelbert recounts,
doth wel declare, happening in
his time in Hungary, and recounted vnto him by a Religious man
of worthy credit, and it is this:

A

A Religious of the ſame Order was accuſtomed euer at the *Aue Maria* bel, or *Angelus Domini*, to riſe out of his bed at the houres of night, and humbly on his knees ſalute the Queen of heauen; This deuout cuſtome once, being perſwaded by ſlouth and lazines, he omitted, when behold, being falne a ſleepe againe, he ſeemed in his ſleepe to ſee, the Church ſteeple euē incline it ſelf vnto the ground; which ſight three times being repreſented vnto him in ſleepe, at laſt he imagined that he heard theſe words; Miſerable and negligēt creature as thou art, art thou not aſhamed to ſee euen ſenſleſſe creatures thus bow down themſelues in reuerence to the Mother of God, whilſt thou ſenſible as thou art, neglecteſt it? by
which

which vision touched with a liuely sorrow for this neglect, he became more feruorous thereafter in his deuotions.

These interiour Reuerences then, although of themselues they be of neuer so high worth and dignity, yet when commodiously they may be done, we are neuer to neglect the exteriour, but stil accompany the one with the other, that the feruour of the one ioyned with the other payne may render them more meritorious; and the best place for the exercising these deuotions *is*, when the commodity of some Chappel or Oratory is offred vs, at which time we are vpon our knees, in a more particular manner to commend our selues to Alm. God and his B. Mother; And

of

of this we haue for paterne our
Sauiour Chrift, who as often as
he afcended to Hierufalem, repayred euer to the Temple, the
firft thing he did, to offer vp to
his eternal Father his prayers and
adoratiōs. In imitation of which,
thofe of the Capucines Order
haue a conftitution, that when
they arriue in any place, they are
firft of al to refort vnto the
Church, and there to adore the
Bleffed Sacrament: the words of
the Conftitution are thefe: Being
arriued to the place where we are
to goe, to fhew our felues true
fonnes of the Eternal father, we
are firft to vifit the Church,
where hauing don reuerence, &c.

And diuers by thefe meanes
haue efcaped imminent dangers;
as appeares by this following
holy

story, recounted by the Illustrious Iames Voragius Archbishop of Genua, in his history of the B. Virgins Assumption.

There was (sayes he) a person of quality, whose wife excelled in al vertues, but principally in deuotion to the B. Virgin, so as no day past that in some reuerent and Religious manner she did not honour her. Now it happened that her husband through his excessiue prodigality, at last fel into want and misery, in so much as one day some noble men inuiting themselues to dinner with him, and he wanting meanes to entertayne them, in that splendid and aboundant manner as he was wont, to avoyd the shame went forth into a wood, where he intended to absent himself while
they

they might be come and gone
without taking notice of their
visiting him; whilst in a Melan-
coly passion he wandred vp and
down then revoluing in his mind
into what misery he was falne,
behold a person of a horrible afpect, mounted vpon ꞙ horse no
lesse horrid then he appeared vnto
him, requesting him to let him
know his cause of discontent; To
whom the Gentleman (after he
had recollected his spirits which
feare with its dismay, had putt to
flight at first) declared his whole
fortunes; at which ⟨ quoth the
other) if that be al, take comfort,
for I wil promise you (grant me
but one request) to reduce you
to an estate more riche and opu-
lent then euer you were in before;
It must be a strange request (sayd

the Gentleman) I fhould not
grant you vpon that condition;
nay, it is but eafy in performance
fayd the diuel) for it was he dif-
guifed in that fhape) to witt, that
on fuch a certaine day and houre
you bring your wife along with
you , and meete me in this
place:& this being agreed vpon,
the diuel directed him to a caue,
where he foûd a mighty treafure,
by the helpe of which, recouering
out of his neceffity, he liued in a
more noble way then euer. Now
it hapned, the time drawing nigh,
when (as he had promifed) he
was to take his iourney with his
wife vnto the place appointed.
and she perceiuing that fom-what
extraordinary was in hand, by his
hafty warning her to prepare to
take horfe with him, and the trou-

ble

ble of his Countenance, when she
could by no meanes gett out of
him what it was ; she recom-
mended the matter to the B.
Virgin , & presently tooke horse
so obedient to her husband, as neuer to examine further his inten-
tions ; Now it hapned on their
way, that passing by a litle Chappel dedicated to our B. Lady, the
Lady by the consent of her husband lighted and went in , only
in mind to do her deuotions , and
returne againe; but behold, whilst
with prayers and teares she commended to the Queene of heauen
the good successe of her affayres,
she was diuinely cast into a sleepe
meane while the B. Virgin assu-
med her shape , and with her husband went on her way.

They were no sooner arriued

at the entry of the wood, but the diuel with great noyfe and furie appeared vnto the Gentleman, not daring to approch vnto him for feare of our B. Lady (whom prefently he knew) but cafting on him a fterne regard in this manner he fpake vnto him; vngrateful and perfidious as thou art, is this al the reward I haue, for thofe great benefits thou haft receiued of me? didft thou not promife to conduct thy wife hither vnto me, and in her fteed had thou brought heer the mother of Alm. God? It was againft thy wife (fince againft this I cannot) I intended to auenge my felfe, for her being fo diligent in the honour and firme affection to the Queene of heauen.

Wherunto the B. Virgin thus
an-

answered him : and whence is this temerity thou abhominable Feind, that thou shouldst dare to offer any iniury to those who loue and reuerence me? goe hence to Hel againe, and desist from malicing them, vpon payne of a greater hel, then euer yet thou feltst; When the diuel with a violent clatter, as if al the wood had been torne vp by the rootes, strait vanished away, and left the Gentleman in such affright, as he fell flatt to the ground before the B. Virgins feet, beseeching her pardon for his offence; who sharply reprehending him for it, commanded him to goe back vnto the Chappel, to awake his wife out of her trance, and returning home with her, to discharge his house of al those il gotten goods, so dam-

Cc 3   nable

nable to keepe : Al which he
punctually did , and quitting
both thofe goods and his euil
together , he became in short
time of more plentiful fortune,
then euer he was before , by the
fpecial fauour of the Queene of
heauen; who is alwayes fuccou-
rable and merciful to thofe , who
implore her ayde in their neceffityes , and aduantage them with
high graces and priuiledges , who
endeauour to honour her with
this excellent fort of Adorations,
as wel exterior as interior, which
hitherto we haue largely treated of ; together with the rea-
fons , difcourfe , authority , and
wondrous examples , which
should induce vs to the embracing of it , which is the principal fcope and ayme of al this
worke.

And now at laſt , we haue brought it to an end, by the particular fauour and aſſiſtance of Alm. God , obtained through the interceſſion of his glorious Mother , our moſt benigne and B. Lady ; whom we beſeech by the ſame interceſſion , to render vs worthy of the participation at laſt of eternal good , which being only that , which can ſatiat indeed , can only render vs on al parts happy and content.

FINIS.

Faults escaped in the Print.

PAge 8.line 1. read vvhich God p.13. l.2. the
cauſ⸗, p. 16 l. 14. vaniſhed, at ſight of, p.
17 l. 17 al vvhi.h, p. 36 l. 18 at his, p. 38 line 9
Soueraigne, p. 48 l.1. the Dungeon, p. 51 l. 9
Confeſſour, p. 59. l. 15.freed, p. 61 l. 7 heare
our, l. 10.ſupplicat p. 63.l.7 vvas a, p. 64 l. 12
at the, p.65. l. 2 tendernes p. 71 l. 9 conclude,
p. 88 l. 3 ⸗ffered, p. 98 l. 10 Sauiour, p. 103 l.
19 curiouſly, p. 109 l. 12 abiectly, l. 13 at the
vvorlds p. 111 l. 1 they preſently vndertocke,
p.115 l.8. moneths ſpace, p. 121 l. 12 adorning,
p. 123 l. 7 title of, p. 131 l. 8 not ſuch, p. 147
l. 11 choſe, p. 148 l. 8. the like, p. 157 l. 9 that
p. 164 l. 17 vvords, p 169 l. 3 execution, p. 178
l. 8 high nobility, p. 182 l. 13. them moſt, p.
186. l. 1 neere the, p. 189 l. 1. altar, p 210 l.
18 guſt, p. 218 l. 4 holy man, 131. l. 14 man of,
l. 15 may vvel, p. 236. l 22. theirs there, p. 237.
l. 2. them, p. 260. l. 5 this deed, p.261 l. 11. af-
tervvards, p. 284 l. 15 at al, p. 289 l. 16 then,
p. 315 l. 4 protection, p. 322 l. 3 earth, l. 6
could I alleage, p. 329 l. 19 better, p. 338 l. 17
at each: p. 349 l. 3 at Paris, p. 374 l. 15 them,
l. 20 he ſayes, p. 390 l. 22 houre, p. 400 l. 8
fiercenes, p. 416 l. 8 bovved his knees, p. 446 l.
18 he vvas, p 455 l. 5 aske, p. 463 l. 6 and the,
p. 464 l. 5 lavvyer, p. 473 l. 16 of his, p. 487
l. 17 enuironed, p. 491 l. 2 he hath, p. 510 l.
12 ſhe vvas, p.534 l. 19 fell, p.553 l. 16 mediatrix, p. 581 l. 11 conceiued.